PRAISE FOR
EXPERIENTIAL MARKETING
SECOND EDITION

'A very clearly written and inspiring guide, demonstrating a unique approach to integrated experiential marketing that carefully explains the methodology in a concise and effective manner.' **Hamish Millar, Marketing Manager, Pernod Ricard UK**

'The must-read guide on experiential marketing that covers the changing world of the retail landscape, with simple models and objectives, in order to execute winning solutions for the increasing demands of consumers.' **Mark Robinson, Retail Sales Director, Silentnight Group**

'This book is amazing. It's more than just a how-to guide – it's also a "what is" and a collection of great case histories. Need answers, guidance or inspiration? Look no further. It's essential reading for any modern marketer!' **Kevin Jackson, Editor-in-Chief, *Live Communication Magazine***

'In presenting experiential marketing as a methodology, rather than a channel, Smilansky offers advice and insights relevant to B2C and B2B businesses of any size. One-way communication channels are the way of the past; learning how to foster authentic two-way conversations is the next challenge. Anyone interested in building a strong and lasting relationship between their customers and their brand needs to read this book.' **Lynn Morrison, Marketing Director, Opus Energy**

'In today's ever-changing consumer and media landscape, this book demonstrates how to truly engage and create a deeper emotional connection with modern audiences; a must-read for senior brand marketers, CEOs and their teams.' **Maria Hatzistefanis, President/CEO, Rodial Group (Rodial Skincare, NIP+FAB)**

'Practical, pragmatic and succinct. Seasoned marketers and people just starting out will find something of use in this book. Something for everyone and written and styled for the 24/7 world we live in.' **Tony Cooke, HR Director, adidas Group**

Second Edition

Experiential Marketing

A practical guide to interactive brand experiences

Shirra Smilansky

KoganPage

First published in Great Britain and the United States in 2009 by Kogan Page Limited
Second edition published in 2018

2nd Floor, 45 Gee Street
London EC1V 3RS
United Kingdom
www.koganpage.com

c/o Martin P Hill Consulting
122 W 27th St, 10th Floor
New York, NY 10001
USA

4737/23 Ansari Road
Daryaganj
New Delhi 110002
India

© Shirra Smilansky, 2009, 2018

The right of Shirra Smilansky to be identified as the author of this work has been asserted by her in accordance with the Copyright, Designs and Patents Act 1988.

ISBN   978 0 7494 8096 7
E-ISBN   978 0 7494 8097 4

British Library Cataloguing-in-Publication Data

A CIP record for this book is available from the British Library.

Library of Congress Cataloging-in-Publication Data

Names: Smilansky, S, author.
Title: Experiential marketing : a practical guide to interactive brand experiences / Shirra Smilansky.
Description: 2nd Edition. | New York : Kogan Page Ltd, [2017] | Revised edition of the author's Experiential marketing, 2009. | Includes bibliographical references and index.
Identifiers: LCCN 2017043565 (print) | LCCN 2017052182 (ebook) | ISBN 9780749480974 (ebook) | ISBN 9780749480967 (alk. paper)
Subjects: LCSH: Branding (Marketing) | Target marketing.
Classification: LCC HF5415.1255 (ebook) | LCC HF5415.1255 .S55 2017 (print) | DDC 658.8/27–dc23

Typeset by Integra Software Services, Pondicherry
Print production managed by Jellyfish
Printed in Great Britain by Ashford Colour Press Ltd

CONTENTS

An online-only bonus chapter – 'Outsourcing versus in-house' – and other resources are available at the following URL

(please scroll to the bottom of the web page and complete the form to access these):
    www.koganpage.com/EM2

ABOUT THE AUTHOR

Shirra Smilansky is CEO and Executive Creative Director of Electrify Worldwide Ltd. She was a Visiting Professor at London Metropolitan University and helped them develop the first master's degree on Experiential Marketing in the UK – 'Experiential Meets Digital'. She has been a guest speaker on BBC Radio (*Wake up to Money*, BBC Radio 5 live). Smilansky has travelled around the world to host workshops and seminars for global brands such as L'Oréal Luxe, San Miguel, LEGO and adidas, covering topics such as the neuroscience behind creativity, and teaching her proprietary methodologies – the BETTER creative model and SET MESSAGE planning system. She often hosts talks that focus on the relationship between live brand experiences and social media, as well as exploring how brand experiences can sit centrally in the marketing communications planning process.

A marketer, writer, strategist, creative, educator and entrepreneur – Smilansky is a recognized player and pioneer in the Experiential Marketing field.

FOREWORD

My first truly in-depth look at the world of experiential marketing (ExM) was around 10 years ago when I was writing my master's dissertation and read Shirra Smilanksy's first book. I had been working in 'the field' as an Event Manager for a variety of leading agencies and loved the idea that targeting the five senses and giving people a brand experience meant you could change somebody's buying habits.

Reading the second edition of *Experiential Marketing* is a reminder of how much things have changed since the start of my career. At that time, Facebook and Twitter were in their infancy and Instagram did not exist. Today, planning an ExM campaign without considering content creation, shareability and hashtag is unthinkable. The dream of content creation is virality, with videos of the very best campaigns able to achieve millions of views across social networks and spread brand awareness on a global scale. But harnessing this and truly creating something great that captures people's imaginations requires a level of creativity and authenticity that many brands can struggle to reach.

Social media has enhanced the power of ExM; advertising is no longer a one-way street. You can go on to Twitter or Facebook and converse with brands from anywhere in the world. And due to this, brands don't just have personalities, they have voices – and you can take these voices to the world through ExM, embodied in a creative and memorable real-world brand experience and by skilled brand ambassadors.

This book is the perfect companion for any marketer who wants to get the very best from a campaign and develop an authentic and relevant creative idea. Having been on the forefront of this ever-evolving industry for 12 years, I still find that I am learning every day.

The evolution of ExM, with focus on both present and future practices, is expertly crafted into the following pages. Whilst guiding you through the systems, processes and measurement tools necessary to design, plan and execute experiential campaigns from start to finish, this is also likely to be the most informative book on experiential marketing you will ever read.

Liam Dixon
experiential marketing expert,
and Client Services Director at Equals Agency

PREFACE

It has been about 10 years since I wrote the first edition of this book. At the time, even the term 'experiential marketing' was little known, and even the most experienced of marketing directors at brands would often answer our introductory calls with 'Experimental, what!?!?'

As we progress towards a world where bots and computerized intelligence rapidly fulfil most human jobs better, faster, and with increasing creativity, these are interesting times indeed. How the accelerating evolution of technology is impacting and disrupting the most mundane of industries (from laundry to banking and everything in between) and what this means for brands and marketers, is the most compelling question on the tip of everyone's tongue.

This is a time where convenience and function are overtaking the glitzy, glamorous allure of the synthetic and contrived brand advertising we were once brainwashed by. And where design and image-led brand 'fantasies' are increasingly meaningless, given that everyone and their cousin (via a free mobile app) can now create their own reasonable corporate/brand identity; the commoditization of a decent visual brand image is truly commonplace. As a result, in this experiential era and digital age, only real and authentic, socially conscious and relevant brands will survive. The 'added-value' brand experience is the only relevant form of activation to achieve 'cut through' in our ever-fragmented media and consumer culture.

Big data and artificial intelligence are enabling forward-thinking companies to create truly personalized and increasingly relevant customer experiences, tailored en masse. With the internet of things (IoT) upon us, an intimate and relevant brand experience at scale is increasingly influencing the product offering itself, thereby demonstrating that experiential marketing goes – and must go – far beyond 'promotions in the real world', and deeper; as an ideology, influencing a firm's central business philosophy and offering to create an experiential, tailored product or service, not merely an experiential campaign. This is symptomatic of the consumer era we live in, where the customer is king (or queen!) and content is becoming the ultimate currency.

ACKNOWLEDGEMENTS

Writing this book has been an incredible journey. I initially set out to update the first edition, and instead wrote a completely new book – so much had changed in 10 years, not least of which my perspective and I have many people I wish to thank for their support, contribution, encouragement and friendship during that evolution.

Thank you to everyone who contributed, with special mentions to: Nick Kingsnorth for working on the book launch and marketing, Jack Rose for coordinating the interviews with industry experts, Zoe Louizos for proofreading and copy-editing, Charlotte Owen, Philippa Fiszzon, Natasha Tulett, Chris Cudmore and the team at Kogan Page for their feedback, guidance and putting up with me, as well as for all their encouragement at the right moments, which enabled us to bring the book to completion in time. Thanks to all of those interviewed, quoted and referenced throughout the book, and to all the wonderful marketing industry sources and agencies who are showcasing fantastic experiential work, flying the flag for beautiful and immersive experiential marketing projects, products and services around the world.

Industry experts, membership clubs and networks/events have been so important to me in the development of my career and this book (both editions), and for that I give special thanks to: Spencer Gallagher, Duncan Cheatle, Katy Howell, Kevin Jackson, Dani Caplin, Ruth Wrigley, The Supper Club, The DAFD, Digital Podge, and the ExM Forum, Live Com, *Event Magazine*, NESTA, and The Funemployed.

Thanks to Sketch London, where the book launch took place 10 years ago for the first edition and again for hosting the launch of this book – a truly spectacular and artistic location and by far one of the most experiential and immersive venues in the world, and thanks to Henry Bennett of Sultan Shakes for making it happen.

I'd also like to thank my family: Jonathan Smilansky, Errica Moustaki, Alex Smilansky, Booboo, the seven wonders and the Cantaladies; Portia Barnet Herrin, Victoria Vaughan, Roxanne Jones, Nelly Curtis, Lisa Colleran, Clare Coultas, Jade Keane, Katie Lazell. My oldest best friend Lauren Jones. My spiritual family: the devotees of the Quintessence Hashram. My inspirational and supportive partner: Jack Nutter. Jedi Ben, Tom Eales, and

The Knowledge Book, for providing the universal magic and connecting me to the collective consciousness and my inspiration. Big shout outs to the vibes cartel and broader vibes massive. I'd like to give thanks especially to all who featured in the summer of 2017 while I was writing the book, and provided me with an ongoing reminder that despite the increasingly technical world we live in, life is really one big multi-sensory experience joined by a narrative across a sequence of immersive events. In no particular order, big-up: Jack Nutter, Lisa Andronova, Lucas Daniel Barnfield, Joe Andrews, Jamie Nesbitt, Lauren Spiteri, Finlay Simpson, Lizzie Waite, Jonathan McCabe, Nick Kingsnorth, Rachel Chudley, Jonny Kerr, Cassie Beadle, Mickey Voak, Jolyon Varley, Rhi Davies, James Kelly, Nadia Barak, Ross Harrison, Oli Goss, Louise Dooey, Toby Regbo, Josie Naughton, Isobel Driscol, Elnaz Niknani, Rosie Browning, Lyndsey Critchley, Dave Ashby, Daphne Hall, Michelle McLaughlin, Roisin Reilly, Grace Egan, Tom Frog, Naomi Parry, Doug Booth, Felix Bos, Margherita Visconti, Alice Felgate, Hayden Kayes, Rosie Bones, Lucy Fitzgerald, Nutty Williams, Cassidy Burcher, Annie Mackin, Katie Langridge, Catherine Eldridge, Belle Powley, Fee Greening, Dan White, Matt Smith, Toby Southall, Paddy Corrigan, Nico Kaufman, Elin Hill, Miguel Koch, Chris Gepp, Ann Henderson, Asher Clarke, Adam Browning, Johanna Carle, Will Skillz, Jesse James, Sean Cunningham, Kate Heath, Caroline Little, Mark Day, India Rose James, Georgina Burden, Laina Farmer, Henry Bennett, Sarah Roco Barnes, Dulcie Horn, Holly Hood, Steph Voisey, Polly Stenham, Steph Hamil, Alice Vandy, and Jessi Brown. Also thanks to Miquita Oliver and Jazz Domino Holly – inspirational women who I've known for over 10 years, were there at the launch of the first book, and who are still smashing it and representing today, and thanks to all women who believe in themselves and know to never give up while striving for their dreams; girl power!

PART ONE
An experiential revolution

The accelerating transformation
of business and marketing

What is experiential marketing?

Experiential marketing is a methodology, not a channel

Marketing communication messages, through media or other marketing channels, exist to communicate with different consumer groups or business sectors. Marketing communication channels traditionally include: advertising, direct mail, packaging, sales promotion, sponsorship, public relations, digital and live brand experiences. These have all seen rapid transformation as technology accelerates change in the creative industries and 'Next Gen-ers' (a mix of millennials and Gen Z) grow up to represent enormous chunks of society's purchasing consumers and influencers.

Integrating your live brand experience

Live brand experiences should not be created in isolation without consideration for how they and their content will translate through other channels. It is always best to explore how to replicate them digitally and integrate them with the rest of your marketing efforts, utilizing and considering the formats of a selection of your available channels to help support its effectiveness. Marketers deploy each channel to achieve different goals and objectives, and each platform has different considerations in terms of how to best produce appropriate content and personalized creative.

Advertising: raising awareness of a live brand experience

Within an integrated experiential marketing strategy, advertising is usually implemented to create or raise brand awareness of a live brand experience.

> ## Interview excerpt: experiential brands win the race
>
> Rodolfo Aldana, Director of Tequila, Diageo
>
> There are brands that are now selling millions and they never put an ad on TV. These brands, they're experiential. From a PR and experiential perspective, we are more and more certain that if we keep doing that and we add amplification through digital, we actually are going to get a greater result.[1]

Mass traditional advertising has high 'reach' and is typically effective at raising awareness, but can be expensive to implement on an effective scale. When used on a large scale, traditional advertising can have a low cost per thousand (CPT), but overall it *can* be a very expensive tool, one traditionally effective for market-leading brands that can afford to run very large-scale awareness campaigns.

However, since the rise of programmatic, digital advertising, and the ability for laser-sharp targeting and personalization, this is changing. These days, it is far more common to see the use of targeted social media ads to drive participation in a live brand experience. Facebook provides such rich audience-targeting options that it is often a great tool for driving localized event registrations using its geo-targeting capabilities, and can prove extremely lucrative in marketing strategy.

Direct mail: a physical moment in a digital world

Direct mail, which can involve posting marketing materials directly to people's homes, can be used as part of customer relationship management (CRM) programmes, in order to engage consumers for a direct response or sale at home.

Despite having historically been perceived as a channel reserved for junk mail and takeaway menus, a lot has changed. The opportunity to create a physical interaction and achieve cut-through is increasingly valuable in this digital age.

The phenomenal rise of subscription-based businesses such as Dollar Shave Club, and Birch Box, which offer a tailored product experience in a box, is testament to how an effectively designed product experience delivered by post can be disruptive, modern and exciting.

Packaging: an intimate brand experience with scale

Consideration of packaging is essential to every brand, as it communicates their brand identity to the consumer through the colours, shape and overall 'look and feel' of the product. As 'merged reality' technologies such as augmented reality (AR) and virtual reality (VR) continue to rise and become available through packaging in the form of products such as Google Cardboard, the packaging of a product can now offer the customer a window into a world of branded content – both interactive and shareable.

Even though many of these technologies have been around a while, it often takes time for brands to work out how to apply them with relevance for the occasion, rather than appearing to be gimmicky or simply opportunistic.

Sales promotion and retail: an omni-channel world

Sales promotion involves driving sales in the retail environment through special offers, discounts, rewards and vouchers. Field marketing activities (such as in-store promotional staff, field sales, auditing, mystery shopping, merchandising and sampling) are generally classified within the sales promotion channel. In today's ever evolving omni-channel/omni-experience retail environment, the role of the physical store is changing.

Customers are now starting, stopping and completing the sales loop across multiple touchpoints. Physical stores provide an opportunity for shoppers to have a sensory experience with a brand or product. The best stores immerse consumers in a world that brings the *Brand Personality* to life, and give the customer a chance to touch, smell, taste, hear and feel what the product or brand is all about. Often a customer would prefer to complete the sales process via mobile online or tablet and at their own convenience.

With the increasing popularity of 'click and collect'-style services/'reverse showrooming', and overlaying shopping experiences onto social content, forward-thinking businesses are taking the omni-channel future retail reality into account, making it easier for the shopper to start buying in-store and finish online, or start online and finish in-store.

Invisible interfaces to take over with the rise of the internet of things (IoT)

There are now numerous opportunities to shop 'whilst living' or socializing, and many variations of the new shopper journey are opening up, as the role of the 'bricks and mortar' store is evolving into an important marketing channel; a permanent space for live brand experiences. As technology starts to blend seamlessly 'into the background' and the dawn of invisible interfaces allows us to almost forget technology is even there, shopping opportunities can become increasingly personal, authentic and relevant. The future of tech retail allows the possibility for brands to add value through content, offering 'opt-in' shop-able moments elegantly interweaved into consumers' lives in ways that feel participatory, rather than invasive. This topic is explored in great depth in Chapter 4 of this book.

Technology is increasingly providing brands with the ability to personalize their sales promotion messages through using iBeacons or geo-fencing, to engage with users on their mobile devices. Some examples of this include Unilever providing money-off coupons through a combination of iBeacons and the Magnum Mpulse app and global brands such as Coca-Cola also make use of the technology to drive local promotions.

Sponsorship and branded properties

Sponsorship is a great tool for brands that target niche audiences. It can earn credibility and communicate with an audience in their preferred environment. Traditionally, sponsorship is a practice that involves branding at sporting, cultural and other events, at which there is a desired association with the event or people. Sponsorship aligns the brand directly with people's current perceptions of the company or event in question. Traditionally brands would pay hefty price tags for the rights to place their logo on a sponsored event's marketing materials. They would also still need to shell out extra budget to then 'activate' that sponsorship effectively and integrate the live brand experiences within a sponsored event, such as the Olympics, or Wimbledon, but these opportunities often come with a number of rules and restrictions.

There is room, however, to a certain degree, for non-sponsor brands to align with the event in a clever way. It depends on who is sponsoring the event, and what brands can do off the back of things. There are always guerrilla opportunities, and brands like Paddy Power often use clever stunts and pranks around events without breaking any laws or regulations. Brands can still tap into the spirit and culture of an event, to be part of the story and feeling, without having to make a large investment into an event via sponsorship.

Since experiential marketing and guerrilla tactics have matured, and technological advances have made it ever easier to ambush or 'hijack' major sporting and public events, with or without the hefty price tag associated with traditional sponsorship, it has become increasingly important for brands actually paying up for rights to really add value and leverage them for proper impact. An official sponsorship of a major sporting event should pave the way for experiential and digital innovation not a corporate logo-plastering exercise that any millennials will run a mile from. With assets like talent, players and influencers being offered up within sponsor deals, there is a wealth of opportunity to create interesting and relevant content that will resonate and engage emotionally with fans.

Evian #wimblewatch

At Wimbledon 2016, an interesting content-driven campaign was created by Evian where a daily online video series that was hosted by VIPs, bloggers and fans showcased reactions to the tennis events on Wimbledon's courts under the #wimblewatch campaign umbrella. Participants also shared their emotions via social media using the #wimblewatch hashtag.

Technology accelerates geo-targeting and hyper-localization in brand communications

Technological advancements at concert halls, stadiums and venues are also expanding the possibilities for many brands to improve the audience experience and bring fans closer to the action; and more venues becoming Wi-Fi, Beacon and pre-pay enabled as standard, with digital and mobile engagement and sales promotions to support physical real-world experiences, are becoming increasingly accessible to sponsors.

In Campaign Insight sponsorship report 'is official dead?' they state:

Brands will continue to invest in official sponsorship deals, but they will demand more from rights holders in terms of access to content and flexibility in order to provide value to customers. As a result fans can expect more relevant, interactive and personalized content that will enhance their overall experience of events.[2]

Creating your own branded property

Many challenger brands, and those with an experiential philosophy at their heart, have spent years perfecting the art of *creating their own* branded properties and events from scratch; a route that in contrast to sponsorship offers enormous flexibility and economic opportunity. Red Bull, The Sonos Studio, House of Vans and The Heineken Experience are great examples worth looking into.

According to agency Sense in 2015, consumers are four times more likely to trust a brand that does things in the real world, and 7 out of 10 people said they would buy the products of such a brand over a competitor who didn't (Figure 1.1).

Figure 1.1   What do people really think of brands and ads?

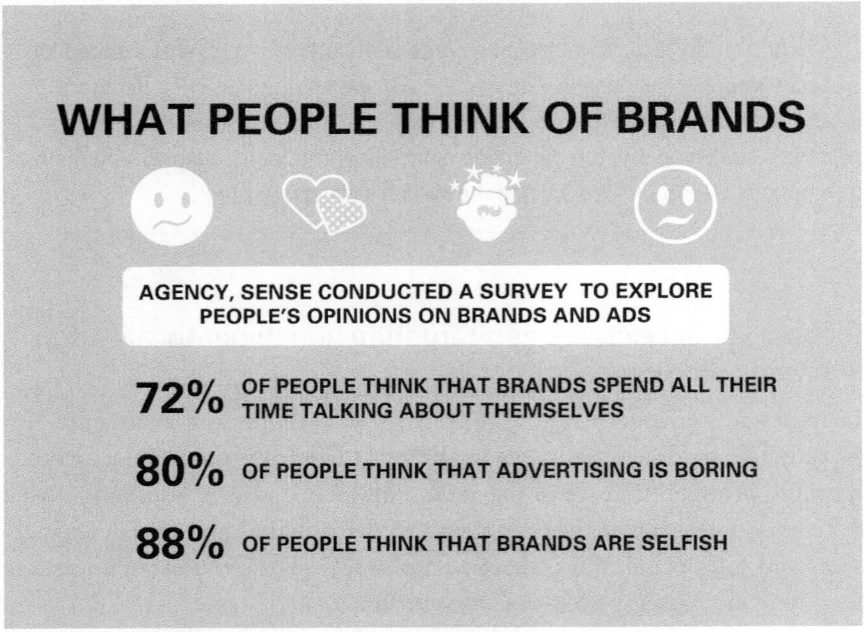

WHAT PEOPLE THINK OF BRANDS

AGENCY, SENSE CONDUCTED A SURVEY TO EXPLORE PEOPLE'S OPINIONS ON BRANDS AND ADS

72% OF PEOPLE THINK THAT BRANDS SPEND ALL THEIR TIME TALKING ABOUT THEMSELVES

80% OF PEOPLE THINK THAT ADVERTISING IS BORING

88% OF PEOPLE THINK THAT BRANDS ARE SELFISH

SOURCE Based on research by Sense agency (2016) *Psycho Brands!*

PR – driving participation in a live brand experience and expanding its content reach

Public relations (PR) is the process of managing the flow of information between an organization and its public. Its activities include award ceremonies, celebrity endorsements, press and media relations, and events that aim to project a positive image of an organization to its key stakeholders. As printed publications lose popularity and consumers demand their media and content to be consumable in a more instant and temporary fashion, the role of PR is changing. Live brand experiences provide a great opportunity for brands to invite journalists, bloggers, vloggers and influencers to partake in a total brand and product immersion, much richer than the traditional press release, and with enormous scope for unique content and unprecedented social media following. Instagram for example now leads in social engagement, with brands using Instagram picking up 1 million followers in 2015, almost five times higher than in 2014.

PR can also be very effectively used prior to a live brand experience, in order to raise awareness of it and generate interest. It is quite common to see live brand experiences, pop-ups and events run with an overlay of varied event programming, often ticketed via sites and apps such as EventBrite, YPlan etc. PR coverage can be effective at driving traffic and registrations to these pages, thereby increasing attendance, even during 'off-peak' times with low passing footfall.

Digital – redefining for today's connected world

There have been numerous definitions of 'digital' and, as we become ever more immersed in a connected world, the term's continuous evolution is inevitable. In the past, digital was often about technology. Within a marketing context, digital was a new way of engaging with customers. Though it can be both, what it really represents is an entirely new way of doing business. Digital has become less of a 'thing' and more a way of '*doing* things'.

The IoT and the omnipresence of smart products has opened up opportunities for disrupters to use unprecedented levels of data precision to better understand their customer experience. In the automotive industry, for example, cars connected to the outside world have expanded the frontiers for self-navigation and in-car entertainment. Brands need a better understanding of each step of the customer journey, regardless of channel. They need to think about how both digital and human touchpoints can deliver the best possible experience, across all of the business and its marketing. Digital interactivity gives us a better opportunity to understand how a consumer is interacting with a brand and we can then gain insights from those interactions to better improve the customer experience.

For example, the content and experience may adapt as a customer shifts from a mobile phone to a laptop, or from evaluating a brand to making a purchasing decision. The rising number of customer interactions generates a stream of intelligence that allows brands to make better decisions about what their customers want. The rapid rise of wearable technology and the IoT represents the latest wave of touchpoints that will enable companies to blend digital and physical experiences ever further.

Brand advocacy

Although brands and companies benefit from using these channels, marketers worldwide are looking for new ways to utilize these channels to their full potential in order to engage their *Target Audiences* on a deeper level. They want to build relationships that create loyalty (if it can be said that such a thing still exists) and every marketer's dream: brand advocacy and, ultimately, evangelism. True 'Experience Brands' are converting their consumers from shoppers (who are now proven to be disloyal and promiscuous with their choice of brands) into brand evangelists who praise and preach about the brand, its personality and core message or features to their friends, families, colleagues and communities. Brands that succeed to invite and join their fans in co-creating and sharing in the brands' development, innovation and content produced are winning hearts and minds on a vast scale.

Figure 1.2   Most valuable brands of 2016

We can see that Forbes Most Valuable Brands of 2016 are those who have formed a 'golden brand bond' with their customers:

#1 Apple
#2 Google
#3 Microsoft
#4 Coca-Cola
#5 Facebook
#6 Toyota
#7 IBM
#8 Disney
#9 McDonalds
#10 GE

SOURCE Based on research by Forbes (2016) *The World's Most Valuable Brands!*[3]

These brand evangelists are building brands at the speed of light. They are not only communicating messages that traditional marketing could likewise do, but are creating something unique: a personal recommendation (Figure 1.2). This 'golden brand bond' is priceless.

Word of mouth and personal recommendations

Experiential marketing creates brand advocacy. It drives word-of-mouth communication through personal recommendations that are the result of consumers feeling that the brand experience added value to their lives, and connected with them through relevant interaction. The clear results of this are strengthened brand relationships and increased customer loyalty, and therefore a more long-term strategic approach to gaining and maintaining market share.

Sometimes the product itself is truly superior to its competitors, with innovative features and benefits that can only be communicated through experience. This is why experiential marketing campaigns often have the objective of driving product trial. When you choose a restaurant, it is often a direct result of a personal recommendation or word of mouth. Word of mouth increases sales more effectively than advertising, and experiential marketing drives word of mouth better than a traditional approach to marketing can hope to.

Think back to the last time you went to eat in a restaurant. Did you go there because you heard it was good, or because you saw an advert in a magazine saying it was? Or when a friend rants and raves about a new miracle cleaning product that removed seven stains from his white tablecloths, and you pass that same cleaning product in the aisle on your next supermarket visit – do you think you will give it a try? The answer is most likely, *yes*! Word of mouth is priceless, and leads us to the all-important question: which marketing communication channel or approach drives consumers to spread word of mouth? Today's consumers are bored of being inundated with endless invasive adverts and messages urging them to buy products and being drowned in a sea of noise. They want brands to engage with them authentically; to add value to their lives and to give something relevant back. Consumers aspire to lifestyles that their favourite brands portray; they want to be a part of the brand and what is associated with it, and they want to immerse themselves in the brands they love. Once they become advocates, they start to do your marketing for you. This is why the marketing world of today has been redefined as the era of the customer, and leading 'experience brands' are communicating in a new era: the era of experiential marketing.

What is experiential marketing?

Experiential marketing is the process of identifying and satisfying customer needs and aspirations profitably, engaging them through authentic two-way communications that bring brand personalities to life and add value to the *Target Audience*.

An integrated experiential checklist:

1 Experiential marketing is an integrated methodology; always engaging *Target Audiences* at their will through authentic brand-relevant communications that add value.

2 An experiential marketing campaign is built around one big idea that should involve a *Two-Way Interaction* between the brand and the *Target Audience* in real time, therefore featuring a live brand experience at its core.

3 The 'other' marketing communications channels and social media platforms that are selected and integrated are known as the 'amplification channels', which amplify the impact of the big idea (the live brand experience and its content, through seamless and authentic storytelling).

Experiential marketing is a methodology. It is a customer-centric approach to effectively communicating with your *Target Audiences*. 'Experience Brands' are those that embrace the customer experience wholly, gaining significant competitive advantage by deploying this *Two-Way Interaction*-focused, experience-oriented strategy across everything they do in an authentic and real way that has relevance to their audiences.

The growth of experiential marketing

Experiential marketing spend often comes from other allocated budgets such as the PR, events or below-the-line budget, or the sales promotion budget. Increasingly, many decision makers are realizing that experiential marketing is an integrated methodology to marketing communications and offers considerable advantages when combined with social media and PR, compared to advertising.

Interview excerpt: creating impact through experiential marketing

Barbara Bahns, Head of Regional Marketing Planning
and Communications CEE, Visa Inc

Whereas 15 years ago marketers would still go for a high-reach above-the-line campaign, and some of them still do, obviously, that doesn't create brand engagement any more, not on the scale that it did maybe 20 years ago, for example, when advertising on TV was fairly new and was kind of exciting. It's not that exciting any more, is it?! Now the TV spots that you remember are the TV spots from the 1990s, because it was new, and it was new storytelling.

Experiential marketing on the whole is opening up – well it is actually allowing me as a marketeer to be able to talk to my audience and to drive impact with them, something that is increasingly difficult if not nearly impossible with an above-the-line.[4]

Increasing budgets

Budgets are increasingly moving towards experiential marketing initiatives and plans. Many marketers are therefore moving significant portions of budget to experiential marketing, in favour of 'above the line/advertising'-led approaches. They find experiential marketing to be especially useful in achieving objectives that the others find hard to accomplish, such as creating brand advocacy, encouraging word of mouth and bringing the *Brand Personality* to life through multisensory expressions that lead to long-lasting memories and a deep emotional connection, as explored throughout the *BETTER* chapter of the book (Chapter 6).

The investment in experiential marketing by brands has risen again according to the 2017 Bellwether Report from the Institute of Practitioners in Advertising (IPA).[5] The figures again reveal experiential marketing to be outpacing other disciplines in terms of brand spending. Live brand experiences (classified as event marketing) were predicted to see the greatest increase against other disciplines.

Focus on measurement

Measurement is a high priority to justify increased investment in experiential. However, a lack of suitable and consistent methods for evaluating experiential marketing has been a major criticism faced by the industry. This means experiential marketing is often measured using similar metrics to traditional marketing and advertising (such as opportunity to see) – methods that are far from suitable in measuring the success of the campaigns. If you consider that the value of a truly engaged consumer – who has been educated and immersed in a brand and what it stands for – is far greater than one who merely 'was exposed to the brand', then you realize how inaccurate it is to quantify the value of the reach in the same way.

Experiential future

At first glance, and after failing to impress in the respect of huge numbers, some people perceive experiential marketing as a limited tactical tool, rather than as a key strategic approach that marketers should consider central to their integrated marketing communications plan. In fact, word-of-mouth reach and brand advocacy are so valuable – and can expand the brand's reach to such a massive scale – that if experiential marketing were to be measured according to its unique benefits, marketers would find that it is hugely successful in impacting unprecedented numbers of people. As with all marketing, this is not always the case if only last-minute tactical activities are implemented. To gain maximum benefits, customer experience and experiential marketing should be central to the long-term marketing strategy of any brand.

Traditional channels aim to increase brand awareness, market share and sales. Experiential marketing can achieve these objectives, but the live brand experience must be at the core of the integrated marketing communications strategy in order to gain maximum results. Experiential marketing brings a great deal more than brand awareness or a quick sale from a promiscuous customer. To gain maximum benefits from implementing experiential marketing, we should look at the more sophisticated results that it can achieve when properly integrated, invested in and planned well in advance.

An immersive and experiential era

Some companies have implemented experiential marketing strategies for years and confidently differentiated themselves from the competition, forming long-lasting relationships with their *Target Audience*, maintaining customer loyalty and incubating fans into advocates.

They have tantalized the five senses through live brand experience events *in real life* (IRL), and amplified them, extending the reach of their content through other marketing communication channels and social media. Immersive brand experiences add value to the consumer, and give something back, paving the way for innovating, market-leading brands to create longer-lasting and deeper connections with customers.

Consumers have visited amusement parks such as Disneyland, Sea World and Universal Studios for decades, revelling in the universe of their favourite characters and brands. By allowing consumers to touch, smell, taste, see and hear, Disney has created immersive experiential environments that generate an emotive response. For years, this has propelled guests to talk and rave about those memorable events to loved ones and acquaintances alike.

A world of experiences

It is no surprise that while the experiential revolution is occurring and marketers are shifting focus from one-way to *Two-Way Interactions*, the same thing is happening in education. World-class educational experts (from kindergarten teachers to quantum physicists) are concluding in unison that when learning, the best way to truly understand and absorb information is through experiencing the problem, the process and the solution. Teachers have always taken children on field trips to lakes and forests to help them understand natural biology through engaging with the true environment. They regularly facilitate experiments as a key part of learning.

However, it is not only schools and teachers that believe engagement is the key to successfully educating and informing students. London, along with many other cities worldwide, is home to a fascinating science museum, which allows visitors to touch, hear, see and taste, taking them through a journey of staged experiences and interactive tools, all the while communicating key messages. They succeed in educating, informing and achieving their objectives within a creative exploratory environment.

Similarly, MOMI (the Museum of the Moving Image) has captured the attention and wonder of film fans for decades, allowing them to immerse themselves in a movie-themed environment, which is at once interactive, entertaining, informative and educational. This shift marks why establishments such as these spend so little of their budgets on traditional marketing. They know that the consumers who provide their revenue execute their most effective word-of-mouth marketing.

Consumer trends shift towards 'experiences as entertainment'

There has been an experiential revolution across so many sectors, from food, to theatre, to arts, to sports, to retail and to entertainment. It is now the gold standard expected from consumers and a long-term global shift towards experiences has transformed the way we choose to eat, drink, play, sleep, travel – in fact transact and share in every way. When you apply the same deeply considered and immersive, experiential principles applied by 'interactivity gurus' and cultural pacemakers – such as Punch Drunk Theatre, Secret Cinema, You Me Bum Bum Train, Immersive Zombie Experiences and countless more coveted immersive entertainment experiences purveyors – to a business and marketing context, not only will you generate immense consumer advocacy and achieve glorious commercial results, but you will also truly add value to your consumers' everyday lives, giving back through authentic real-world experiences that generate social currency and build long-lasting, deep emotional 'golden bonds'.

Two-way communication and interactive engagement are the keys to creating memorable experiences that drive word of mouth, and transform consumers (and trade/media/employees/other stakeholders) into brand advocates and brand evangelists. The power of a personal recommendation is unbeatable – 84 per cent of people say word-of-mouth recommendations are the most trusted source of brand discovery. So, delivering an exceptional brand experience is one of the most effective ways to turn customers into vocal promoters of a brand. The value these advocates bring goes beyond social engagement and retention (Campaign Insight, Marketing in the age of the customer).[6] Brands are being shaped by word-of-mouth marketing generated by socially connected customers.

Experience brands build two-way relationships

We can all agree that if a consumer feels strongly about your brand – strongly enough to personally recommend it to many others – you have succeeded in achieving the golden brand bond. The trust and powerful connection between your brand and your customer is an indicator that a genuine relationship has been established. For example, if you went to a dinner date and were not able to 'get a word in', you would assume the person you were with was not interested in you. Likewise, from a consumer perspective, brands that only talk *at* people, not *with* them, are not going to develop long-term relationships with their consumers or drive brand advocacy. There is a sense that the brand doesn't care. Two-way engagement experiences are the key to establishing deep and long-lasting relationships with people who trust and recommend brands to their peers.

Summary

We looked at:

- traditional tools and why some are losing effectiveness;

- increasingly tech-driven generations X, Y and Z and acceleration of innovation in tech;

- how the 'internet of things' (IoT) and a notable shift towards data analysis is driving increased personalization and bespoke experiential communications;

- how integrated marketing communications can work so well together when applied in an experiential style;

- budgets – increasingly shifting away from advertising and towards an experiential approach to marketing and activating brands;

- consumers – making higher demands from brands in terms of the authenticity and transparency of their communication.

Notes

1 Smilansky, S (2017) Excerpt from an interview with Rodolfo Aldana, Director of Tequila, Diageo

2 Campaign Insight and ESA (2015) [accessed 23 May 2017] Sponsorship Report: Is Official Dead? [Online] https://sponsorship.org/resources/brand-republic-esa-expert-report-is-official-dead

3 Forbes (2016) [accessed 2 January 2017] The World's Most Valuable Brands [Online] https://www.forbes.com/powerful-brands/

4 Smilansky, S (2017) Excerpt from an interview with Barbara Bahns, Head of Regional Marketing Planning and Communications CEE, Visa Inc

5 Bellwether Report (2017) [accessed 27 August 2017] *Institute of Practitioners in Advertising, IPA* [Online] http://www.ipa.co.uk/page/ipa-bellwether-report#.WaIXZiiGNPYv

6 Campaign Insight [accessed 29 August 2017] Marketing in the Age of the Customer [Online] http://www.campaignlive.co.uk/insight/marketing-in-the-age-of-the-customer

A whole new world

Millennials, brand experiences and social media

Millennials, Gen Z and beyond

Marketers are finding, through extensive research, that traditional media channels and one-way communications are losing their effectiveness. This can be attributed to many different factors such as generations X, Y and Z, media fragmentation, noise/clutter and the emergence of interactive technologies. Millennials, aka 'the internet generation' or generation Y (those born between 1980 and 1995) now account for over one in three working adults. They are a media-savvy generation adverse to obvious marketing and advertising ploys.

Interview excerpt: media fragmentation and the rise of experiential marketing

Barbara Bahns, Head of Regional Marketing Planning and Communications CEE, Visa Inc

If you look at how fragmented the world has actually become, in terms of media consumption, in terms of how consumers interact with brands, what I'm seeing more and more is that in order to actually cut through it is virtually impossible, because it is very expensive. Experiential marketing actually allows you to make an impact on a much smaller scale but with a much higher brand engagement.[1]

This is the social media generation. While mass media and traditional advertising are being shunned by this demographic, social networking media such as Instagram, Snapchat and YouTube are growing in their importance exponentially, and demonstrate the power of content and influencers in driving word of mouth. Gen Z (those born after 1995) are cut from a truly digital cloth, as they were born during a time that 'the net' prevailed. They could be said to literally 'speak internet', often using social media terminology within their speech during everyday conversations and through the increasingly sophisticated language of emoticons and emojis. They are a consumer group who live in the moment, and have contributed to the growth of disposable, temporary and instant content, as advocated by platforms such as Snapchat.

They also demand a far greater degree of transparency from brands, leading to an increased focus on authenticity and the importance of corporate social responsibility (CSR) within brand strategy. As marketers, we must think creatively and engage with consumers in ways that make them want – and allow them to opt into – brand communication. We want them to choose not only to receive and partake in messages, but to communicate back with the brand and their immediate peers and networks.

'For Gen Y/millennials, shopping is top entertainment, it's all about emotions and experiences.' Gen Y consumers are definitely emotional consumers. When Van den Bergh and Behrer did a study of Gen Y attitudes to brands, they carefully examined over 5,000 stories and said: '72 per cent contained positive emotions such as happiness, surprise, excitement, peacefulness, etc. Compare that figure to the poor 29 per cent of stories that referred to functional product characteristics, and you'll understand the point' (Van den Bergh and Behrer, 2013).[2]

In 1982, Scott Fahlman became the first to propose the use of :-) 'for jokes' in e-mails and :-(for 'things that are no joke' in a message to the Carnegie Mellon university computer-science general board. Things have definitely come a long way since, and real life and social life are increasingly merging inseparably.

Live brand experiences combined with social media

Experiences in the real world are engaging and memorable. For this reason, live brand experiences drive brand differentiation, brand equity and business results. We know social media is everywhere. It seeps into our daily lives: we are snapping, posting, tweeting, pinning and Instagramming our everyday lives on social networks and then sharing it. But what is the value in combining the two activities? Katy Howell representing social media consultancy Immediate Future, and Shirra Smilansky representing experiential marketing agency Electrify, joined forces to commission a (2013) study and find out.

#LIVEBRANDSOCIAL study: detailed research, deeper thinking

Katy Howell from Immediate Future worked with Electrify to design a questionnaire that asked 1,000 people for their thoughts in the first comprehensive, nationwide survey of how, what and why live experiences and social media work together. We talked to those who have been active in both social media and live experiences. Our aim was to answer the big question: *By combining social and live experiences what more can we do to deliver better value for brands?*

Helping you plan

We have dug deep to uncover nuggets that will help you plan the optimal triggers for sharing and motivations for attending live experiences – data that helps you to evaluate the combined impact, delivering value right across the purchase path.

Beyond mobile

Nine out of ten people in the UK have a mobile phone, and over 80 per cent of 18–44 year olds have a smartphone. How does this influence the way we consider designing a live experience? Especially when over 20 million Brits use mobile smartphones to connect to social networks – giving you a chance to reach a wider audience. This research, based on survey data, gives you a rock-solid foundation for planning and evaluating when integrating social with live experiences. Live brand experiences combined with social media generate greater results than each on their own. Identifying and understanding this beautiful relationship creates a number of valuable opportunities for your brand.

Do live brand experiences combined with social media deliver tangible results?

The short answer is yes! Over half of the consumers questioned said they would buy a product or service as a result of live brand experiences combined with social media. Whilst those who participated in the experience may have the opportunity to buy on site, many (45 per cent) went on to purchase at a later date. The propensity to purchase was also stimulated in those who just heard about the live experience through social networks, but didn't attend; 42 per cent bought after the experience as a consequence of seeing the live experience on social media.

Loyalty and relationships

Over one-third (38 per cent) of consumers told us that they become regular customers as a result of live brand experiences combined with social media (Figure 2.1). One-third (33 per cent) will go on to write a positive review about the brand. Customer retention is paramount in today's competitive landscape. It is satisfying to note that the live experience, when coupled with social, drives longer-term behavioural change – ultimately delivering extended value.

Figure 2.1   Brand experiences and social media drive repeat business

SOURCE Immediate Future and Electrify (2013) #LIVEBRANDSOCIAL study

Applying the integrated experiential methodology to the purchase funnel

AIDA is an acronym and a long-standing hierarchical model used in marketing since the 19th century. It describes a process that marketers aim to take the consumer through when marketing a product or service:

AIDA

Awareness: the attention or awareness of the customer.

Interest: we traditionally raise consumer interest by creating public conversation or demonstrating features and benefits.

Desire: convince customers that they want the product or service and that it will satisfy their needs.

Action: the all-important stage leading customers towards a purchase (communications with a call to action (CTA) are mostly used here).

There have been other additions to the AIDA model, such as 'S' for satisfaction: satisfy the customer so that he or she becomes a repeat customer and recommends the product. This shift is in line with the emerging focus and emphasis on advocacy – word-of-mouth and personal recommendations that come from building deeper relationships, and ideally 'golden bonds' with your customers. Referral strategies that have grown businesses – such as Uber – organically and with very little or no advertising are demonstrating the power of word of mouth and recommendations.

'A' for awareness

Live brand experiences, especially when integrated into a broader experiential marketing strategy and combined with social media, can be effective for achieving each of the AIDA stages. Take 'A' for awareness. Live brand experiences are sometimes accused of being ineffective at reaching large numbers of consumers, but this is far from the truth. In some situations, the live brand experience – which is at the core of the experiential campaign (in many cases the live brand experience is delivered face to face) – may only have a reach of around 500,000 people. This figure should not be taken at face value, because it has been shown that consumers who engage in a live brand experience are likely to tell many others. Therefore, that 500,000 can quickly grow into millions. Word of mouth is truly the most effective marketing tool of all.

'I' for interest

Live brand experiences can certainly be used in the 'I' stage of AIDA, in order to create interest by engaging consumers; not only demonstrating features, advantages and benefits of a product, but more importantly interacting with the *Target Audience* through brand-relevant, authentic engagement. There is no better way to stimulate interest and convey a *Brand Personality* or message than to allow consumers to immerse themselves in the essence of the brand as well as to try the product, play around with it, eat it, drink it, touch it or press it.

It does not matter what the product is: if you can convey its core brand values and transport the product or service into the everyday lives of your *Target Audience* through pleasant interaction, and at the same time engage them and let them try it, then you can truly demonstrate your brand positioning, and your unique selling propositions (USPs), converting a customer into an advocate.

'D' is for desire

Likewise, you can also use live brand experiences at the 'D' stage in AIDA, to provoke desire by creating experiences that communicate the aspirations of the *Target Audience*, creating the subconscious sense that using the product or service will bring them the lifestyle that they desire.

'A' is for action

Sales promotion is traditionally a tool that is effective at driving people to action and leading the consumer towards taking a final purchase decision (especially when that decision to purchase is primarily influenced by cost). Statistics show that live brand experiences (which should be placed at the core of the experiential marketing strategy, especially when combined with social media) are more likely to drive purchase decisions than almost any other marketing channel.

An experiential approach to channel planning

When planning your marketing channels around the AIDA or AIDAS model, it is important to approach every channel with an experiential marketing ethos. If you embrace *Two-Way* experiential marketing communication and place the live brand experience (delivered face to face or remotely) at the core of your broader marketing communications strategy, the results will speak for themselves.

Viral efforts related to events

Freeman XP Viral Study findings show the primary social engagement goals are to drive attendance and then reach attendees on site during events.[3] A secondary, emerging trend that many leading companies are already focused on is to reach applicable industry members, prospects and influencers who may not attend the events. The importance of marketing social content is also suggested in the finding that 50 per cent of leading event marketers and exhibitors have a specific budget for viral efforts (see Figure 2.2). In addition, 53 per cent of brands and exhibitors are increasing their spending on social efforts, and 44 per cent expect their spend to remain at the current level in the next budget cycle with almost no brands decreasing their spend. Also, 53 per cent of the survey respondents say they measure their event-related viral impact.

The survey respondents are from large companies in consumer products, tech, pharmaceutical, financial services, automotive, entertainment and

Figure 2.2   The impact of events going viral

According to a study by Freeman XP, viral efforts combined with events are important to top marketers, but a small percentage feel they are currently being deployed effectively.

SOURCE Based on research by Freeman XP & Event Marketing Institute (2015) The Viral Impact of Events Extending and Amplifying Event Reach via Social Media

media: 70 per cent have total revenue over $500 million; 37 per cent have over $10 billion in annual sales; 62 per cent are consumer focused (or both); and 38 per cent are primarily business-to-business (B2B) brands.

CASE STUDY

Taco Bell Snapchat lens

Contagious I/O reported on how to celebrate Cinco de Mayo in the United States, Tex-Mex restaurant Taco Bell partnered with Snapchat to create a branded lens that let users turn their face into a giant taco shell. Ryan Rimsnider, Taco Bell's senior manager of social strategy, told Contagious I/O: 'The brief was about finding something that is contagious, something that drives playtime and makes people use it not just once, but multiple times. Ultimately, we were hoping this would be something they would want to share and talk about. We didn't want it to feel like an ad because that wouldn't be right for the Snapchat community.' The lens was viewed 224 million times in just one day, and is the top campaign in Snapchat's history.[4]

Figure 2.3   Brand experiences with social media drive sales

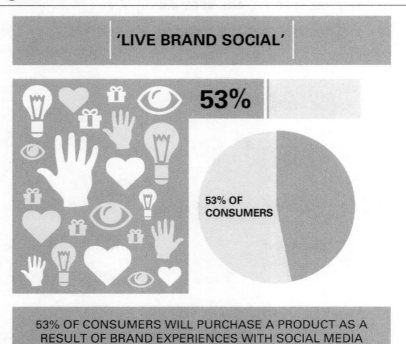

SOURCE Immediate Future and Electrify (2013), #LIVEBRANDSOCIAL study

#LIVEBRANDSOCIAL study summarized

Before, during and after

Social fits snuggly into a live experience. During the event you can extend the reach by increasing the brand chatter with live content (see Figure 2.3).

Tell them about it

Useful information. You can actively impact social media coverage and raise awareness beyond the physical event. But what about before and after?

Before – digital influence is social

When asked what online material has influenced attendance at a live experience, social networks came out top. Almost-two thirds (61 per cent) say that they find out about an event because a friend told them about it. But over half (56 per cent) find out about a live experience because of social media.

After – it's a chance for a long-lasting relationship

Your customers want to connect. In fact, 37 per cent of consumers said they had joined a brand's social networking page or profile following a live experience. And one-quarter have asked their friends and family to join a brand's social page. But more than this, the relationship is a truly positive one and the emotional connection formed is deep, the multisensory experiences have imprinted long-lasting memories, and tapped into unconscious fantasies and aspirations. Around half (49 per cent) of all respondents we asked tell us they felt more positive about brands when they took part in live experiences with social. The opportunity exists to extend the activity into social media after the live experience, to enlist positive, more engaged brand followers and giving you a chance to continue speaking to customers on an ongoing basis.

How do we continue that dialogue?

What do we do to continue our dialogue with live brand experience participants effectively, after they have engaged with the brand? This is possible once these groups of engaged participants are in some form of 'club', and where all the data we gathered about them and the content we created with them during the live brand experience is now stored.

Interview excerpt: impact of continuing dialogue with live brand experience participants

Barbara Bahns, Head of Regional Marketing Planning and Communications CEE, Visa Inc

The power of one advocate is greater than say just 100 generic engagements.

I would rather have continued dialogue with an educated (brand-experienced) participant who knows what my brand is about. I would rather have one of those who are like advocates and 'get it', rather than having 100 who have signed up to a product or service but actually they don't really know what they have signed up for. The advocate will be so much more valuable: 1) this person will actually use the product because he/she understands it; and 2) at some point this person will influence maybe knowingly or unknowingly other people, by using the product or maybe talking about it, or friends seeing it.

The really big question is at the moment, because ultimately every business wants to know, what is my return on investment (ROI) on doing something like this? So when I do experiential, and let's say I did do the follow-up individually with participants with Facebook or Snapchat or whatever it may be, and I really can engage with these people – what is really interesting is looking at how we can evaluate the ROI behind this.[5]

Further to this, a 2016 article in *Marketing Week*[6] features Rachel Kavanagh, the UK and Ireland Managing Director for beauty subscription business Glossybox. Her following three quotes for them give a clear picture:

- 'How did the new wave of brands that have gone from zero to huge with no advertising budget build advocates? Community, personalization and *involving* these mini clubs or groups in further co-creating and influencing the brand with us.'

- 'One Glossybox subscriber speaks to five other people about what they got in their box, which is the new ROI – return on influence. We know user-generated content will drive our business.'

- 'Having a strong community is crucial for beauty subscription business Glossybox, where 80 per cent of acquisition comes via word of mouth on social media.'

Her predictions are for the next steps in influencer marketing to begin combining user-generated content with loyalty, following a gamification style or rewards mechanic. The Amazon model is leading this already, allowing customers to gain points in return for sharing reviews and influencing other shoppers. Kavanagh's discussion with *Marketing Week* closes with a succinct description of its merits:

- 'The Amazon loyalty programme is not based on purchase, but on whether what you write is helpful to the rest of the community. This encourages customers to create their own influence, which will be the next big step in e-commerce.'[7]

Interview excerpt: creating an influencer pyramid

Rodolfo Aldana, Director of Tequila, Diageo

We have an influencer pyramid where at the top you have either big celeb events or celebrities, then in the middle you have social media influencers who help propagate all that content, and create their own content. Then at the bottom, at the base, it is the consumers who want to receive and enjoy fast content.[8] (See Figure 2.4.)

Figure 2.4   The influencer pyramid

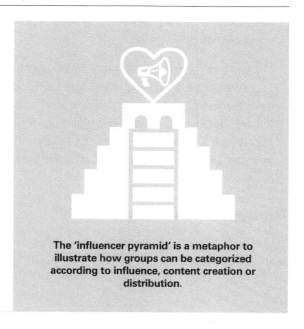

**celebrities/
talent
creators
sharers**

The 'influencer pyramid' is a metaphor to illustrate how groups can be categorized according to influence, content creation or distribution.

Translating a brand experience into the small screen

There is such a fantastic opportunity to consider the content carefully and truly design set/venue/event production with it in mind. Marketers and event producers alike are often guilty of forgetting that one of the most important goals of the physical environment design in a live brand experience is to be captured beautifully by what is most likely to be, a mobile phone.

Consumers today live on their mobiles, with more than half of UK smartphone users (53 per cent) checking their devices within five minutes of waking. Over half of smartphone owners regularly use their devices on public transport, at work and while shopping, according to Deloitte. Moreover, the increasing sophistication of smartphone's camera technology has established them as the primary device for personal recording and image making.

Vice President (VP) of global brand and creative Dany Atkins at Kodak states in an interview with *Creative Review*:

> David Bailey famously said 'the best camera is the one you have on you at the time' [and] the device most people have on them today is a phone.[9]

Interview excerpt: combining live brand experiences with social media

Max Abbott, National Brand Advocate Manager, Cellar Trends (global drinks brand portfolio)

The last few years has seen a real development in how much time and effort we put into these kind of experiential marketing initiatives and into trade marketing, and how much time and effort we spend on extending the experience onto social media platforms. All are areas of growing importance and I believe that we can use those platforms to communicate an experience in a very, very cost-effective way.[10]

Transparency is everything

In the Jack Morton report on the best brand experiences at Cannes, Tom Manion, Creative Director of Jack Morton in San Francisco states:

Event marketing brands that are naked win – brands that expose themselves to the world beyond just revealing their product are winning awards at Cannes – and winning the hearts and minds of the consumer. Today, people want to see meaningful action from brands, and they want to see it from within the organization. At Jack Morton, we believe that how brands act is more important than what they say, and events continue to be a powerful way for brands to expose themselves in an authentic way. Events bring us closer not just to the brand but also its people and its purpose.[11]

In an Eventbrite report by Booker, titled 'How to Plan Successful Experiential Marketing Campaigns', Adam Azor, Managing Director, Curb stated the following:

Experiential has become one of the most effective marketing disciplines. Its symbiotic relationship with content and social media has seen it become not just an alternative to traditional media but a powerful tool of modern marketing.[12]

Summary

The younger a consumer is, and the faster their network, the more likely they are to use their phones as they go about their day. These quick glances add up collectively, as UK consumers check their smartphones over 1 billion times per day. As mobile becomes their most important medium, it is unsurprising that brands are following them there, delivering experiences increasingly developed for mobile.

Notes

1 Smilansky, S (2017) Excerpt from an interview with Barbara Bahns, Head of Regional Marketing Planning and Communications CEE, Visa Inc

2 Van den Bergh, J and Behrer, M (2013) *How Cool Brands Stay Hot: Branding to Generation Y*, Kogan Page, London

3 Freeman XP and Event Marketing Institute (2015) [accessed 15 August 2017] The Viral Impact of Events, Extending and Amplifying Event Reach Via Social Media, Viral Study Summary [Online] http://cdn.freemanxp.com/documents/1382/the_viral_impact_of_events_study_freemanxp_and_emi_final.pdf

4 Raakhi Chotai (2016) [accessed 15 August 2017] Most Contagious 2016 Summary [Online] https://contagious-assets.s3.amazonaws.com/issues/20141218T115015-6715/Contagious-X.pdf

5 Smilansky, S (2017) Excerpt from an interview with Barbara Bahns, Head of Regional Marketing Planning and Communications CEE, Visa Inc

6 Rogers, C (2016) [accessed 7 July 2016] What's Next for Influencer Marketing? *Marketing Week*, 16 June [Online] https://www.marketingweek.com/2016/06/16/whats-next-for-influencer-marketing/

7 Rogers, C (2016) [accessed 7 July 2016] What's Next for Influencer Marketing? *Marketing Week*, 16 June [Online] https://www.marketingweek.com/2016/06/16/whats-next-for-influencer-marketing/

8 Smilansky, S (2017) Excerpt from an interview with Rodolfo Aldana, Director of Tequila, Diageo

9 Steven, R (2016) [accessed 25 April 2017] From The K to The Super 8, Why Kodak is Looking Back to Move Forward, *Creative Review* [Online] https://www.creativereview.co.uk/kodak-looked-past-new-logo-smartphone/

10 Smilansky, S (2017) Excerpt from an interview with Max Abbott, National Brand Advocate Manager, Cellar Trends (Global Drinks Brand Portfolio)

11 Jack Morton Worldwide (2016) [accessed 20 August 2017] Best of Brand Experience at Cannes Lions [Online] http://www.jackmorton.com/blog/the-best-of-brand-experience-at-cannes-lions/

12 Azor, A, featured in Booker, B (2017) [accessed 5 May 2017] How to Plan Successful Experiential Marketing Campaigns, *EventBrite* [Online] https://www.eventbrite.co.uk/blog/experiential-marketing-campaign-planning-ds00/

The experience economy is here   03

The importance of branding as a differentiator

In the business world, commoditization is a process where unique brands and products compete. As a result, standards are raised and equalized, forcing brands into undifferentiated price competition. In the early days of marketing and advertising, companies used to focus on differentiation based on the product features and benefits.

As competition forced rival brands to create competitive products, price wars began lowering the cost of products and driving consumers to make cost-based purchase decisions. Thanks to innovators in the mid-20th century such as Ogilvy, advertising was revolutionized and brands evolved, taking on unique personalities. Through customer-centric marketing communications, they encouraged consumers to aspire to a lifestyle that the brand represented. Thus began the shift from a product-focused era to the customer-focused, brand- and lifestyle-inspired advertising era. This marked a shift from a rational message to an emotional message, or a combination of both.

The service era

As competitive brands were increasingly positioned similarly to each other, and differentiation became difficult again, consumers started to demand more than just great branding. Successful companies realized that high-quality service was an excellent way to add value and differentiate themselves from their competitors. For example, by adding free delivery to a video chain or picking up customers from their home to take them to the car rental shop. As time went on, fierce competition snowballed with competitors all offering relatively similar added-value services with their products, or by adding relatively similar added-value products to their services. Lifestyle branding and differentiation through service became the norm. Again, once there are no clear points of differentiation, price becomes a primary differentiating factor. Clearly, this is not desirable from a marketing perspective.

Customer experience

The growing popularity during the late 20th century of relationship marketing, which focuses on long-term relationships with customers and customer retention, saw increased investment into customer relationship management (CRM) programmes that aim to drive customer loyalty through frequent communication and reward programmes. The next level of thinking on the subject of driving customer loyalty (and beyond loyalty towards advocacy and evangelism) is customer experience management (CEM).

CEM is defined as 'the process of strategically managing a customer's entire experience with a product or a company'. CEM is at the frontier of successful advocacy-driven relationship management programmes, taking companies into an era where the primary and most valuable way they can differentiate themselves is through an immersive, authentic and relevant brand experience at every customer touchpoint.

Successful CEM carefully orchestrates the consumer's experience with an organization and its brands, ensuring that every step of his or her journey (from the retail environment to the app to the packaging to the customer services) is brand relevant, authentic, differentiated and positive.

Real business growth

Experiential marketing allows brands to engage with their *Target Audiences* through initiatives and engagements that aim to achieve marketing communication objectives, and add value to consumers' lives. When CEM is partnered with experiential marketing (the innovative methodology that facilitates positive brand-relevant *Two-Way Interactions* with *Target Audiences*), astonishing business results can be achieved.

By successfully implementing a CEM orientation throughout every department of an organization, and then reaching out and communicating with *Target Audiences* through integrated experiential marketing, organizations can successfully convert consumers into brand advocates and ultimately evangelists. Today, products that are trying to differentiate through additional free services, or services that are trying to differentiate by additional free products, along with traditional CRM programmes, are all beginning to look like commodities. This is largely due to the full circle that business and marketing have made on their way back to human engagement and *Two-Way Interactions*. Experience is the new currency of the modern marketing landscape, because experiences are what make up our lives and we talk about our experiences every day.

A positive customer experience at every touchpoint in the journey

CEM is becoming one of the highest priorities in customer-centric organizations, where an experiential strategy is leading the way. Therefore, when you think about the volume of resources that you will want to invest in CEM and in experiential marketing, you should think of the overall scale of your organization and how to shift its orientation as a whole.

CASE STUDY

Apple continues to pioneer exceptional customer experience in-store

Another pioneering organization in terms of customer experience is Apple, which created a truly added-value, simplified and design-led experience for its customers. The simplified experience starts from the very beginning of their relationship with the brand, to every touchpoint along the way, from in-store, to online, to its customer service. It tackled several classic pain-points and ensured a positive added-value experience in the form of brand-immersive stores, free in-store workshops that bring to life all the available software, and staff who are themselves brand advocates. All of its efforts are designed to create lifelong advocacy inspired by its interaction with customers.

In this case, the consumers are not just shoppers who purchase the products, they are the people who sing the brand's praises, converting endless computer users by preaching the benefits of an alternative. When customers go into one of Apple's stores worldwide, they are made to feel as though they are in a music and gadget candy store, with the cinema-style screens and beautiful sets. Apple have built a playground for the modern adult and teenager alike. By educating and informing consumers through brand-relevant, engaging experiences, they create brand evangelists. The word of mouth, inspired through personal recommendations and lifestyle aspirations, is priceless.

Apple has managed to hit the nail on the head; not only because it has an experiential philosophy at its core, but also because it uses it as part of its retail environment. With cutting-edge design, education, added service and sensory elements, its stores are the platforms for inspiring customer experiences, and the store staff act as the *Brand Ambassadors*.

Customer-experience journey planning

Companies like Apple are not the only brands to take experiential marketing to the next level and continuously place the experiential strategy at the core of their overall strategies. Increasingly, countless other global brands such as adidas, Red Bull, Singapore Airlines, Sony, Bombay Sapphire, Asahi, Diageo, and Smirnoff, position brand-relevant experiences at the core of their entire communications strategies.

Customer experience journeys provide a deeper understanding of customers, their feelings, and how they engage with brands. Observing, documenting and analysing the customer experience through the customer perspective enables brands to understand customer interactions throughout the customer experience and how best to strengthen their relationship with that individual customer. This applies not only to areas such as customer service, but also to the pre-purchase and recommendation stages, enabling companies to present relevant, contextual content and personalized experiences to customers, also supporting advocacy, referrals and word of mouth.

Customer-experience journey work requires a positive and collaborative culture of cross-functional collaboration. Sharing responsibility for customer journeys across functions can help companies to modernize their customer journey efforts and transform their organizations. This means adopting a higher-level journey strategy that will focus on understanding customers. An analytical mindset will help companies to identify and optimize opportunities to retain customers, drive incremental purchases and encourage positive word of mouth.

Data gets smart and drives real-time behavioural insights

A Forrester and IBM report, Customer Journey Study Marketing, talks of how pioneering businesses with forward-thinking perspectives on customer experience are using real-time insights to drive accountability across functions.[1] Such companies see the fantastic potential impact of truly engaging customers, understanding them deeply, and demonstrating that experience mapping and journey work requires strategic cross-functional collaboration and accountability from different departments within the organization such as marketing, customer experience, customer service, sales, and business technology professionals. But the report highlighted how the marketing function should take the reins and lead the way for other departments to follow suit – almost 60 per cent of respondents, said that marketing leads journey mapping and analysis in their organizations.[2]

CASE STUDY

Experience as a point of difference

Sam is a marketing director at a leading petrol company that has recently opened a coffee shop in each of its larger outlets, but was struggling to differentiate without competing on price. Service was originally its key differentiator and is what allowed it to charge a higher premium for its services in the past. Its competitors had become wise to this, and improved their service, providing little room for differentiation and lack of justification for the higher price.

By adding a positive added value and brand-relevant experience, Sam hoped that he could appeal to the commuter who spends long hours on the road and wants to stop for a refreshing, high-quality cup of coffee on their way home.

The challenge

Sam knew he would have to position the brand as a quality choice for premium coffee and sandwiches, as well as petrol – three things that traditionally do not go hand in hand. He knew from the market research that their agency conducted that when consumers refuelled, they often sought a little caffeine to help them stay awake on the road.

Yet, the research also uncovered that consumers wouldn't trust the quality of the coffee, and historically have been less likely to purchase coffee from a petrol station than other outlets. Therefore, customers tended to visit the petrol station with the cheapest petrol rather than the best coffee.

Approach

The agency creative team came up with the suggestion of creating a live brand experience that could be rolled out across most of the stations.

Sam had overlooked the importance of the fact that the coffee beans they used were purchased from fair-trade sources. The experiential campaign would position the coffee brand as being one that cares for people and the environment, adding credibility by only using fair-trade organic coffee beans and freshly grinding the beans for each cup of coffee.

Putting it into action

As an authentically environmentally friendly brand that gives back to the community, the coffee bar was redesigned to show photos of the rainforest farmers who harvest the coffee beans, and gave consumers the chance to win trips to visit the rainforest coffee plants, by answering questions about fair-trade coffee and endangered regions.

The consumers were also provided with a free sample of coffee when they purchased their fuel, and were encouraged to sign up to a 'care and share' loyalty card that donated money to relevant charities every time they filled their tanks.

The broader Digital Outdoor Media campaign was also designed to reflect this initiative, focusing on the fact that the brand and its customers were working hard to counteract and offset the negative effect that the petroleum industry has on the environment and labour.

The petrol stations were also fitted with scent machines that emitted the smell of freshly ground coffee beans, further strengthening the front-of-mind affiliation between fair-trade quality coffee and the petrol outlet.

Outcome

Following this integrated campaign there was a dramatic uplift in the number of customers who bought coffee as well as fuel when visiting this chain of petrol stations. At this point, the premium rate they were paying became less significant, and the competitive pressure and commoditization on the brand eased.

The reason that this petrol-station company wanted to position itself as a caring, environmentally oriented brand was to try to counteract the perceptions that consumers have of the negative effects that petrol and oil cause to the environment, and also the affiliation with lower-quality food.

By using the live brand experience concept as part of a creative integrated campaign – designed to bring the consumers closer to the brand personality of its coffee shop – it also managed to reposition the brand as a whole. This brought it one step closer to succeeding in its corporate goal of increasing sales and differentiating itself from the competition.

A raised level of business consciousness

This raised level of business consciousness we are experiencing around the world has elevated business into the experience economy, as originally predicted by Pine and Gilmore.[3] The experience economy and the dawn of the experiential marketing era is here; the consumer and the employees of a company are equally part of its marketing efforts as its agencies and marketing department (see Figure 3.1).

Figure 3.1 Investing in customer experience as a top priority

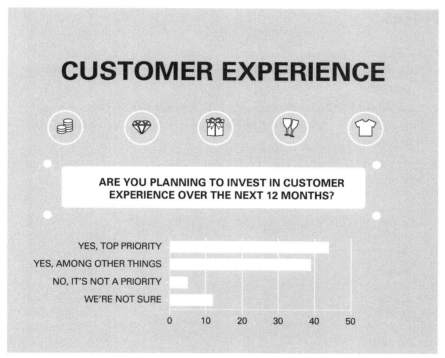

SOURCE Campaign Insight, 2016 [Online] http://www.campaignlive.co.uk/insight/taking-back-control

Summary

We have noted the change in the business era we have entered, from one where added service meant added value, to an era where the traditional product and service concept has gone through its own commoditization, and that this has resulted in the dawn of the new business era.

Experience-driven organizations are now rising to the top due to:

- offering their consumers great products and services;
- providing a superior customer experience at every touchpoint;
- using authentic brand-relevant experiences effectively, which act as a unique differentiator.

We have seen how this enables a competitive market to maintain stand-out players that can get away with premium prices, and maintain a loyal customer base and stable market share.

Notes

1 Forrester/IBM [accessed 27 August 2017] Customer Journey Study [Online] https://www.ibm.com/think/marketing/why-journey-maps-lead-to-improved-engagement/

2 Forrester/IBM [accessed 27 August 2017] Customer Journey Study [Online] https://www.ibm.com/think/marketing/why-journey-maps-lead-to-improved-engagement/

3 Pine, B J and Gilmore, J H (1999) *The Experience Economy*, Harvard Business School Press, Boston

Concept stores, the future of retail and pop-ups 04

The changing face of retail

Retail has changed enormously over the past 15 years. The financial crash of 2008 saw countless household names go bust, leaving their once shiny, busy stores looking like depressing, empty shells. With recession killing off not only stores but also businesses, even offices started to vacate, leaving building owners footing the rates and bills in the absence of tenants.

The doom and gloom, post-apocalyptic-style barren movie scene of the high streets and business districts in major global cities did not last long, and like a plant growing from the cracks in broken concrete, the once desperate state of the commercial property scene paved the way for creativity and independent players. Pop-ups from start-ups replaced high-street chains, co-working hot-desk spaces filled empty offices with ambitious and inspired millennials, and fusion retailing where anyone from a barber, barista and bedroom brand would team up, created fun and unique 'destination' shopping.

Rise of the smartphone era

As the demise of the few was superseded by the rise of the many, another phenomenon was taking place. Smartphones with friendly interfaces and accessible internet became so prolific that accessing the internet from mobile phones overtook the desktop, and with 2.1 billion adults owning a smartphone worldwide,[1] e-commerce became a must for every brand. Digital shopping gave brands direct access to their consumers in ways that were previously reserved for only those with their own expensive bricks and mortar, who could finally skip out the retailers who stocked their products, giving them access to the masses, and the rise of direct to consumer (D2C).

With millennials and Gen Zs – in contrast to Gen X and baby boomers – intent on consulting each other and reverting to reading online reviews before making even quite simple purchase decisions, what is to become of the physical store environment? Once one might have argued that it was the immediacy provided by a physical store, where you could walk out with the item on the spot – rather than wait for its delivery – that kept stores alive. Nowadays, the logistical revolution and rise of speedy one-day and even one-hour delivery slots has arguably killed that dream.

Store-y telling

Retail across the board has become a deeper, more entertaining and customer-relevant experience – from Rapha cycling clubs to IKEA dining-club pop-ups – despite the convenience of clicks over bricks, research from Deloitte confirmed the high street still retains a far greater portion of all transactions (above e-commerce). Interestingly they also reported conversion is 20 per cent higher when shoppers use digital interactions alongside their store visit.

The goal is to bring our digital and physical worlds together, allowing them to complement each other harmoniously and deliver on the expectations of the empowered and demanding customers of today and tomorrow.

The new question has become – if it is so much easier and more convenient to purchase online – and if even luxury, pricey products that once one would have been so confident needed to be seen and touched in person (think Net-a-Porter) were flying off the virtual shelves – then what is the point of stores at all? The question invites us to envisage 'the store of the future', a destination by choice and driven by our basic needs to be entertained, educated or amused, to be social, to escape the mundane and immerse ourselves in a 360-degree, multisensory 4D interpretation of the brand who invited us there.

Interview excerpt: brands must add value and engage

Beatrice Descorps, Global Vice President of Marketing, Molton Brown

The luxury customer wants to see brands that have depth, the same depth you would expect when you are talking to someone. If you want communication to be meaningful, you have to discover more, remove the layers and see there is a real core substance – that is what they are after really and the way you demonstrate this is through the overall experience.

There has been a big shift; before it used to be that you had your luxury brands and the customers had to fit in. They had to 'comply with', they had to 'bend to fit in' whereas now the customer is central. He or she expects that brands adapt to be relevant to them, to be almost bespoke to them, to have a relationship with the brand rather than 'serving the brand'.[2]

An omni-experience retail future

The store of the future must offer more than products and the opportunity to touch, feel, try on and take away. These functions are increasingly fulfilled by ever-developing conveniences, and enhanced e-commerce customer experience is becoming a mandatory prerequisite for being a player in the retail landscape.

In 2017, 60 per cent of the expected \$3.7 trillion in US retail sales will take place on PCs, mobiles or tablets, or be influenced by research on devices, and 35 per cent of mobile device owners who said they are 'not recent shoppers' accessed mobile phones while in-store to check prices.[3]

The role of the store of the future goes well beyond the facilitation of purchase, and has becomes more akin to inviting consumers to enter the personal home of a new or old friend: an invitation to enter the personal and expressive world where every scent can trigger a memory and associated emotion – where the personality shines through with every design choice, decor and in the objects curated in the space.

The accessibility of convenience shopping creates a greater demand for great experience

Shopping has become an intimate opportunity to experience through the senses, through participation, and to spend time by choice *not* necessity. The store of the future is in fact far less of a shop and more of a brand *space*. A space with a purpose, a blank canvas not so different to the 20 metre by 20 metre floor areas in malls that brands can hire to create an event. Really, these spaces offer brands with a home that can play host to live brand experiences that express an authentic truth and can be invented and reinvented as necessary to stay relevant and exciting. These experiences are made to add value to their consumers in the same way experiential marketing initiatives have always set out to do.

Multi-brand collaborations capture hearts and minds

Multi-brand collaborations with complementary lifestyle services are also thriving already. From eating and drinking, to playing and learning, stores of the future do not just do one thing, they do many – lifestyle destinations that offer brands an opportunity to collaborate with each other, joining forces with other complementary services and products to carefully curate a physical reflection of their 'inner brand worlds'.

The main purposes of the stores and shopping malls of the future are:

- To provide customers with an added-value, brand-relevant, positive experience.
- The experience itself can be designed to invite the consumer to explore, be entertained, amused, inspired and educated – or a mix of them all.
- The experience will – as all experiences do – ignite feelings, inspire action and fuel word of mouth.

Manufacturing and technological advancements change corporate mindsets

This shift to a customer-centric approach has also been fuelled by the vast improvements in manufacturing that have led to a rise in speedy, on-demand production. This was pioneered by Zara who sacrificed some margin in favour of less wastage and the ability to react to trends quickly and give customers more of what they *really* want, and therefore, buy. Stock manufacturing by such players is often handled more locally so it can be scaled up or down according to real-time purchasing data. Therefore, despite higher costs per item, they are winning, thus revolutionizing and rapidly accelerating the journey from 'factory to fashion'.

The four key facets of the retail-experience revolution

This chapter explores how this experience and customer-led retail revolution is expressed in four key facets and how they apply, with examples from leading and emerging brands across all sectors, from fashion to fitness, to automotive, tech and luxury (Figure 4.1).

Figure 4.1   The retail-experience revolution: four key facets

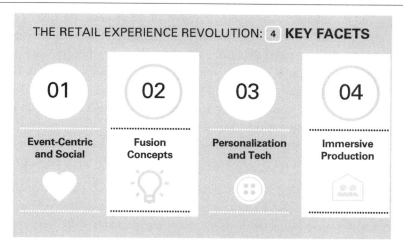

Key facet #1: 'event-centric and social'

Many disruptive, event-oriented stores are winning the race by generating brand advocacy, and even brand evangelism from their customers by creating activity programming and production that inspires content, social sharing and positive PR. It is still shockingly apparent how many bricks-and-mortar retailers are still behind the times, and you will find that, in a large majority of chain retail stores, customers will be chastised and ejected from the shops for taking photos of their retail set-ups (for fear they are in fact rival brand spies).

It is understandable that brands would not want their competitors or their competitors' retail agencies spying on their hard work and unique set-ups, but at what price? In the age where customer is king, content is social currency and enticing customers to capture, snap and share is the ultimate goal, this stern approach to taking pictures and videos is unmistakably old-fashioned and one would expect a practice reserved for retail stalwart. However, that is not the case, and content-friendly stores designed with social media as the priority, not as an after-thought or impossibility, are still reserved for the forward-thinking, disruptive and experientially minded few, and it is they who are taking over at lightning speed.

The following few examples from a variety of global brands demonstrate facet #1: 'event-centric and social'. These unique store environments are bringing their brands to life and mobilizing their visitors, resulting in brand love and devotion.

Missguided #IRL – example

Missguided is a global online fashion retailer, aimed at 'generation Snapchat'. It is truly loved by its fashion-forward fans. Missguided was founded in the UK in 2008 with the view that fashion is 'a right not a luxury' and offers affordable prices to 160 countries worldwide. The brand inspires its young clientele with fast-changing trend-led fashion and inspiration from an array of global influencers, from the A-list to sometimes unexpected fashion icons (Pamela Anderson had her own range in recent years).

The brand has a strong alignment with social media (its ad campaign messages are almost always delivered through colloquial 'internet speak'):

- Dispelling myths that the future of retail is purely digital, Missguided made a reverse 'clicks to bricks' move with a high-impact debut into physical retail, creating an Instagrammable, Snapchattable, fun, inviting and fast-changing store experience.

- Their 'On Air' store concept was designed to provide shoppers with a live, experiential version of the brand's online social media-led vibe, naturally welcoming their 16- to 35-year-old target customers to capture the unique and interactive environment.

- The space delivers a dynamic live stream of real-time social media content, fashion and inspiration. The space features a series of bold and visually impactful and wow-factor installations that create naturally shareable moments.

Dalziel and Pow, the designers of the space, explain that it has:

> Social interaction at the heart of the concept, Missguided makes the brave move of bringing fitting rooms to the front of the store – recasting this area as an interactive lounge space, complete with emojis and tongue-in-cheek signage. Inspired by a glamorous Miami Beach pool party, palm trees surround the space and a swimming pool animation is projected onto the ceiling, while a concierge adds to the VIP feel. Comfy seating areas encourage groups of friends to spend time showing off looks and exploring their personal style.

> With this empowering, bold and accessible destination, Missguided offers a seamless online/offline retail experience for its hyper-connected, fashion-hungry fans.

adidas Studio LDN – example

This east London-based fitness studio located in Shoreditch's trendy Brick Lane is much more than just a store:

- The space invites women to 'Unleash their Creativity' while it brings its brand to life, communicating the *Message – Key Communication* for the event-led concept store: 'Be Powerful, Kick Ass, Defy the Status Quo'.

- The studio welcomes participants to co-create and share their passion for sport, fitness and life with workshops that include inspiring fitness classes, local-run clubs powered by adidas runners, creative sport and nutrition talks, and new product testing, amongst other innovative event initiatives.

- Classes and event attendance can even be registered via conversing with their Facebook messenger chatbot.

Lululemon – example

Canadian athletic apparel retailer Lululemon's stores, which often spread over multiple floors, aim to transform the traditional retail experience – with a cafe, complimentary yoga classes and even an in-store concierge on standby to assist in their lifestyle and shopping space:

- Visitors are welcomed at the in-store concierge desk, which is designed to tailor each shopper experience to their personal desires. Advice is not limited to products on sale, as the concierges can advise on other local interest activities and events that reflect the healthy, active and fit Lululemon brand personality and their customers' lifestyles.

- Changing rooms feature seamless technology that includes features such as digital installations that detect movement from the yoga mats positioned in front.

- These transform participants' yoga poses into beautiful, bold and colourful digital art impressions. As if that wasn't futuristic enough, the reflective fabrics on their garments are even highlighted by striking laser beams!

Uniqlo London – example

Uniqlo's London flagship store spans six floors and features a rooftop terrace designed exclusively for events:

- Two of its floors show off concept space 'Life WearHouse', which acts as a separate cultural activity hub and boasts its own street-level entrance.

- The two floors are regularly transformed to showcase changing themes and reflect Uniqlo's LifeWear range while using futuristic technology to give guests a chance to interact with the brand's new products and ideas before they are rolled out en masse.

- This is a great example of how inviting brand fans to interact and input into a brand taps into the human desire to influence, which in turn creates brand advocacy and drives positive word of mouth, creating a powerful relationship and the magical golden bond.

Key facet #2: 'fusion concepts'

By fusing seemingly disparate products, services and experiences, multi-brand retailing is setting the pace for added-value customer-centric lifestyle experiences. In London's Redchurch Street, it is now more unusual to see a menswear brand without a barista and a barber than one with. This makes sense as they have found that getting men to shop for expensive clothes in person is easier with the added allure of a rare-roast artisan coffee or a cut from a qualified coiffure!

The examples that follow examine some of the world's most forward-thinking and pioneering retail brands, effectively demonstrating Key facet #2: fusion concepts', and showcasing 'how to do multi-brand, right'.

Colette – example

Colette in Paris is a figurehead for concept stores, and a fantastic example of a pioneering multi-brand, lifestyle destination and concept store that has long captured the imagination of countless visitors and influenced tastemakers across the globe:

- The Parisian store features three levels of the latest avant-garde art, tech, fashion and desirable 'stuff'. Appealing to the kid and collector alike, its display has everything from the beautifully unnecessary to the futuristic and functional.
- Colette boasts a stunningly curated collection of 'stuff' in its iconic and eye-catching staple design style. The space includes a gallery, candle bar, beauty department and even Japanese-style lucky-dip bags.
- Colette is also home to a water bar, which serves over 90 different brands of water.

Graanmarkt 13 – example

Graanmarkt 13, located in an Antwerp townhouse, is a true global pioneer in fusion concept and multi-brand retailing, featuring a restaurant, gallery, and even an apartment and store in one home-like setting:

- The ground floor houses a store with fashion, collectibles and carefully curated items and there is a gallery space that is styled like a home and used to host events.

- The space has a welcoming feeling, having once actually been the home of owners Ilse Cornelissens and Tim Van Geloven.

- The top floor is now an apartment available to rent, while an award-winning chef hosts the basement food offering.

Seven Rooms – example

Seven Rooms, also located in Antwerp, comprises a large, white loft space that has been partitioned into seven different spaces, each representing different lifestyle areas:

- There is a bedroom, kitchen, living room, library, garden, bathroom and walk-in closet. Each houses a small selection of curated items from fashion to homewares and fragrance. The purpose of the layout is to give shoppers a relaxed, slow and enjoyable experience, even offering drinks and snacks from the kitchen.

- The white plinth and podium product displays create a fresh, clean gallery-style atmosphere; a perfect backdrop for the independent and high-end designer items on show.

- Despite a definite understated elegance, Seven Rooms makes visitors feel they would happily move in and live there, a sign its guests are certainly right at home.

- The space plays hosts to regular events and exhibitions, collaborating and showcasing innovative artists, musicians and designers.

H&M Barcelona – example

H&M's Barcelona flagship store is huge, and the brand's first-ever store to feature a food offering, thanks to a partnership with Flax & Kale:

- With all of H&M's clothing, kids, home and beauty ranges displayed via unique fixtures and fittings made from a mix of premium and unusual materials, it forms a mini H&M world under one roof.

- It is a complete one-stop experience for the whole family, and one that demonstrates how fusion and concept retailers are starting to appear less like shops and more like members' clubs meet destination department stores.

Topshop London – example

The iconic Topshop and Topman flagship store sits at the heart of London's Oxford Circus. A real pioneer in global concept multi-brand retailing, the store has famously welcomed an enormous array of global A-list style icons. This was not an easy feat for a mid-range high-street fashion brand, which as far as the mid 1990s had almost entirely lost relevance with its audience:

- Long gone are those days, and the three floors at Topshop have anything and everything you could dream of, from nail salons to fashion shows and blow-dry bars, the store even famously helps break emerging fashion designers with its much-loved independent fashion and vintage concessions.

- Its in-store experience is second to none, and it pioneered added-value services such as personal shoppers and VIP lounges well before the counterpart rival chains attempted the same.

- Topshop and Topman appeal to a wide age range and a global clientele, with the flagship store even offering a cafe lounge area to rest tired legs after a long day shopping. It truly exemplifies destination shopping, and after a visit to Topshop (which could easily span an entire day), it would be surprising if a visitor felt the need to go anywhere else.

Hermes Singapore – example

Hermes's Singapore flagship at Liat Towers marked a real metamorphosis for the brand after it relaunched the revolutionary concept store:

- The space fuses luxury shopping with art, following 15 months of renovation. The window displays feature an art installation from artists around the world, turning its fascia into a show-stopping cultural attraction.

- The top floor named 'Aloft at Hermes' is also a fusion art gallery and exhibition space, while the third floor is named the Hermes Home Universe.

- The flagship store shows off a beautiful exterior blue facade and its iconic Hermes firework-maker on horseback. With his hands raised to the sky and his silk scarves fluttering in the wind, he is featured as a proud sculpture on the roof of the building.

- Boasting limited-edition items through coveted collaborations, it veers away from what could have been 'yet another' Hermes luxury product display, melding its luxurious products (everything from the usual clothing and accessories to writing and stationery products and the brand's equestrian range) with art and installations.

- The Singapore delight is a bold, disruptive world inviting guests to enter and discover the Hermes lifestyle as a unique and inspiring cultural destination.

O2 – example

O2 is Britain's second-largest mobile telecommunications provider, counting over 23 million customers. It runs 2G, 3G and 4G networks across the UK and operates over 450 retail stores. O2's concept stores invite customers on any mobile network, not just their customers, to reimagine the once hair-raisingly frustrating experience of shopping for a mobile phone, to one where they can in fact skip the shopping entirely:

- A true 'destination' concept, fusing a home-style, large community workspace table that offers complimentary coffees, with what has become a physical counterpart to the brand's experience-led 'O2 Priority' world, this acts as a gateway for members to gain exclusive access to events and entertainment.

- The space has a modular and changeable format, including digital screens and areas dedicated to hosting interactive brand takeovers with partner content from other brands such as movie studios and other content partners.

- The 'inspiration zone' invites consumers to 'discover' and enjoy, as interactive messaging and illustrated animations are projected onto the community tables, where visitors can relax, socialize, work or charge their phones and laptops.

- 'Expressing local culture', another theme emerging frequently amongst future retail pioneers, is a central part of the O2 concept and embedded into every execution, including local storytelling on hoardings, used for pre-promoting store openings as they arrive in each city.

Notcutts Garden Centres – example

Notcutts is one of Britain's leading garden centre chains. Once a traditional garden store, Notcutts wanted to transform the garden centre experience, and turn their spaces into a complete lifestyle destination for families:

- It did so by uniquely creating 'The Kitchen' a 190-seat rustic, country-style restaurant concept, which overlooks 'The Plateria', a beautiful and lush green section to the store. The vintage, mismatched, homely furniture adds to the shabby chic, local feel.

- There is even a farm shop with local, regional, artisanal produce served from market stall-style counters and a real local butcher concession to boot.

- The Notcutts flagship is a real celebration of the country lifestyle, and one that turned a (plant shopping) and potentially mundane chore into a fun, family day out.

- The fusion and collaboration with local independent partners brings to life the charming Notcutts *Brand Personality*, thereby storytelling and engaging its guests while adding value to their day.

Key facet #3: 'personalization and tech'

The omni-channel/omni-experience retail revolution has created a dramatic shift from separate, siloed channels and an evident disconnect between online, own-brand stores and third-party retail, to a seamless, cross-channel shopping experience that sees customers dipping in and out of the exploratory purpose many times across each touchpoint, before finally purchasing at any one of them. In the age of ultimate choice, and the conversion of an excellent customer experience into a hygiene factor, consumers are no longer impressed by personalization – they now demand it.

As advancements in retailers' technological capabilities are allowing for ever-increasing volumes of data to be gathered on customer purchase behaviour, the ability to personalize anything from ads served, to offers on screens in-store, the expectation from the customer that you only 'show me what I like and want' will become ever more prolific and commonplace.

The internet of things (IoT) is perpetuating the disappearance of screens and creating the rise of 'invisible digital', where technology is hidden in everyday objects, and behavioural triggers can generate data or output. For example, physically moving a product into your shopping basket in-store results in relevant product information and content being stored into the store's apps on your mobile. The following few examples demonstrate the rise of personalization and tech, paving the way for stores of the future around the world.

Amazon Go – example

Amazon Go launched with a disruptive global 'retail first'. The world's first machine-enabled store knew exactly who you were (so long as you had the Amazon Go app installed on your mobile):

- It was linked to customers' accounts in such a seamless and invisible way that they could simply browse the grocery goods and items on offer, fill their bag, and enjoy the truly frictionless retail experience of simply walking out of the store without queuing to pay.

- Without any sales counters, staff or tills, the store used computer vision, machine learning and AI (artificial intelligence) to process the goods taken against its inventory and bill directly and seamlessly via its app.

LEGO London – example

London's LEGO flagship is the iconic family brand's biggest store ever, spanning across two storeys:

- The store shows off life-size replicas of a London tube carriage made from hundreds of thousands of bricks, and even has a 20-foot replica of Big Ben!

- The store is not just a visual spectacle, it is truly a mark of the brand's position at the forefront of the digital and experiential world in which we live, with its 'mosaic portrait system' upstairs in the store offering guests the chance to enter a photo booth and receive an instant box kit, which allows them to build an accurate replica of their face made entirely from bricks.

- The staff are even fitted with 'smart watches' to receive requests from browsing customers, allowing them to better serve shoppers as they move around their innovative and iconic, *truly* 'bricks and clicks' flagship.

In an interview with Forbes, John Goodwin, Executive Vice President and Chief Financial Officer of the Lego Group said:

> We believe that physical stores are a really important part of our overall Lego brand proposition. These stores are so much more than just a way to see the face of the products that we have to offer – they are environments for people to immerse themselves in and see and experience models and fantastic constructions first-hand. It's not that we think online shopping is not important, but we think it is all about providing multiple touchpoints for consumers.[4]

IKEA – example

IKEA's Toronto pop-up allowed the Swedish home retailer to bring to life its global theme 'It all Starts with the Food', entirely streamlining and simplifying the shopping experience:

- By eradicating tills completely, and allowing shoppers to add items to a virtual shopping cart by simply tapping their barcodes with a limited edition, RFID-enabled wooden spoon.
- This was a great example of a simple way to effectively bridge the physical and the digital, through innovative and excellent application of a readily available technology.
- The pop-up store was designed based on a series of room layouts, each of which was designed to challenge consumers to rethink existing food conventions, trying new things and breaking from tradition.

adidas Knit – Bikini Berlin – example

'adidas Knit For You' was a temporary pop-up retail concept, located in the uber trendy 'Bikini Berlin' – an alternative 'hipster mall':

- The pop-up space invited consumers to convey convention in collaboration with adidas as it explored local manufacturing and pushed boundaries, allowing shoppers to make their own 'sport to street', unique merino wool jumper.
- Using innovative manufacturing and creative technologies, visitors to the store could design their own knitwear, which would be produced on the spot and be ready to wear within just four hours, demonstrating the forward-thinking brand's commitment to delivering with speed, efficiency and personality.
- The exacting fit was achieved through the use of body-scan technology, while motion-responsive projectors allowed customers to try on patterns.

Make Up Forever – example

Make up Forever's tech-fuelled concept store has successful outposts located in New York, Paris, Singapore and London:

- The New York stores aim to educate and entertain the customer with an array of personalized make-up-oriented experiences throughout the customer journey, facilitated by technology and innovation.
- Customers can pick up products (grouped by trend) from a rotating conveyer belt, each inviting them to explore trends, tips and application techniques.
- A make-up master stands in the centre of the conveyer belt and personalizes the products on each tray for each customer before giving them a leaflet explaining the products they tried that day.

- The desire to learn the secrets of make-up artists has been fuelled by the social media-led rise of beauty influencers, and the store plays host to make-up lesson events and activity programming by such experts on a daily basis.

- The schedule of events and lessons appear on giant digital boards, updating attendees on what activities are taking place in store that day.

- Every detail is considered, from the lighting, which is set at the perfect temperature to create a flattering hue, to a seven-seat GoPro make-up installation located in the centre of the store, and tablet devices that allow shoppers to virtually 'try on' false lashes.

Hyundair Rockar – example

Hyundair Rockar has been redefining automotive retail, doing away with the traditional out-of-town showrooms known for their bad carpets and pushy salespeople, and replacing them with bright, modernized and tech-driven immersive experiences:

- These are staffed by Rockar Angels who are *Brand Ambassadors* (who are not on commission) and based in newly defined experiential stores.

- Immersive digital technology creates a 360-degree, personalized automotive experience in the stores, while the entire customer journey has been redefined so that customers are able to drive in with their old model and literally drive straight back out in their brand-new car.

- Test drives take place from a dedicated brand area in the carparks, making the entire experience of car shopping as quick and easy as an afternoon browsing new clothing fashions at the mall.

In 2016, The Drum stated: 'The significant portion of companies looking to deliver a personalized offline experience (25.5 per cent) demonstrates that the line between digital and offline personalization is ever blurring as customers demand a highly consistent brand experience.'[5]

Key facet #4: 'immersive production'

We perceive the world around us as it is filtered through the senses. The sum of all these perceptions combined creates what is ultimately our experience. The part of the brain, the hippocampus, which is responsible for interpreting our surroundings through the five senses, is also the same part responsible for our memories and imagination.

That is why we remember what we experience across numerous or all senses better than when exposed to one sense alone – just seeing, or hearing, for example. By adding a positive emotional component to our experience, we link our sensory and emotional systems, which give rise to unconscious fantasies in this way and in fact begin to romanticize our memories, connecting them to heightened positive emotions over time, as they blend with our inner-world dynamics and aspirations (see Figure 4.2).

Figure 4.2   We romanticize our memories of multisensory experiences

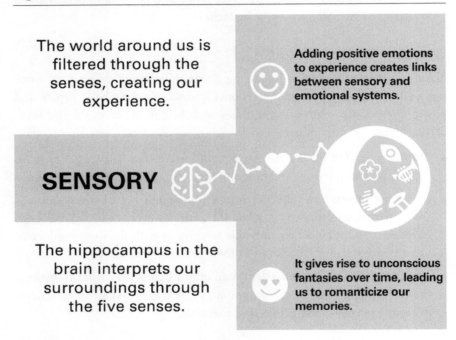

It is no wonder therefore that retailers who create immersive, multisensory environments and treat their customers as the priority, creating positive feelings and memorable experiences, are winning hearts and minds alike, leading to lasting business results. Multisensory, production-led brand storytelling environments – which also retail – are the output.

Lush cosmetics – example

London is home to Lush's flagship store, featuring three floors of sensory explosiveness, in an inviting world of natural, delicious and beautifully scented products:

- The store even features a spa where visitors can experience the products more deeply, while staff take on the role of *Brand Ambassadors*, demonstrating a second-to-none, in-depth product knowledge, and the ability to build strong rapport through natural, relationship-building interactions with the customer.

- Lush takes the curation of its brand-relevant, immersive retail experience to heart, and reinvents the concept of the space regularly, testing new ways to engage the senses and appeal to its target audiences creatively, while always aiming to break the mould.

- Lush created the Gorilla Perfume gallery concept, which was a new way for their customers to experience their fragrances. Each smell is inspired from a wide range of real-life events, evoking a mixture of feelings and emotions, from 'stories of ex-boyfriends who look like one of the Bee Gees to wanting to re-create the smell of Dad's garden'. Suzie Hackney, Creative Director for Lush, explained: 'The gallery enables customers to become immersed using many senses and connect with the fragrance in a different way to only having it on the skin, creating a lasting memory and connection.'

- Lush adeptly creates environments that merge retail and evocative storytelling, as with its Parisian-inspired cafe where customers have perfume consultations, and can have fun under a giant talking hat. There is also the option to visit a 1970s-inspired disco, dress up and take a photo with friends while listening to music on silent-disco headphones.

- Lush also previously experimented with a pop-up concept for a Scented Cinema experience, which involved turning the store's lower ground floor into a cozy 16-seat cinema. Cult classics and favourite Christmas movies were scented with Lush perfumes and specially produced snacks and drinks with fragrance-inspired flavours were provided, alongside a box of props to smell and wear during the film.

- Lush's immersive store concept is a great testament to the power of the multisensory experience and immersive production in creating lasting impact and a deeper customer connection.

Virgin Holidays – example

Virgin Holidays ended its relationship with travel agents in order to adopt a direct to consumer (D2C) strategy. The totally redefined 'in-store approach' 'plays a massive role', according to Claire Cronin, VP of customer and marketing:

- The 'V room' stores offer a totally immersive brand experience, where consumers are invited to experience the world of Virgin – both visually, as the store design reflects the Virgin *Brand Personality* 'to a T', through to the virtual reality (VR) and immersive tech that shows off the company's destinations.

- The store design appeals to all the senses, with each step of the customer journey beautifully communicating everything from the in-flight beverage service, to an appointment with a Virgin Holidays travel consultant and premium seating options so customers can physically experience how much room they will have on a flight.

Ralph Lauren New York – example

Ralph Lauren's mansions are the epitome of effortless all-American chic. The New York flagship mansions (one for women and one for men) have their own elegant designs, which echo the prominent, expressive architectural features of each building:

- The unique spaces are truly immersive and a pleasure to the senses, offering visitors an experience closer to that of visiting a luxurious personal home than a fashion store.

- The flagships effortlessly bring to life the Ralph Lauren *Brand Personality* and products through a sensory journey, offering relevant services to complement the brand, including their very own Ralph's coffee shop within the mansion.

adidas 5th Avenue – example

adidas's 5th Avenue flagship is its biggest global store, and its immersive design – which takes inspiration from a US high-school stadium – is nothing short of breathtaking:

- From a tunnel-style entrance, and giant screens to watch live sports, to locker-style changing rooms and its own juice bar, it is a fully immersive and creative sports lifestyle destination.

- The track-and-field areas allow customers to actually test the products in action before they buy, while the store uses the latest technology in manufacturing to allow shoppers to personalize their items, customizing and creating their own sneaker designs. Even tourists are catered for with same-day hotel delivery slots, enhancing their customer experience and encouraging ease of purchase.

- The 45,000-square-foot wondrous brand destination is a true testament to adidas Group's strategy, which celebrates cities and the trend-creating, social catalyst hubs that they are.

Sonos – example

Sonos, which promises to revolutionize sound in the home through a socially connected wireless listening experience, has an innovative and immersive retail concept:

- Their iconic design features several 'home-like' set designs. There are seven soundproof pods in the New York flagship store, each shaped like houses, and each have their own design, where customers can test out the different speaker types.

- Lounge areas where guests are invited to chat and chill are also spread throughout the store, while additional products from Sonos are on display in their unique and visually eye-catching Wall of Sound.

- An immersive and multisensory environment, it looks far less like a store and thus creates an impactful and welcoming brand environment where consumers can enjoy the brand and product offering, without the pressure of needing to buy on the spot.

Perrier-Jouët's L'Eden – example

A pop-up champagne bar concept held during London Design Week was 'L'Eden' from champagne brand name Perrier-Jouët:

- The pop-up featured a creative and immersive experience in collaboration with designer Noé Duchafour-Lawrance that used 3D printed elements in the design.

- The pop-up's design engaged all the senses through a unique journey that invited guests to experience the world's first bio-responsive garden – created by culinary luminaires 'Bompas & Parr' – where the plants moved in response to human movement.

- By associating with the natural and botanical elements of the immersive experience, Perrier-Jouët stimulated positive associations that left a deep and lasting impression in the mind of the visitor.

Tiger Beer – example

Tiger Beer launched its first New York pop-up store with a creative concept inspired by an insight the brand had identified – 'its need to overcome the stereotypes and the clichés of products made in Asia'. Tiger Beer wanted to explore and portray a variety of more innovative and unexpected fields not traditionally associated with Asia, and they found that Asian creativity was traditionally confined to association with food and technology, while it was more surprising to showcase its creativity through design, art and fashion. Iona Macgregor, Chief Strategy Officer at Marcel, told Contagious I/O: 'The challenge was to surprise people enough to get their attention, and at the same time be single-minded and clear enough to build a consistent brand.'

- The Tiger Beer brand capitalized on these insights to open a truly immersive brand world, in place of a traditional retail outlet or bar activation.
- It launched the Tiger Trading Co – a pop-up store in the heart of New York's Chinatown on Canal Street, famed for its discount shops that sell plastic knickknacks imported from Asia.
- Despite perceptions of its Canal Street location, the shop was filled with a curated collection of over 700 unique items, each chosen to reflect the best in Asian technology, fashion, art and design.
- The store was immersive and design-led with a 118-square-metre glass floor filled with stereotypical Asian-made products sourced from the Canal Street area. New Yorkers could attend the shop by presenting a limited-edition Tiger Beer coaster from one of 30 participating bars local to the store, thus driving footfall from/to the 'on-trade'.
- The coaster not only granted consumers entry, but also could be exchanged for one of the items from the shop and a free Tiger Beer, driving product trial for the beer.

In 2016, Contagious Communications stated: 'By contrasting the designer products with the stereotypical cheap knickknacks, Tiger cleverly repositioned Asian-made goods – including its own beer – as desirable and stylish. In total, the pop-up garnered more than 28.8 million social impressions and sold out of its stock every night.'[6]

Summary

As the rise of mobile phones has changed the face and convenience of shopping, retailers have reinvented and innovated, resulting in a drastic reinvention of bricks-and-mortar retailing. The newly defined retail-experience revolution is summarized with four key facets to the store or pop-up concept of the future:

1 event-centric and social;

2 fusion concepts;

3 personalization and tech;

4 immersive production.

In this new omni-channel/omni-experience age for retail, brands must look holistically at the entire retail experience, without seeing each retail channel as competition to the next, but rather aiming to seamlessly weave their brand touchpoints into a beautiful journey that provides storytelling, entertainment, education and inspiration for its customers.

A unified experience

A unified, truly experiential and hospitality-focused physical retail experience that fuses content, digital and tech, allows data to help better serve the customer through added-value personalization that increases relevance. The store of the future fulfils an important milestone within an overall 360-degree brand journey that has a global view for today's global customer, while not forgetting the importance of authenticity and local tailoring in achieving resonance and relevance.

The way that the modern consumer interacts with brands has to be reflected upon through an omni-channel lens.

An opportunity for real-time data

While offline data sources such as point-of-sale or in-store have historically been focused on top of funnel engagement, it is now increasingly possible to leverage those physical touchpoints to gather real-time data points and, in turn, build a far better and more holistic view of a customer's behaviour. This analytical angle complements a wonderful opportunity to immerse a visitor in a brand's world, creatively expressed through each of the senses.

This will leave an impactful, long-lasting sensory impression (even from a fleeting pop-up!) and brand memory to be imprinted upon their psyche and lead to action and create the golden brand bond, achieving the ultimate goals – brand advocacy, evangelism and personal recommendations.

Notes

1 4 INFO (2016) Mobile Fact Pack, Advertising Age

2 Smilansky, S (2017) Excerpt from an interview with Beatrice Descorps, Global Vice President of Marketing, Molton Brown

3 AdAge [accessed 27 August 2017] Omnichannel Retail, White Paper [Online] http://adage.com/trend-reports/report.php?id=95

4 Samuelson, K (2016) [acessed 11 January 2017] In the Age of Digitalization, Lego Just Opened Its Biggest Store Ever, *Fortune*, 19/11 [Online] http://fortune.com/2016/11/19/lego-store-london/

5 The Drum (2016) [accessed 11 January 2017] The Pressures of Personalisation [Online] www.http://www.thedrum.com/marketinsightreport/data-activation

6 Contagious Communications (2016) [accessed 4 May 2017] How Brands Can Change Attitudes [Online] www. http://resources.contagious.com/how-brands-can-change-attitudes

Digital experiences, artificial intelligence in marketing and merged realities

The ascension of artificial intelligence (AI), robots/bots and personalization driven by data have spurred one of the key creative renaissances in history, allowing enhanced relationship building and one-on-one experiences between brands, products and consumers, all of which have been driven by technology. From the invention of the printing press in the 1400s that allowed 'scalable' transmission of stories, to the 1960s where tech facilitated musicians to fabricate new sounds in the studio that had not been possible for artists playing live, technology has been about transforming ideas into art. An ever-increasing convenience of goods and services, and the incredible ability of technology to facilitate the immediate and efficient meeting of our consumer needs, mean that demands to brands on delivering impeccable customer experience have skyrocketed.

Disruptors are innovating at the speed of light

Tesla's Elon Musk continues to reveal to the world incredible eco-technology that raises hopes for a sustainable future and marks the way for a class of corporations whose values and mission bring promise to humanity, and with driverless cars on the immediate horizon, man and machine have never felt more like partners.

Secretive Chinese automotive brand Faraday Future, whose senior management are predominantly 'ex-Tesla', launched its fully electric vehicle very soon after the company's inception. The company has implied that they have plans to explore other aspects of the automotive and technology industries, such as experiential ownership and usage models, in-vehicle content and autonomous driving.

Disruptors such as Tesla and Faraday Future are essentially experiential, interactive, branded products, changing the world of physical goods into one of digital experiences. These futuristic breakthroughs mark a change where the concept of experiential marketing starts to broaden beyond the remit of marketing communications, beyond branding, and into every silo of a business. From manufacturing and design to customer service, HR and distribution, the experience needs to be considered, cohesive and simple.

Technology is becoming increasingly invisible

A great UX today usually means great 'user interfaces' in web design or apps. It is claimed, that, in time, 'technology will disappear' as many increasingly claim the human body will eventually become the ultimate interface. Until then, as the everyday objects (and even kids toys!) in our lives become 'smart', they come to life – opening up a world of interactive brand experiences and setting us on an experiential journey into the future of virtually invisible, and totally personal, marketing. As we increasingly experience our lives simultaneously online, and in real life (IRL), every channel has been redefined by our ascension into a new digital and experiential world. It is more important than ever for brands to produce and co-create authentic brand experiences, in collaboration with their audiences and their respective influencers.

Boundaries are blurring

There can be seen to have been three key shifts showing that the boundaries between the physical, the digital and the human and the robot are increasingly blurring, and impacting brands dramatically (Figure 5.1).

Figure 5.1   Three key shifts

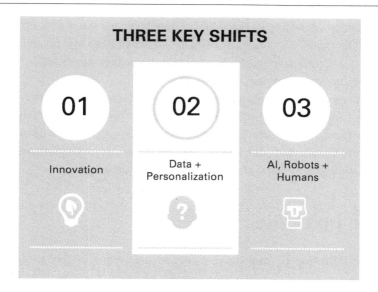

Innovation

Innovation pushes brands beyond their core commercial remit to communicate their brand personalities laterally, and address additional consumer needs and desires. As Jeremy Basset, Head of Unilever Foundry, stated in the WARC Innovation Casebook 2016: 'The need for brands to evolve and innovate has never been more critical. Innovation entails ideas that fuse innovative technology, product and creative solutions to create genuinely fresh executions.'[1]

CASE STUDY

The Rip Curl Surfer GPS Watch

The WARC Innovation Casebook 2016 covers a truly innovative case study: it discussed how the Rip Curl Surfer GPS Watch enabled users to track their waves, and brought the brand – which had been worried about meeting their consumers' changing demands – closer to their hard-to-reach and discerning 'Surfer' *Target Audience*. The watch experience generated data that in turn created an engaged community and united surfers from around the globe, demonstrating how technology can bring together both people and brands, igniting positive sentiment and performing functional duties that add value, with relevance and authenticity.

Alex Altman, Managing Director, MEC Global Solutions stated in the casebook that, 'The Rip Curl GPS is a fantastic example of a brand totally in touch with consumers and developing a product that both meets their needs and, at the same time, further strengthens brand love.'

It has become increasingly feasible for products to be 'smart', gather intelligent data, draw conclusions and take actions, thereby entirely reinventing the notion of what a 'live brand experience' can be. The data gathered results in consumer benefit, and often opens up plenty of commercial opportunities by enabling marketers to better identify and fulfil customer needs.

Speed up or die

It can be daunting to step outside the normal remit of day-to-day business and strive to break new ground, make what can feel like risky changes through innovation, and embrace technology's evolution at this incredible snowballing pace. In fact, the true risk lies in being left behind in the blink of an eye.

At the time that Netflix was transitioning from DVDs by post, to live streaming, CEO Reed Hastings was featured in a report by The Drum Works 'The Next Digital Transformation'. He said:

> Companies rarely die from moving too fast, and they frequently die from moving too slowly.[2]

The report commented on how even the most successful brands often do not really seek out their customer needs and desires as they are scared that what they might find would hurt their core businesses. Harvard Business School Professor Clayton Christensen called this phenomenon the 'innovator's dilemma'. Christensen said, 'Disruption is so problematic for the incumbents because their processes and business model that make them good at the existing business actually make them bad at competing for the disruption.'[3]

Data and personalization

The innovative application of data to develop personalized and tailored brand experiences is more important than ever. This shift is touching every channel, with especially notable executions being specifically tailored advertising in the digital-out-of-home (DOOH) sector. This is because the ability to react to real-time circumstances, such as weather, demographic and facial recognition, and news headlines, allow for increasingly relevant and positively surprising messaging.

AdAge's Marketing Fact Pack predicts data will continue to create opportunities.

'The data is creating unprecedented opportunities. It is creating new challenges, and challenges that you are not even aware of yet. Connection transforms every industry, business and customer experience. More connections creates more data.' The report continues: 'More data creates more complexity and more risk. In the connected world, we need more than data science. More than ever, you need to know how to connect people, places and things. And the key to connection is authoritative identity.'[4]

The importance of personalization is most definitely a huge priority, for 99 per cent of marketers surveyed in the 'Market Insight Report: The Pressures of Personalisation', by The Drum.[5] Challenges have shifted from budgetary to operational, technical and structural, with finite resources limiting the scope of personalization roll-out.[6]

The majority of marketers noted increasing sophistication emerging across their businesses, and a growing investment in the core strategies needed to deliver better customer experiences and truly to embrace an experiential marketing philosophy at C-suite level. Despite the budgetary, technical and organizational considerations, businesses are increasingly investing in new creative strategies to innovate and create more personalized customer experiences across business units.

Personal storytelling opportunities

High production-value, real-world content can provide brands with magical storytelling opportunities that can adapt effectively to suit and maximize effectiveness of the digital channels they use. The selected channels need to be integrated well, and use data to drive personalization, thus merging the physical and the digital. By using data to drive personalization, brands can maximize their impact, and more effectively achieve marketing communication objectives and generate ROI

> Millennials have even gone as far as to say they'd prefer to *experience* things than to buy products – or even own a home. If you're a brand, offering exciting, unique experiences to your potential and existing customers is therefore an incredible opportunity.[7]

Interview excerpt: millennials seeking immersive experiences

Beatrice Descorps, Global Vice President of Marketing, Molton Brown

There is a big expectation for consumers and especially for millennials to understand more through rare experiences and to discover the naked truth through the senses.[8]

Adapt creative messaging to suit the format – top-down creative is dead

It has therefore never been more important to adapt and personalize 'creative' messaging, personalizing it to suit the individual and the delivery format. The old-school approach of top-down, glossy TV creative – meant for broadcast – being adapted for other channels is no longer cutting it, creating an ever-increasing and often overwhelming number of considerations and options for brand marketers, who now need to consider both the real-world experience that will generate the content and the digital format into which it needs to translate.

Kristin Lemkau, CMO from JPMorgan Chase, states:

> The playbook – I tell my team that while the banking and payments industry we are in is being disrupted, marketing is being disrupted much faster. People are still expecting interruptive forms of advertising – which were created when there were only three TV channels and no remote – to work. Do we seriously think pop-ups and pre-roll are going to build more consumer love for our brands? Focus on reinventing your tactics, don't rely on false positives from old measures, and remember the riskiest thing you can do is sticking with the playbook you have.[9]

Real-time data feeds are accelerating intelligence

For ads to resonate, they must respond to the zeitgeist and be relevant to the here and now. Many participants in Gum Gum and The Drum's – 'Reimagining Advertising' report recommended using real-time data feeds and world events to dictate an ad's narrative, including weather, sporting events, and even data streaming from the NASA Opportunity Rover on Mars![10]

The sheer enormity of data now available is revolutionizing the face of the advertising world '100 terabytes at a time'. It facilitates marketers to deliver personalized experiences to consumers en masse, those same consumers who have come to demand authentic and real-world experiences, and who are more digitally native than ever.

AI, robots and humans

In an article on AdAge.com by Bulik titled 'How Marketers Are Using AI to Improve the Brand Experience' Robert Schwartz, VP of global digital marketing at IBM stated: 'Artificial Intelligence (AI) has moved out of its infancy, with creative and intelligent examples becoming more common-place than ever.' He expanded: 'It's one thing to redesign a digital experience, or make over a website or an app, but it's quite another to add the power of thinking and cognitive computing into embedded experiences.'[11]

Molecular tasting algorithm – example

A start-up in Chile called The Not Company used machine learning to rein-vent the food experience. The Chilean business has created an algorithm that can analyse most food on a molecular level to identify and suggest plant-based alternatives with a perfect taste profile replica, but that are far better for your health.

Professor Einstein, chess and DeepMind – example

At CES 2017, Hanson Robotics unveiled its life-like 'Professor Einstein', displaying realistic facial expressions and able to engage in discussions concerning maths and science, while other robots have gained intelligence from playing online, and chat with the people in the crowds and even play chess!

Google's DeepMind notoriously beat a grandmaster at the ancient Chinese board game Go. The win might appear to be a small display of the computer's capabilities, but its significance sent ripples across the technosphere: 'Go is renowned as the world's most challenging game, with more possible outcomes than atoms in the universe.'[12]

AI is a game changer

The continued development of full AI is posing enormous questions about the future of the human race. There have long been disturbing prophecies about AI from a number of intellectual figureheads, including Stephen Hawking, who teamed up with Elon Musk and 1,000 AI experts in January 2015 to write an open letter highlighting the 'potential pitfalls' of creating 'superhuman' artificial intelligence. However, like it or not, AI is a reality, and one that has huge ramifications for the marketing world.

Domino's Dom – example

According to the Most Contagious Report 2015, consumers are now expecting increasingly seamless, bespoke experiences.[13] Domino's pizza app users can 'speak their order to Dom' who is based in the brand's app and uses voice recognition to converse with hungry customers. It allows people to create their own toppings, add items and explore sales promotions. Dom was created by AI agency Nuance Communications and CP+B, Boulder. The report explained that the app and AI tool combined contributed towards a 12.8 per cent quarterly sales increase, against the backdrop of a category enduring stagnant growth.

Creative industries are harnessing AI too

AI is being used creatively too, and these developments into the artistic functions are proving to have enormous impact already. AI-created movie hits have not yet hit the silver screen, but a computer has made a movie trailer. Contagious reports how, in August 2016, IBM Watson created an advert for 20th Century Fox sci-fi thriller *Morgan* by analysing the film and then selecting the 10 best scenes to include.[14] A Beatles-style pop song was created using AI in 2016 too. The program, by Sony Computer Science Laboratory, analysed a database of 13,000 tracks to create a new melody and harmony. Sony announced the follow up, an entire AI-written album for 2017.

As Kate Hollowood stated in the report: 'your creative department may seem reasonably human right now, but things may change.' She was referring to a recent surprising turn of events where McCann Japan's AI creative director created a fairly convincing ad for Clorets mints that was preferred to the human-generated ad by a panel of British advertisers. Hollowood said: 'These examples of AI-generated creativity don't yet compare with their man-made counterparts, but as the tech improves, we would expect the work to also become more impressive.'

AI and bots creating interactive and personal dialogue

Let's take a look at some examples of brands that have been exploring the use of AI in their marketing.

CASE STUDY

Tommy Hilfiger's TMY.GRL messenger bot

Fashion brand Tommy Hilfiger ran several campaigns across Facebook and Instagram during New York Fashion Week. On Facebook, it released a shoppable video allowing people to purchase items seen on the runway and set up a chatbot, TMY.GRL, using Facebook Messenger:

- The Messenger bot asks users questions to establish the type of content they would like to see. The chatbot was launched to promote the brand's collaboration with model Gigi Hadid.

- Created in partnership with AI platform msg.ai, it then displays tailored and interactive content based on their answers, showcasing behind-the-scenes imagery, shopping opportunities and fun facts about Gigi, their ambassador.

- The bot offers an 'add to cart' button within the app, thus completing the loop and driving social engagement and sales all at once.

Puneet Mehta, founder and CEO of msg.ai, commented:

> The consumer and brand relationship is on the cusp of the most significant change since the smartphone. Messaging is becoming the new browser and the gateway to consumer life, with artificial intelligence bots being the new user interface. With TMY.GRL, Tommy Hilfiger is providing consumers with the digital commerce experience of the future: immediate, individualized, entertaining and seamless across the entire customer journey.[15]

Hospitality sector harnesses new tech and AI

The introduction of AI, bots and machine learning in various formats is making fast progress in the leisure, hospitality and food sectors. The human feeling is a crucial touch in what makes hospitality businesses special, and it's unlikely bots or AI will ever replace the human touch.

Another innovative use of AI was launched by Knorr, the well-known food company who used AI technology to generate individual flavour profiles and personalized recipe experiences, through their 'Love at First Taste' campaign.

These examples demonstrate how a variety of industries and brands are using AI to build better customer experiences, and it is evident that they are just getting going. IDC predicts that global spending on cognitive systems will reach US $31.3 billion by 2019. Accenture found that AI could double economic growth rates by 2035 and boost labour productivity by 40 per cent.[16]

Whilst the public may still feel reticent to fully accept the idea of self-driving vehicles or dealing face to face with AI in customer service roles, this technology is fast becoming an everyday reality, and an accepted part of today and tomorrow's marketing landscape.

Live brand experience participation in real life (IRL) and remotely

This book focuses on experiential marketing as a key approach for achieving marketing objectives. The experiential approach is focused on a *Two-Way Interaction* in real time and a live brand experience, and thereby a significantly deeper consumer bonding process. Live brand experiences usually manifest in the form of live events IRL that allow the consumer to live, breathe and feel the brand through interactive sensory connections and activities. The activities are usually designed to add value to *Target Audiences* in their own, natural environments.

Remote live brand experiences are increasingly accessible to brands

Live brand experiences are simply immediate, two-way branded experiences, and can be equally successful across many interactive technologies and platforms that facilitate communication between consumers and brands *in real time* and remotely. For example, consumers can participate in live brand experiences on live TV or digital channels where the shows' content is fluid, and they participate in and contribute to it in real time. Likewise, a live brand experience or event can be activated online with 'live streaming' participation via social media networks such as Snapchat, Periscope, Facebook Live and Instagram Live.

Summary

Real-life experiences have replaced simulated ones, and now both are increasingly merging. Whilst once upon a time, consumers accepted simulated narratives, authenticity rules the roost now as today's consumers are less receptive to this approach and expect honesty and transparency from brands. People today want real experiences that affect real people.

Therefore, the future of the most prosperous brands lies in the combination of real, authentic IRL experiences, with innovation, personalization and the intelligent fusion of robots, AI and humans as collaborators in the delivery of these experiences. It is the recommendation of this book that, for best results across all channels, marketers place live and interactive brand experiences, focused on authentic real-world content, at the core of their digital and product experiences, and at the heart of their creative campaigns.

Notes

1 WARC (2016) [accessed 27 August 2017] WARC Innovation CaseBook, WARC Innovation [Online] http://content.warc.com/read-the-2016-innovation-casebook-summary-from-warc

2 Richard Robinson (2016) [accessed 27 August 2017] The Next Digital Transformation, Turn, The Drum Works, 8 [Online] http://www.thedrum.com/whitepaper/digital-transformation

3 Richard Robinson (2016) [accessed 27 August 2017] The Next Digital Transformation, Turn, The Drum Works, 8 [Online] http://www.thedrum.com/whitepaper/digital-transformation

4 Neustar (2017) [accessed 21 February 2017] Advertising Age Marketing Fact Pack [Online] http://adage.com/d/resources/resources/whitepaper/2017-edition-marketing-fact-pack

5 The Drum (2015) [accessed 27 August 2017] Market Insight Report, Pressures of Personalisation, 20 [Online] http://www.thedrum.com/marketinsightreport/personalisation

6 The Drum (2015) [accessed 27 August 2017] Market Insight Report, Pressures of Personalisation, 20 [Online] http://www.thedrum.com/marketinsightreport/personalisation

7 Event (2016) [accessed 27 August 2017] Brand Experience Report, *Event Magazine*, 24 [Online] http://www.eventmagazine.co.uk/event-brand-experience-report-2016

8 Smilansky, S (2017) Excerpt from an interview with Beatrice Descorps, Global Vice President of Marketing, Molton Brown

9 Neustar (2017) [accessed 21 February 2017] Advertising Age Marketing Fact Pack [Online] http://adage.com/d/resources/resources/whitepaper/2017-edition-marketing-fact-pack

10 The Drum (2016) Reimagining Advertising, The Drum and Gum Gum

11 Bulik, B S (2016) [accessed 27 August 2017] How Marketers are using AI to improve their Brand Experience, AdAge [Online] http://adage.com/article/cmo-strategy/marketers-ai-improve-brand-experience/306483/

12 Most Contagious Report (2015) [accessed 3 February 2017] Contagious Communication's Ltd [Online] http:11www.2015mostcontagious.com

13 Most Contagious Report (2015) [accessed 3 February 2017] Contagious Communication's Ltd [Online] http:11www.2015mostcontagious.com

14 Most Contagious Report (2015) [accessed 3 February 2017] Contagious Communication's Ltd [Online] http:11www.2015mostcontagious.com

15 Arthur, R (2016) [accessed 21 October 2017] How Tech Stole the Show at Fashion Week, *Guardian* [Online] https://www.theguardian.com/media-network/2016/sep/23/tech-fashion-week-burberry-tommy-hilfiger-virtual-reality

16 IDC (2015) [accessed 27 August 2017] The Programmatic Guide, Oracle Marketing Cloud [Online] http://demand.eloqua.com/LP=6309?elqct=SocialMedia&elqchannel=OMCBlog&elqoffer=ProgrammaticGuide_16&sls=OMCGSU_DG_WP_ProgrammaticGuide_0316&elqcname=OMCGSU_DG_WP_ProgrammaticGuide_0316

The *BETTER* creative model

How to create unique experiential marketing ideas

Adding method to the magic

'Creativity' is a fascinating faculty. It is, however, often misunderstood in many ways, in part due to the misinformed messages conveyed by society and the media of the 'left/right brain' concept. We are made to believe that a lucky chosen few of us possess this vague and indefinable quality, benefiting from sudden 'light bulb' flashes of genius and inspiration.

When we dig deeper and explore the science behind the art, it becomes apparent that the parts of our brain responsible for generating creative ideas and solutions are in fact working as a team, dancing in a choreographed routine that is in fact quite systematic and accessible to us all. By learning to better understand and perform the steps we go through, both consciously and subconsciously, we begin to identify how to better facilitate and lead a better thinking process. Creativity involves characteristics of *both*: 1) reasoning; 2) imagination. The left/right brain idea is a myth.

Introducing the *BETTER* creative model

Creative thinking is a process in which one generates an original, unusual and productive solution to a problem. The *BETTER* model is a creative process designed by the author, which has now been used for over 10 years with brand clients to develop authentic, ideas for real-world, interactive live brand experiences. It goes through several stages, covering conceptual development, social storytelling, weaving in a brand narrative and high-reach content opportunities – pre, during and post each brand experience.

The *BETTER* model can be utilized as a brainstorm or workshop format, and also as a planning process over time.

The *BETTER* model was developed in order to create a systematic methodology for experiential marketing ideation. Using the model, you can develop creative concepts that are:

- authentic;
- positively connected;
- personally meaningful.

BETTER enables you to bring the *Brand Personality* to life and create ideas that are experiential in nature and dazzle your *Target Audiences*. Ideas must also be built around *Multi-Sensory* expressions of the brand; driving word of mouth and generating content that creates an *Emotional Connection* with great storytelling abilities.

This is best achieved when the big idea for the integrated campaign is centred on *Two-Way Interactions*, and through communicating the brand story via the live brand experience, which focuses on engagement that drives advocacy, gaining maximum *Reach* for the content and overall experiential campaign.

Each letter in the *BETTER* acronym represents a different stage to be considered in order for the optimal creative development process.

> The *BETTER* model
> **B**rand Personality
> **E**motional Connection
> **T**arget Audience
> **T**wo-Way Interaction
> **E**xponential Elements
> **R**each

The first three stages: **BET**

Brand Personality, *Emotional Connection* and *Target Audience* populate insights and relevant materials (such as multisensory elements, *Target Audience* insights and authentic, brand-relevant activities), which then incubate in the mind and develop.

Preparation, incubation and illumination for creative ideas: the resulting ideas that form become inspiration for a Two-Way Interaction, which in turn brings these inspirational elements to life through immersive and interactive brand experiences and activities that are authentic to a brand and relevant to its audience.

Creating a far-reaching impact

The *Exponential Elements* and *Reach* stages explore word-of-mouth triggers and build the narrative of the content, pre, during and post the *Two-Way Interaction*.

The three networks of the brain work in tandem and complement the BETTER model

The *BETTER* model follows a process that is entirely complementary to the way that our brain's natural creative process works. Graham Wallace in *The Art of Thought* in the 1920s first coined the four creative stages as: preparation, incubation, illumination and verification. These stages closely reflect the way the brain works according to the latest research in neuroscience.

Figure 6.1   The four stages of the brain's creative process

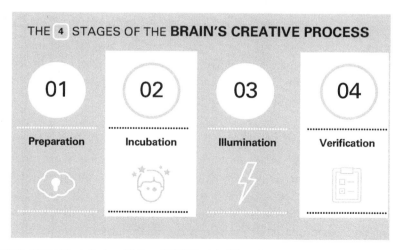

SOURCE Adapted from Graham Wallace (1926) *The Art of Thought*

Creativity, not purely a left or right brain function after all

Wallace's approach debunks 'left–right brain myths that purely imply creativity as a random art', demonstrating how in fact the main three networks of the brain – the executive network, the default network and the salient network – in fact work together operating with both rational/analytical and imaginative functions on the left *and* the right sides of the brain.

Illumination stage of the creative process

After first going through the 'preparation and incubation stages', filling the mind with facts then visualizing outcomes and relaxing the mind, the illumination stage and 'eureka moment' follows due to the salient networks that work as our trusty assistants in the background, synthesizing our internal and external experiences and options (as generated by the four earlier stages in the *BETTER* process: '*BETTER*').

Verifying the idea and planning the mechanics

This leads us perfectly into the verification stage, embodied as we review and narrow options before finally integrating commercial thinking, mechanics and *Exponential Elements*, and packaging our content narrative for optimal *Reach* (the final two stages of *BETTER*). It has been suggested that we are entering a creative renaissance in terms of the creative strategy paradigm. This next level is now about holistic, contextual experiences that encompass 'one to one', 'one to brand' and 'brand to one'.

The neuroscience of creativity and the creative process

First, you have to throw all your previous notions of the right and left brain out of the window – consider this myth debunked. Several sections of the brain must play their part in a coordinated team-like game, over the course of the four 'movements', or stages of the creative process, as explained by Wallace, to conceive an idea and bring it to life.

Three large-scale networks

There are three large-scale networks of the brain that work together throughout the creative process (executive, default, salient networks). 'Creativity is not strictly confined to the right side of the brain, nor is analytical thinking only borne of the left. The brain is an orchestra working together harmoniously to perform the imaginative symphony that is creativity and ideation.'[1]

As Steve Jobs once said:

> Creativity is just connecting things. When you ask creative people how they did something, they feel a little guilty because they didn't really do it, they just saw something. It seemed obvious to them after a while. That's because they were able to connect experiences they've had and synthesize new things.[2]

Live brand experiences for every market

Brand personalities can differ regardless of sector

Utilizing the *BETTER* creative model, one could easily develop very different experiential marketing ideas for two similar products in the same sector. The ideas would be different if the creative process is executed correctly and the two brands had different *Brand Personalities* (even if the products and services were similar). This may seem obvious in somewhere like the drinks sector, for example, where branding is everything, but not necessarily as apparent in areas where communication and advertising ideas are traditionally inspired by rational, product-focused messages. Experiential marketing can be implemented successfully across all sectors, from financial services to FMCG, from drinks to music, from technology to leisure. No single sector (whether product or service) is more or less appropriate for an experiential marketing strategy, because the key inspirations for the best experiential marketing ideas come from: the *Brand Personalities*, provenance, heritage, authentic product truths, and the *Target Audience*s themselves.

Bring the authentic product truths that resonate with the audience to the forefront of ideas

The *Emotional Connection* (stage two in the *BETTER* model, Figure 6.2) that can be created through brand-relevant, participatory experiences can transcend the functional selling points of the product, its features and benefits. This is not to suggest that the product and its features and benefits do not play a role in the campaign – they do, as the consumer usually has the opportunity to trial the product, especially in the live brand experience when executed face to face. It does not really matter which sector or industry the product belongs to. As long as you understand the brand values and which of your authentic product truths and heritage resonate with the *Target Audience* and influencers, you have what is needed to generate spectacular concepts for high *Reach* (the final stage), engaging brand experiences.

There are some products that compete in a saturated or commoditized sector, where differentiating through the product features is difficult and ineffective. By creating a large-scale brand experience programme, which facilitates the brand forming an *Emotional Connection* with its *Target Audiences*, those consumers are more likely to become brand advocates, allowing stand-out in a cluttered sector, and rely on word of mouth rather than implementing discounts to drive sales.

Brand Personality

Bring your Brand Personality to life

Live brand experiences offer a fabulous opportunity to bring your *Brand Personality* to life, and appeal to the participant's desires and aspirations. When developing the big idea for an experiential marketing campaign, the *Brand Personality* should be brought to life at the heart of the live brand experience. Brand experiences, when executed in the real world, also provide an ideal platform for demonstrating a product's (rational) features and benefits, because the product can be trialled by the consumer in real life (IRL) and the experience with the product itself can complement any interaction with activities that convey the *Brand Personality*. By bringing a *Brand Personality* to life, an experiential marketing campaign conveys sophisticated messages that traditional approaches cannot easily achieve, and it is especially effective at communicating complex *Brand Personalities* and values to create an emotional appeal. This can connect with the aspirational lifestyle of the customer, enhancing a subliminal perception that by aligning themselves with that brand it will bring them closer to their inner fantasy world.

Using the BETTER creative model

The *BETTER* model is an acronym

- *Brand Personality*
- *Emotional Connection*
- *Target Audience*
- *Two-Way Interaction*
- *Exponential Elements*
- *Reach*

Figure 6.2   The *BETTER* creative model

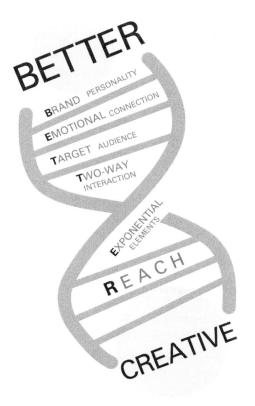

B is for *Brand Personality*

Figure 6.3   *Brand Personality* in the *BETTER* creative model

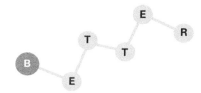

Identifying the human-like characteristics of the brand

The first stage requires us to whittle down our DNA and human-like characteristics into a select few core attributes. Some people might find the concept of a brand having a personality slightly confusing and may not differentiate between the brand and the product. For example, if you look at a brand such as Coca-Cola, the product itself is Cola, so from a consumer perspective there is confusion regarding the difference between the product and the brand. To understand more about what is meant by a *Brand Personality*, we should first think about personality in the context of people. Marketers are used to thinking in terms of *values*, these are more akin to our *morals*, while our personalities are so varied and the possibilities for bringing them to life are plentiful. By first of all identifying up to three *Brand Personality* attributes that we will bring to life, we complete the first stage in the preparation phase of the *BETTER* model.

Everybody is different

Remember that different people have different personalities. We may all know someone who is chatty, bouncy and happy, yet we may also know people with a wide variety of other personalities or human-like characteristics such as sophisticated, smart, glamorous, brash, innocent or direct.

Now we must try to humanize and look at brands in the same way in order to be able to build real relationships with our customers in real life and beyond, we need to understand our *Brand Personality* and consider how it comes to life, and how we translate it into the human and multisensory dimensions.

What personality combination does your brand have? Is your washing powder's *Brand Personality* fragrant, natural and caring? Or does it have an exciting, bright and energetic personality?

Think of three different Brand Personality *pillars*

Try to identify the three '*Brand Personality* pillars' you wish to combine and bring to life, ensuring you remember to be authentic. If you take your existing (probably static or video) brand identity and imagery, advertising and packaging associated with a brand, try to consider the company mission and vision and the tonality of the brand's communication, aiming to extract three core *Brand Personality* pillars to form the *Brand Personality* – these three human-like *Brand Personality* attributes facilitate the 'B' stage of the *BETTER* model.

Extracting Brand Personality *pillars*

All brands across all product or service sectors have personalities. Take, for example, cars: what *Brand Personality* does your car have? What personality does your husband's, wife's, girlfriend's or boyfriend's car have? Do both your cars have the same personalities, just because they are cars? If you were asked to compare the personality of a Volvo to the personality of a Mercedes, would they be the same? Even in a situation where you compare two family cars that are similar in product specifications, one car's adverts and appearance communicate a *Brand Personality* of trust and reliability, while the other has a pragmatic, logical and simple *Brand Personality*.

The core personality pillars embedded and encoded in existing brand communications should be decoded and extracted, forming the *Brand Personality*. This will be the first point of inspiration for the experiential marketing idea.

Decoding Brand Personality *pillars from traditional brand identity or advertising 'creative'*

As a marketer, you are likely to be very familiar with the concept of brand values and you probably have a good understanding of branding. What was the agency responsible for the last ad you saw attempting to communicate? Next time you see an ad, regardless of whether it is for a financial services product, a travel brand or a candy bar, brainstorm which different human-like personality attributes come to mind, as if the brand itself were a person with its own unique personality. Try to think, what person do I know who this brand would be if it was human? Is the person in this ad the type of person I want to be friends with? Is this brand representative of values or a lifestyle to which I aspire? Or is this brand like someone else I know, someone I like, or someone I don't like? Is this brand endearing? Is it honest? Is it sexy? Is it smart? Is it trustworthy? Is it aspirational? Is it adventurous? Is it fun? Is it sophisticated? Is it comical? Is it active? Is it laid back? There are many different personality facets to take into consideration, and many different characteristics that a brand can have, because *Brand Personalities* can be as complex as human personalities. They can have their own intricate personalities and unique mix of archetypal human-like brand pillars for activating when expressing themselves through interactive brand experiences in real life.

Personality types and unspoken associations

When Carl Jung (1968) published a study of Hans Christian Andersen's fairy tales he wrote, 'Any viable work of poetry (and work of art in general) rests on archetypal foundations.' The power of archetypes in great stories is their ability to tap into a rich vein of unspoken associations, in the same way that our limited conscious memory taps into the rich vein of our experienced world. The associative basis of memory is why metaphors and archetypes are so powerful. Metaphors allow us to associate a rich vein of ideas and memories in our minds through one central 'idea', making that idea a powerful trigger of behaviour.

The three Brand Personality *pillars, forming the 'B' in* BETTER

The first stage of *BETTER* is about figuring out which core personality pillars hold up the brand, and how they fuse together to represent what it stands for. Try to analyse and dissect the existing brand identity and other marketing communications that have been most effective, to extract its core human-like characteristics. This process will help you to get into the habit of extracting the most important *Brand Personality* attributes, which you will then use as inspiration throughout the rest of the *BETTER* creative development and storytelling process. You can then further refine into activation planning during the more detailed planning process (using the *SET MESSAGE* model, to be outlined later in the book).

After completing the first step of the *BETTER* model, you should have narrowed down three 'human-like attributes' that you will then use to bring to life the *Brand Personality*. For example, Brand Z, a fruity breakfast cereal, has a healthy, fit and natural *Brand Personality*.

Examples

The following examples illustrate how brands in varying sectors with different audiences can have a wide assortment of core *Brand Personality* pillars, regardless of their market.

Energy Drink – example

If you have an energy drink that targets sporty, energetic people and the *Brand Personality* is 'active and bubbly', then the live brand experience could be focused on a similarly energetic, active and bubbly interactive activity:

- The experience could be captured using Intel's real-sense technology, which creates a superior and instant green-screen effect allowing the app to superimpose the content on to any background, allowing you to transport participants into any environments.

- Take for example a game that involves jumping on a branded trampoline whilst surrounded by blown bubbles from 360-degree bubble machines with a real-sense video clip of the person 'bouncing in the sea of bubbles', superimposed on to a silhouette outline of the energy drink bottle. This would be embedded into the brand's imagery, and instantly transmitted through to the participants' smartphone to keep and share.

- The product could be trialled as part of the experience through sampling, and the brand imagery could be represented through the colour scheme, look and feel of the experiential set and its content.

- Importantly, the actual interaction is inspired by the *Brand Personality*. Therefore, once a consumer has engaged with the brand experience, he or she is left with a memorable impression of that brand's DNA; its specific blend of personality values will automatically affiliate the product with those attributes.

- If this experience were targeted effectively and reached its *Target Audience*, it would connect with the aspirational and lifestyle aims of the consumer (namely, energetic and active) and result in a genuine 'golden bond' that represents a deeper and more meaningful connection, strengthening the relationship between the brand and the customer.

- This live brand experience, which is focused on an interactive game in real life, can also be amplified through all the marketing communications channels, for example re-creating the IRL experience as a digital video filter app, and using the video content captured within its social media ads.

Beauty brand – example

In the beauty sector, there are many products that focus their *Brand Personality* on values such as attractiveness, freshness and glamour. There are some beauty products that have a more complex *Brand Personality* and positioning. There is a Japanese brand from the beauty sector whose brand story is inspired by the concept of **beauty secrets** being passed from **generation to generation**. It was hard to convey its *Brand Personality* attributes effectively through, for example, traditional billboard or print advertising:

- Experiential marketing provides the perfect platform for bringing the authentic brand story to life in an integrated campaign, including a live brand experience at its core.

- Consumers and influencers who participate in the live brand experience share their own beauty secrets that they heard from someone else – secrets that have now, in turn, been passed on to others around the world. Winners received a 'beauty secrets makeover' by one of four world-expert make-up artists from previous generations, and the content was filmed as an interactive tutorial for a live-streamed digital event. The *Brand Personality* was the inspiration for the core participatory activity of the experience.

- It would have been near impossible for the consumer to interact with this added-value, brand-relevant experience without learning on an intrinsic level that 'beauty secrets' are a key part of what the product represents.

- Even though consumers will not think about it in terms of a *'Brand Personality'*, they will understand the concept and associate the brand with that idea subliminally or subconsciously.

- Either way, the next time they come across that product, they will automatically associate it with the *Brand Personality*: insightful beauty secrets learnt from wise forebears.

Two different cream liquor brands – comparative examples

Cream liquor brand – example 1 There is a brand of cream liquor that originated in South Africa and uses traditional African symbols in its packaging. It has a **South African heritage** and an **indulgent** and **traditional** *Brand Personality*, authentically inspired by its roots and heritage:

- The brand gained market share quickly after its launch by building an *Emotional Connection* with the *Target Audience* and engaging them through live brand experiences, sampling roadshows, interactive outdoor media and PR competitions.

- The African-themed, branded immersive set features a life-size model of an elephant and a traditional, indulgent African hut.

- The experience features VR with 360-degree safari content, costumed dancers, mixologist *Brand Ambassadors* and traditional African craft-making sessions.

- Consumers find out about the upcoming live brand experience tour dates through articles and ads in the press, which invite consumers to attend the immersive experience and send photos of themselves 'being indulgent', for a chance to win a premium safari trip (to the locations filmed in the VR footage).

While brainstorming the creative, the marketing agency behind this campaign remembered to take the *Target Audience* and their lifestyle into consideration and create an interactive two-way experience, which adds value to them and reflects the African heritage, while communicating the 'indulgence' and 'traditional' *Brand Personality* themes at the same time.

Cream liquor brand – example 2 A completely different cream liquor brand from New York has a **young, urban** *Brand Personality*. This brand also used an integrated experiential marketing methodology:

- Their above-the-line outdoor advertising campaign showed content of glamorous city people from its Instagram ads holding house parties in loft-style penthouse apartments, and gave cocktail tips and recipes, provided by celebrity mixologists.

- The sponsored Instagram adverts invited the *Target Audience* to message back with cocktail ideas inspired by where they live in order to receive a voucher and a chance to win a free 'cocktail party experience' in their own homes, hosted by one of the famous mixologists.

- The winners' events were shown on Instagram live, and content was captured for use in future ads, while everyone who received a voucher was invited to share their own cocktails on social media.

- It is evident how the two integrated experiential marketing ideas were *Brand Personality*-specific and different each time, even though both products (cream liquor) are very similar in composition.

Two different power-tool brands – comparative examples

Power-tool brand – example 1 There is a power-tool brand whose *Brand Personality* and values reflect **powerful, intelligent** people. Its *Target Audience* is affluent DIY fans who 'fancy themselves capable of a bit of DIY at the weekends':

- To bring the *Brand Personality* to life, the agency designed an experiential marketing campaign with a live brand experience that is two-way and interactive, engaging the consumer through sensory activities that represent power and intelligence, allowing the values to be communicated through relationship-building activities that generate word of mouth and achieve objectives.

- In this case, the experiential marketing campaign involved a series of face-to-face live brand experiences with content amplification.

- The live brand experience was held at a series of car shows (frequented by the target demographic), where the *Target Audience* had the opportunity to participate in a drilling challenge that doubled up as an IQ test.

- Every participant had the opportunity to win prizes such as super-powerful and intelligent state-of-the-art computers, and free Mensa membership, thus engaging the *Target Audience* and bringing to life the intelligent and capable *Brand Personality* of the power tools.

Power-tool brand – example 2 A different brand of tools has a reliable, trustworthy, 'family values' *Brand Personality*, and a key communication message that focuses on the fact that you can always rely on its tools to 'last a lifetime':

- Experiential marketing is the approach behind this brand's marketing communications strategy, and the big idea, forming the live brand experience, is amplified throughout all its marketing channels.

- This brand targets labourers who use tools for a living as well as avid DIY enthusiasts. The brand launched an experiential roadshow, which involved a touring vehicle visiting building sites and family areas allowing construction workers to have a quick break inside a branded air-conditioned trailer.

- While they were relaxing in the seating zone, they had a free refreshing drink and watched branded content on the screens provided.

- While they waited, the *Brand Ambassadors* ran a family-tree search for them at the computer bar.

- They received a printout of their family tree, designed inside a 'tool themed' infographic, which also featured a sales discount code for use when purchasing tools, and came with a five-year warranty.

- The real-world branded content was used in their above-the-line advertising, showing the tools being passed from father to son.

- The adverts showed real consumers who used the tools and submitted photos of themselves using the tools, in response to a press initiative.

- The digital ads, which were aired on local DIY and construction job site groups, also featured a list of upcoming dates when the family-search roadshow would be visiting the respective building sites and locations.

A comparison in the same sector

When comparing the two campaigns, it is clear to see how the two power-tool brands use different experiential concepts in their campaigns, even though there is little variation in the actual product itself. One is targeted at a more affluent casual **DIY**-er, concentrating on **intelligence, power** and **challenge**, while the other targets a niche demographic and focuses on **longevity, trust** and **family values.**

Brand Personalities *form the inspiration in every sector*

From FMCG to luxury

This same approach to using the *Brand Personality* for inspiration when formulating experiential marketing concepts can be applied across every sector and *Target Audience*. The BETTER creative formula works in every sector from FMCG to luxury to B2B products, and when targeting anyone from high-flying executives, to parents, niche audiences, opinion formers and influencers. The principle here is that no matter which market your product is in, be sure that you are clear on what your *Brand Personality* pillars represent, how your *Target Audiences* live their lives and what is important to them.

Sparks for ideas come from combining, or synthesizing creative components

You can begin creative brainstorming about how to bring these human-like personality attributes to life through immersive, sensory and interactive activities. The *Brand Personality* and this *Emotional Connection* that will be created with your *Target Audience* will form the core of your *Two-Way Interaction* and participatory experiential idea.

Brand Personalities do not have to be bold, exciting and adventurous for them to become the inspiration for two-way, experiential ideas. You can have a serious and intelligent *Brand Personality*, an intellectual and controversial *Brand Personality*, or a regal and luxurious *Brand Personality*. The unique *Brand Personality* combination can be anything, just like a human being. Some people are fun, some are serious, some are active, some are relaxed, and some are loud and extravagant, while others are subtle and sophisticated. No matter which sector you are in, and no matter what your unique *Brand Personality* blend is, it can represent and be used to bring to life through a storytelling narrative, a deeper metaphor that you can bring to life through brand experiences.

Storytelling patterns and inspiration live in our everyday relationships and lives

Zaltman claims there are a number of 'deep metaphors' that are unconscious 'structures of human thought'. These metaphors manifest themselves below the surface and can be used in marketing to communicate more effectively to consumers about a brand, product or topic, using language that everyone can understand and appreciate. Zaltman uses metaphors as the basis of his research to understand deeper beliefs and thinking patterns. He has written about seven fundamental metaphors that are common across cultures and categories: balance, transformation, journey, container, connection, resource and control.[3] All are related to universal human traits, and our love of stories is really a love of extended metaphors. There are many common themes between these metaphors and the archetypes. The brain is above all a sophisticated pattern recognition machine, designed to make predictions about the world in order to optimize our behaviour to achieve the best possible outcomes. Many scientists have argued that the experience of synaesthesia is linked to the brain's use of analogy and metaphor, and that these processes are also deeply linked to creativity.[4]

Brand and customer-centric ideas

At the *Emotional Connection* stage of the *BETTER* creative model, it is time to weave in authentic product truths via real-world storytelling in a way that resonates with the audience, and feeds mutually back into evolving the live brand experience organically.

The goal is to allow consumers to discover the brand's heritage, and engage with its product features and benefits. The core participatory concept and inspiration for the experiential idea, the *Two-Way Interaction*, should be sourced primarily from the *Brand Personality*, multisensory components designed to form an *Emotional Connection*, and *Target Audience* insights.

It does not make a difference to your idea if your sector or industry is perceived to be exciting, luxurious, dull or sophisticated; what really provides an opportunity to create inspiration for an added-value and engaging experience are the *Brand Personality* and the *Target Audience* themselves. No matter what values that *Brand Personality* consists of, if you follow the creative and planning guidelines in the *BETTER* model and throughout this book, then experiential marketing will be a methodology that will work for you. When the big idea (brand-relevant, audience-driven, *Two-Way Interaction* participation) is integrated into your existing marketing communications, with a live brand experience at the core, it will offer results and benefits that will revolutionize your business and marketing strategies.

E is for *Emotional Connection*

In the *BETTER* brainstorming model, the first E stands for *Emotional Connection*. It is important that we form an *Emotional Connection* with the *Target Audience* since we need to engage them in a way that will impact them beyond their conscious thoughts. The reason why this stage of the creative process is so vitally important is that by appealing to people's emotions and creating genuine *Emotional Connection*s, the experience is likely to embed itself in their memories. Studies have shown that vivid autobiographical memories are usually of emotional events. These emotional events are likely to be recalled in more detail and more often than emotionally neutral events. Emotional stimuli and physical souvenirs associated with an experience can heighten memory retention by triggering neuro-chemical activity affecting certain areas of the brain that are responsible for encoding and recalling.[5]

The *Emotional Connection* stage of the *BETTER* brainstorming model is designed to gather inspiration for emotionally and sensory stimulating elements that will lead to lasting impressions in the mind. These will integrate

Figure 6.4   *Emotional Connection* in the *BETTER* creative model

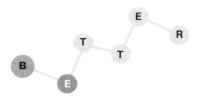

with the results of the *Brand Personality* and combine with the *Target Audience* stage to form the *Two-Way Interaction* part of the brainstorm (the immersive and participatory concept for the live brand experience). The two stages that we consider when we are in the *Emotional Connection* stage are:

Two stages in creating an *Emotional Connection*:

Pt. 1 The 'three key attributes' (authentic, positively connected and personally meaningful).

Pt. 2 multisensory elements (the five senses).

Experiential marketing should always make a deep *Emotional Connection* with the *Target Audience* through formulating a real relationship and positive feelings to create that all-important golden brand bond (where the relationship is strengthened and an individual becomes a brand advocate or even evangelist). To achieve this connection we should apply elements that have the three key attributes to the live brand experience, which have to be orchestrated in real time – 'in the here and now'. These attributes, when integrated into the concepts for all live brand experiences, whether they are delivered remotely (through technology or communication platforms) or IRL, result in experiences that are more memorable.

The three key attributes

The three key attributes that should be thought about during this stage – authentic, positively connected and personally meaningful – are shown in Figure 6.5.

In essence, these three attributes summarize the most important characteristics the concept should have, to ensure that it connects and triggers positive emotions from the participant. If the live brand experience is executed remotely via technology and not delivered IRL, then a fully multisensory approach (which engages all five senses) is less appropriate, but by applying the three key attributes (being authentic, positively connected and personally meaningful) you will still be able to create a genuine *Emotional Connection* and embed a long-lasting memory of the experience (along with its deeper metaphorical associations) into the participant's mind.

Figure 6.5 Three key attributes to create an *Emotional Connection*

To create an *Emotional Connection*, we therefore need to apply the three key attributes to the concept, and if the live brand experience is going to be executed IRL, then we do this in combination with the process of establishing a fully multisensory environment of brand expression and human participation.

Brands are still failing on emotions

While authenticity comes naturally to some brands, creating an *Emotional Connection* with the consumer is proving harder. The creative agency Aesop ran a brand storytelling survey to identify the top brands, finding that 14 of the 180 brands polled 3 per cent or less, struggling to make an impact against the storytelling criteria.[6]

Emotional Connection: authenticity

Marketing Week interviewed Saskia Meyer in 2016, Marketing Director at Fever-Tree, who explains that storytelling is crucial from brand strategy inception. For Fever-Tree it was their authentic idea of having an 'all-natural premium mixer' and uniquely sourced ingredients from around the world by the founders themselves. They maintain that keeping this brand story clear and open is essential, with their success of this storytelling speaking for itself.[7]

Emotional Connection Pt. 2: multisensory elements

> If I eat pink cake, the taste of it is pink. (Jean Paul Sartre, French philosopher, writer and critic)

By immersing the participant of the brand experience in a multisensory environment and storytelling journey (allowing consumers to touch, taste, smell, hear and see) that the product and brand are relevant, they can experience – and, most importantly, feel an *Emotional Connection* – with the brand, one step closer to that ultimate 'golden brand bond'.

Interview excerpt: authenticity and real-world storytelling

Rodolfo Aldana, Director of Tequila, Diageo

What we are seeing is that consumers are now really gravitating towards authenticity and understanding brand stories, caring about how things are made, and where they come from. In bringing to life certain elements that are unique to our brands, we give consumers that point of difference with something to talk about that is really there, and it becomes like social currency for them.

Consumers are gravitating towards real stories, the people behind them and those that may in some way have a positive impact on local communities, and positive impact on the whole country.[8]

By creating a multisensory and immersive live brand experience, we are triggering emotions that traditional marketing and advertising approaches could never provoke. The multisensory approach for creating an *Emotional Connection* is appropriate for live brand experiences that are set in face-to-face environments in real life, and should be applied in combination with taking inspiration from the three key attributes: **authentic, positively connected** and **personally meaningful**.

Neil Gains states, in his book *Brand-esSense*: 'It pays to surprise customers occasionally or provide occasional "big moments". These are the parts of the experience that will be remembered and therefore will guide future decision making.' He continues: 'Perception, memory and action are all part of the same integrated system. We remember experiences that have meaning, in order to make future predictions by matching current perceptions to those past experiences. Meaning comes from predictive ability, emotional salience and context. Our senses help us create meaning.'[9]

By adding product- and brand-related multisensory components into the experience, we utilize elevated platforms that engage emotions through the senses. Experiences that engage the senses affect the right-brain hemisphere and create lasting impressions. Ultimately these memories, which can last a lifetime, can lay solid foundations for a long-term relationship – forming a golden brand bond that leads to action, repeat business, advocacy and, ultimately, evangelism.

Sensory branding is a type of marketing that appeals to all the senses in relation to the brand. It uses the senses to relate to customers on an emotional level. Brands can forge emotional associations in the customers' minds by appealing to their senses. A multisensory brand experience generates certain beliefs, feelings, thoughts and opinions to create a brand image in the consumer's mind.

Synaesthesia: a trait – the power and creativity of connecting different sensory elements

A HubSpot article on the science of creativity highlights some of the key signs of synaesthesia:[10]

- Synaesthesia is a neurological trait that combines two or more of our senses.
- 4 per cent of the population have this trait.
- Having one type gives you a 50 per cent chance of having a second, third or fourth type.
- Extra neurological hooks provide synaesthetes with superior memory.
- Once established in childhood, synaesthetic pairs remain fixed for life.
- Synaesthetes inherit a propensity for hyper-connecting brain neurons, but then must be exposed to cultural items such as food, names or letters.
- Non-synaesthetes can still comprehend metaphors such as 'sharp cheese' and 'sweet person' so we all have the propensity, which is closely linked to our creative functions.

So what does it all mean?

Many recent theorists and progressives have begun to consider the topic of synaesthesia more closely, where they start to wonder, are synaesthetes typically more creative because they are neurologically programmed to understand connections between things that not everyone else can see? Synaesthesia is increasingly being associated to creativity and the creative brain, a phenomena possibly occurring in us all to varying degrees.

Knowing that potentially we are all synaesthetes to some extent truly poses new opportunities in our perspective on how new ideas form, and in turn helps demystify some of the supposed art of creativity, exposing the process for the science it really is. For highly creative individuals who do not yet classify themselves as synaesthetes, there are likely to still be excess connections in the brain that are not as apparent as those classic synaesthetes with more notable traits, such as those who might for example relate the colour pink to the number '7'.[11]

Synthesizing many small parts to make a far greater whole

The *Emotional Connection* phase of the *BETTER* creative model is so important as we begin to populate all these rich sensory components, before our brain then synthesizes the components to generate unique and excellent concepts, fusing ideas that are reflective of a brand's essence and thus expressing its DNA through multifaceted storytelling.

Bring the brand to life and create an Emotional Connection *by touching all five senses*

People often ask, 'How do I decide which of the five senses are most appropriate to bring to life for which live brand experience?' The answer is to refer to the product and the *Brand Personality* for inspiration. Think of all five of the sensory elements: sight, touch, smell, sound and taste (Figure 6.6), integrating those that are appropriate in each case and context, and think of how to take inspiration from the 'three-key-attributes' approach to ideation, making the experience authentic, positively connected and personally meaningful.

This will form the basis of an idea that creates a positive and immersive multisensory brand environment, starting to build an *Emotional Connection*.

Multisensory elements: sight

Visual filters and perceptions tend to be very powerful and trigger strong emotional cues. Just like sounds and scents, colours can trigger very specific

Figure 6.6   Our sensory perceptions are impacted by our total bandwidth

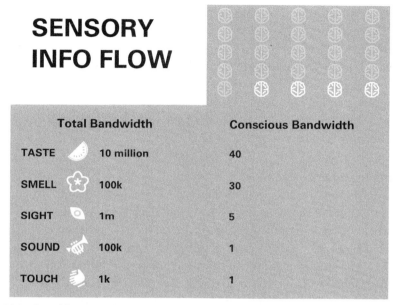

		Total Bandwidth	Conscious Bandwidth
TASTE		10 million	40
SMELL		100k	30
SIGHT		1m	5
SOUND		100k	1
TOUCH		1k	1

SOURCE Adapted from J Van den Bergh and M Behrer (2013) *How Cool Brands Stay Hot: Branding to generation Y*, Kogan Page, London

automatic responses in the cerebral cortex. They can activate thoughts, memories and particular behaviour. Different colours can impact our moods and feelings in varying ways. Yellow, for instance, is right in the mid-range of wavelengths that our eyes can detect. It is the brightest, and it is the colour that most easily attracts people's attention – crime scenes, safety gear and traffic cones often use the colour. Usually, colours with long wavelengths (like red) are arousing and stimulating compared to those with shorter wavelengths (like blue), which lower blood pressure, pulse and respiration rates.[12]

The colour purple – example

Cadbury has long known the power its packaging has had on evoking nostalgia and triggering long-standing memories with associations to childhood and positive feelings.

In 2012, Cadbury won the right to trademark their distinctive purple colour for packaging milk chocolate. Cadbury's purple is a distinctive asset for the brand, with huge importance in making Cadbury memorable and recognizable to customers, hence building mental availability and commercial value.

A British boy in a piece of 'storytelling research' referenced in Bergh and Behrer,[13] described his favourite chocolate brand, Cadbury: 'That familiar purple wrapper. It's almost like a member of my family, something that has been there since childhood. I rely on it for comfort, a treat and a motivator. Cadbury chocolate has seen me through exams, stress and heartache. It has been there when I have a celebration and I hope it will be there for some time to come.' When you read this brand story, it is immediately clear that this boy is not merely talking about the functional features of Cadbury chocolate. You notice a great deal of emotional references, such as being part of the family, helping through stressful moments and being there when celebrating. The *Guardian* reported in 2012 the verdict as, 'the evidence clearly supports a finding that purple is distinctive of Cadbury for milk chocolate'.

Feeling in colours – example

Christian Louboutin has secured the trademark for the distinctive red that marks the soles of the shoes he designs; Harrods has secured its own distinctive shade of green; and Tiffany owns the rights to the distinctive egg-shell blue that wraps every package coming out of their stores.[14]

When colours are intrinsically proprietary to the brand it is crucial to vividly bring those colours to life effectively and with the correct shade, throughout your live brand experience across all materials and formats. Which elements in the real world can you think of during this stage of the *BETTER* model that would reflect your brand colour, product packaging or campaign assets perfectly? Which textures and physical assets would express it in a way that is unusual, relevant and authentic?

Multisensory elements: touch

The tactile sense is crucial. This is where product textures and packaging can be brought to life, brought out of scale and context, or where feelings can be expressed into their physical counterparts, enriching an opportunity for a relevant and immersive connection and thereby deepening the brand experience.

CASE STUDY

Samsung

Samsung created an immersive and multisensory experience, created to support a VR experience of surfing in Tahiti:

- A VR headset, vibrating surfboard, water and air jets all came together to create a transformational experience for the 'participant'.

- This is a great example of how a leading brand is bringing to life its content and advertising through an immersive and multisensory interactive installation that will ultimately leave a deeper and memorable occasion for the consumer than a traditional 'ad' would.

- According to a Jack Morton report showcasing the Best of Cannes from 2016, it was all about creating a profound feeling of 'presence', which the *New York Times Magazine*'s editor, Jake Silverstein, described as the creative benchmark of their new VR content offering.

CASE STUDY

What does Cadbury feel like?

Cadbury Dairy Milk and its experiential agency RPM brought to life a plethora of 'intensely satisfying experiences' as part of its Tastes Like This Feels campaign, which kicked off with a bubble-wrap-popping event as reported by The Drum:[15]

- A giant carpet of bubble wrap invited shoppers to experience the overjoying fun of jumping on plastic pockets of air on a giant scale.

- Dairy Milk chocolate was distributed at the activations and 'joyful' music was played, thereby engaging the 'taste' and 'sound' senses, to complement the primarily 'touch'-led immersive experience.

- The brand showcased the joyful content on their social channels, using a first-person 'point of view' (POV)-style perspective, to further help people 'really imagine the popping of the bubbles in front of them, even if they were not able to get there themselves', Assistant Brand Manager Carly Sharpe stated in the article.

- 'The experience allowed people to evoke the wonderful feeling of intense satisfaction you get from popping bubble wrap and dramatized the joyful sensation that comes from tasting the classic Cadbury Dairy Milk', Carly added.

Multisensory elements: taste

Taste and gastronomical experience can be the most powerful in transporting us both emotionally and experientially into another time or place, whether rekindling nostalgic memories through flavours or tapping into an immediate craving, expression or purely providing us with satisfaction, and in turn creating positive new emotions.

CASE STUDY

Bombay Sapphire

Bombay Sapphire and immersive experts The Robin Collective launched a pan-European campaign called The Grand Journey:

- The activity consists of a 60-minute live experience that immerses audiences in the drink's brand story.

- The brand visited seven European cities with a bespoke tool kit, converting each location into a specially designed avant-garde-style train station and train carriage.

- Passengers 'boarded' the train before going through a mind-blowing virtual tour around the world, combining cultural opportunities to explore the unique art, provenance and flavours, inspired by the 10 botanicals found in Bombay Sapphire.

- Actors interacted with guests to incorporate them into a live theatrical adventure across the globe with the train 'stopping' at each of the 10 locations that Bombay's botanicals originate from, such as Spain, Ghana and China.

- The participants were given a unique cocktail, made by a mixologist, with inspiration taken from the country they had just 'travelled to'.

- Additional unique components to the multisensory experience included illusionists and gastronomical tastings, thus triggering a deep emotional connection through the senses, and authentically bringing to life the Bombay Sapphire provenance, heritage and *Brand Personality*.

Immersive theatre as a vehicle for brand engagement

This blend of brand experience and immersive acting plays into a wider trend where event marketing budgets are on the rise as consumers begin to favour this level of communication over traditional marketing channels. Bombay Sapphire's The Grand Journey is just one of many immersive and multisensory events platforms created by drinks brands that have sought to harness the power of immersive theatre to bring to life their products across global audiences.

Multisensory elements: smell

An important component within the *Emotional Connection* multisensory brainstorming process is considering transmitting emotions through the sense of smell. The limbic brain adds emotions based on the sensory observations of the visceral brain. 'Special attention needs to be paid to smell', Martin Lindstrom stresses in his book *Brand Sense*. There is a direct connection between our emotional brain centre (the amygdala-hippocampus) and the olfactory region of the brain. Scent is never filtered out: it is instinctive and involuntary.

The nose is therefore always pushed into 'evoked emotions and memories'. For many products they can easily recall how they smell and re-experience the stimulated emotion. Think of the artificial scents of Play-Doh modelling compound that bring back childhood memories. Certain perfumes, aftershaves or deodorant scents remind us of people we have loved, for example, or mum getting ready to go to work. Giving your live brand experience or experiential environment a scent that is linked to a positive emotion, or a scent-based journey, can enforce your emotional branding.

T is for *Target Audience*

By now, we have begun brainstorming the human-like activation pillars that create the *Brand Personality*, thinking of authentic, positively connected, and personally relevant attributes, and combined our material with the multisensory elements to create an *Emotional Connection*. The next step is understanding the *Target Audience* and their aspirations, an essential stage towards formulating the *Two-Way Interaction*, which should be at the heart of every experiential marketing concept (Figure 6.7).

Figure 6.7   *Target Audience* in the *BETTER* creative model

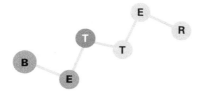

Relevance is everything

It is of the utmost importance to know the *Target Audience* and make sure that the live brand experiences are relevant to them. What they like and what they dislike are crucial considerations. The market research process does not have to be expensive, nor does it always have to be carried out by a market research agency. If you have insights into the *Target Audience* (for example, how they behave and what their needs are), you are part-way there. In this segment of the *BETTER* process, the experiential marketing ideas are inspired by activities that will add value to the audience's lives while exciting them and engaging them with the brand itself.

Punk-rock bankers might not fit

If the product is, for example, a saving bond with a fun *Brand Personality*, and the *Target Audience* are affluent, conservative brokers, it would not necessarily be relevant to bring to life the featured product through a punk-rock-themed live brand experience!

This conservative trade-based *Target Audience* is unlikely to appreciate subversive, underground anarchistic music and, therefore, even if this activity is relevant to the more rebellious *Brand Personality* associated with the bank brand, it is nonetheless irrelevant to the *Target Audience* for this product.

Harness and identify audience insights to inform creative ideas

Thus, before you finalize and confirm the *Emotional Connection* multisensory elements that you will integrate into your concept in order to connect with your *Target Audience*, bring to life the authentic product truths and convey the *Brand Personality*, make sure that your *Target Audience* will find these elements personally relevant to their lifestyle, their aspirations, their goals and their daily lives.

As stressed previously, the ultimate aim is to create a golden bond with the participants of the live brand experience. The *Emotional Connection* with the participants should be designed to create genuine, strong, deep relationships.

Insights from research

How do we create relationships with people in real life? We build foundations for relationships by engaging like-minded people in *Two-Way*

Interaction or dialogue that is relevant and interesting to both parties. It is a 'safe bet' to conclude that talking to people without listening to them would not facilitate a genuine relationship. In fact, this could irritate people and make them want to avoid the brand, or even spread negative word of mouth. Experiential marketing aims to convert consumers into brand advocates who love and champion their favourite brands. By using both qualitative and quantitative research you can learn more about what will appeal to your *Target Audience* in a live brand experience.

Two-Way Interactions are based on trust and relevance

At this stage of the brainstorm, check that any elements you have thought of are relevant to the *Target Audience*, and think carefully about what will drive consumers to be enthusiastic about the live brand experience and inspire them to talk about the brand. The dialogue that you will create in the *Two-Way Interaction* (the talking and listening/giving and creating process) is very similar to how relationships between people are formed, and admiration grows for a loved one or friend. Therefore, any insights into the *Target Audience* should be summarized here for inspiration, and used to contribute to the *Two-Way Interaction*.

Mobile and enhanced data sources are changing the demographics classifications forever

Forrester Consulting surmised in October 2015 that marketing strategies using the traditional campaign logic of demographics-based segmentation are 'so prevalent that they don't feel personal or relevant to consumers'. It is crucial that we identify real behavioural insights and tendencies rather than simply putting consumers into demographic boxes.[16] It is always important to consider all your stakeholder audiences and develop a concept for your brand experience that can engage and satisfy most of them.

Identifying the authentic product truths that resonate with the audience

Pop-up brand experiences and immersive events often play host to different activities or event programming, tailored at different audiences, including: influencers, media, trade and consumers (segmented further at times into individual interest niches).

You have already identified authentic product truths during the *Emotional Connection* stage of the *BETTER* brainstorm, now it is time to focus on which of these are most personally relevant to your audience.

Start to consider how these personally relevant (to your audience) 'authentic elements' could inspire activities for your *Two-Way Interaction*. Successful marketers must use messaging that speaks to the consumers as individuals, addressing their immediate personal circumstances and shopping intent.

Further audience insights

A more in-depth process of analysing your audience for insights and inspiration is elaborated on in the *Target Audience* chapter of the book, including the 'day-in-the-life and aspirational analysis' to be conducted as part of the *SET MESSAGE* planning process.

T is for *Two-Way Interaction*

Consumers and other stakeholders (influencers, media, trade) are likely to reciprocate, as they would if it were a relationship with another human being. In a human relationship, one person must not take from the other person without giving back. Similarly, when creating an experiential marketing campaign, the live brand experience activity must engage, excite and dazzle the *Target Audience*: giving something back (Figure 6.8). You need to make the live brand experience a *Two-Way Interaction* in real time to engage and excite consumers. No matter how exciting and amazing a one-way communication, it will not create as deep and genuine a relationship with the receivers, regardless of whether they enjoy it or not. They will not feel like they participated in it and therefore they will not care or connect on a deep level.

Figure 6.8   *Two-Way Interaction* in the *BETTER* creative model

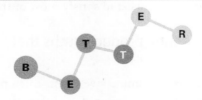

Listen

Just imagine an average Joe who is invariably on his own and one day his luck changes and suddenly he begins dating a model. At first, she seems captivating and beautiful. However, time reveals that she never listens to anything he says. She does not seem to care about him or his feelings, and all she does is talk about herself. Sooner or later, she will start irritating Joe, and his impression of her being beautiful will dissolve. He may stay around and suffer further for some time, but when a new girl at his office turns up, carefully listening to him and laughing at his jokes, making him feel special and personally considered, he would leave the aloof 'stunning model' and appreciate the *Two-Way Interaction* and *Emotional Connection* developing with his **positively connected** beau.

Take input

This example illustrates why it is important to have a positive *Two-Way Interaction* with consumers. It is vital to *listen* to them, *take input* from them and *co-create* with them, otherwise the communication is one-way – and no matter how theatrical or entertaining the campaign may be, it will simply be entertainment at best, disruption at worst, and the consumer will not truly connect with the brand and its personality.

Co-create!

So how does one go about creating a *Two-Way Interaction* within an experiential marketing context? The answer is in the live brand experience. For example, there could be a branded game, service or an interaction in which consumers engage, talk and listen. Experiential marketing has the potential to form the foundations of a life-long friendship and golden brand bond where the participant develops strong feelings – beyond loyalty – for the brand. He or she then becomes a brand advocate who will recommend the brand and spread word of mouth. He or she is your brand evangelist.

Let consumers co-create and at least partially drive the storyline. Armed with myriad devices and social media outlets, they expect to participate in the storyline offered by an advertiser – engage the consumer and enable them to affect the narrative.

Doing rather than being passive

Experiential marketing is the future of marketing because of the focus on brands expressing themselves through 'doing' and involving the customer through relevant and authentic *Two-Way Interaction*. The aim of the *Two-Way Interaction* (the live brand experience) is to create a real-world foundation to your brand story for all your integrated marketing and communications channels that let your *Target Audience* know that your brand cares about them. Consumers increasingly want to be part of the story, to play a role in the unfolding narrative. Brand stories are hardly ever linear, and consumers are no longer just along for the ride.

Rise of immersive entertainment globally

You can see this rise in the form of new and brilliant theatre productions from the likes of Secret Cinema, You Me Bum Bum Train and Punch Drunk leading the pack. These are immersive theatre experiences that put the audience at the centre of the show, integrating them in their world and letting them interact with the show on a level never been done before.

Personalizing storytelling, en masse

It has been claimed that 'one-to-one marketing means a brand no longer tells "a" story' – 'It has to tell its story in the context of each consumer. Instead of telling one story to many, you're telling many brand stories to one.'[17]

The following is an example of how the *Two-Way Interaction* that is individually personalized can develop.

Personalized flavours – example

Harriet is the marketing manager for a natural confectionery product that comes in three basic flavours: strawberry, orange and banana, and is available in fresh new packaging. Harriet wanted to create a *Two-Way Interaction* with consumers and engage them, while discovering which flavours are the most popular (achieving market research objectives):

- Harriet decided that an interactive gaming experience could help establish a flavour and that an immersive sensory experience would then take them on a flavour journey.

- By renaming each flavour so that it formed its own character and identity to bring to life in her narrative, she also hoped to strengthen the impact of the interaction between the brand and the consumers as she humanized the brand.

- The *Brand Ambassadors* invited the *Target Audience* to identify with each flavour by asking them to interact in a personality quiz that determined – if they were a fruit would they be a 'sexy strawberry', a 'brave banana' or an 'organized orange'.

- Depending on their answers, the participants were ushered into the pop-up and allowed into a different secret part of the live brand experience set, which had partitions that unlocked using special triggers, and participated in an immersive and theatrical experience that was geared around their selection.

- It may seem that asking the *Target Audience* to establish their favourite flavour was a potentially lacklustre way to interact.

- But in actuality, the *Brand Ambassadors* discovered something about their identity and celebrated it in an immersive, surprising and entertaining style.

- The consumers were taken on an unexpected, personalized, sensory, whirlwind journey and it made them feel good that the brand clearly cared enough to interact with them as individuals.

Do, tell and sell

Consider that Gen-Y's prefer 'doing', and feel enjoyment and positive emotions through so-called 'gratification activities', which come from taking an *active* role with an opportunity to **impact and influence** the outcome of a scenario or, in this case, brand experience.

Give brand experience participants a chance to mould the outcome of the story

The *Two-Way Interaction* should be built around activities, as personalized as possible to the *Brand Personality*, the *Emotional Connection* components and the *Target Audience*.

Interactive questions, where answers then drive triggers (either human or technological, and either digital or analogue) that create a variation in the live brand experience, and formulate research data (in turn allowing for better, future personalized communication), are excellent methods to building brand advocacy via what is known as the 'Hawthorne effect', getting to know your consumers, developing a real relationship, strengthening connections, making them feel listened to and consulted, helping them to accomplish something, learn something, improve something, which can lead to 'flow' and great happiness, especially amongst generations X, Y and Z.

According to the 'Happiness Hypothesis' (2006) putting ancient wisdom and philosophy to the test of modern science: gratification for millennials will often take place from 'experiences' and Gen Yers will have higher levels of happiness when *experiencing* something. This is not only thanks to the state of flow but also because experiences are mostly social happenings or activities connecting them with other people.[18]

Two-Way Interaction

What activities make millennials and Gen Z happy?

Pleasures:

- Delights with clear sensory and strong emotional components (as we have described in the section about using the five senses to arouse emotions).
- They feel good in the moment BUT sensual memories fade quickly.

Gratifications:

- Engaging activities that relate to Gen Y's interests and strengths and allow them to lose self-consciousness.
- Accomplish something/learn something/improve something/strengthen connections between people, which can lead to 'flow'.[19]

Activities form the core of the *Two-Way Interaction*

During this part of *BETTER*, participatory *Two-Way Interaction* activities and opportunities for the audience to influence and create should be mind-mapped at this stage, tapping into feelings of gratification and joy.

Joyful and personalized experiences lead the pack

An obsession with customer joy combined with a focus on delivering memorable, personal experiences for consumers are the defining characteristics of the companies leading KPMG Nunwood's 2016 UK Customer Experience Excellence top 100, measuring consumer brand perspectives on over 287 brands and 10,000 consumer interviews.[20]

Which real-world activities do your three brand personality pillars bring to mind?

These could be anything, and inspiration should be taken from activities that represent each of your three *Brand Personality* pillars (blue sky thinking is important here!). Combine and integrate one or more of these activities into the interactive part of the brand experience.

How can the sensory components synthesize into an idea?

Multisensory elements can be integrated into environmental design, and by creating physically separate areas and content moments you can lead participants on a multistage brand journey layered with immersive storytelling, designed to communicate the authentic product truths (those you will have identified as personally meaningful to your *Target Audience* from the earlier stages of the process).

Two-Way Interaction is key

As long as the interaction is not a one-way venture, and it takes on board the previous three 'BET' stages (*Brand Personality, Emotional Connection, Target Audience*) of the *BETTER* model, then you are on the right track to creating a fantastic and successful experiential marketing campaign. The *Two-Way Interaction* forms the basis of the interactive creative idea/inspiration for the live brand experience, and will be further developed during the *Experiential Strategy* part of the *SET MESSAGE* planning system.

E is for *Exponential Elements*

So far in the *BETTER* model, you have integrated the *Brand Personality, Emotional Connection, Target Audience* and developed the start of a brand-relevant, *Two-Way Interaction*, which brings the *Brand Personality* pillars to life and adds value to the consumers' lives. Via these means, you are on your way to building valuable consumer relationships, creating brand loyalty and dazzling the hearts and minds of your consumers.

Even though these benefits are superb and yield results that traditional approaches are less capable of achieving, an experiential marketing idea also provides the opportunity to integrate word-of-mouth triggers, integrate social media and tap into a massive buzz-creating opportunity via influencers, as well as providing opportunities for brands to 'incubate participants' into mini clubs, consulting them and co-creating with them, in the process creating deeply educated brand advocates that spread content and positive sentiment for the brand (Figure 6.9).

#LiveBrandSocial – combining word of mouth and social media with live brand experiences

In Electrify and Immediate Future's research 'Live Brand Social', asking which marketing consumers were most likely to share on social networks,

Figure 6.9 *Exponential Elements* in the *BETTER* creative model

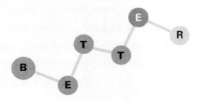

the top answer from participants was live branded experiences (56 per cent). Howell and Smilansky discussed how sharing on social networks appears closely aligned with live experiences in comparison to press ads and TV, which scored much lower.[21] The richness of content found at live experiences is a likely factor in this phenomena. The instantaneous, somewhat disposable and 'live' nature of an experience tends to entice a joyful moment, and trigger a content post, or share, or tweet.

You don't need to be there to get the message

Not everyone can participate in a live experience in person. But that is not the sole purpose of an event, is it? After all, you want to maximize your investment and extend that reach to others – grabbing eyeballs across the nation. When asked, 'How involved have you been in a live branded experience?' it seems that 'seeing' information about, and content from an event, spreads the messages dramatically: 45 per cent have seen a live experience but not participated, whilst 29 per cent have seen live experience content on social networks without attending. Ultimately, combining the two amplifies your efforts. It takes your brand message to a wider audience. A key finding from #LiveBrandSocial was that 56 per cent of consumers found out about a live brand experience through social media.

Driving word of mouth

The experiential marketing idea (focused on the live brand experience) should integrate an *Exponential Element* in which participants, influencers and other stakeholders are encouraged to tell others about the brand experience. As previously mentioned, word of mouth is one of the most powerful tools, and one of the most solid benefits of experiential marketing. The *Exponential Elements* stage in the *BETTER* model is where we look at how to better trigger and track word of mouth and sharing of your *Two-Way Interaction* and live brand experience content, driving the reach of the message to broader audiences, peers of participants and so on; these people are then exposed to your brand in the form of what is essentially a 'personal recommendation' from a trusted source of influence or friend. This is incredibly valuable and personal recommendations have been proven over and over to be the number-one driver in business growth. *Harvard Business Review* says that personal recommendations are over 10 times more effective than TV advertising.

Interview excerpt: increasing content *Reach* through influencers and authentic content

Vivienne Gan, Vice President, Global Public Relations, Langham Hospitality Group (global luxury hotel and resort brands)

There is a whole basket of variables in choosing which influencers to work with; number of followers is definitely one but there is no set number and you could have just 5,000 followers, but if they are good, qualified followers then that's great. There is that and then there is the type of things that they post; we look at the quality of their photographs and the content.

Marketing is more of a two-way relationship than it used to be, the way people talk about authentic experiences and authentic images – that is where I feel that bloggers and influencers come in, the authentic ones. It is not so much a one-way communication any more, it's two-way.

What I would like to see is a lot of companies becoming their own media source. I was thinking why can't we be a media source, where we put content out there first and directly, we put it on Twitter first, we put it on Facebook first, and then the media can pick it up. We are moving more and more away from traditional media, even something as old school as advertising.[22]

In a creative and authentic experiential campaign, exponential word of mouth and content spreading often happens by default, even when not considered properly, as the live brand experience aspect is extraordinarily powerful and exciting. The consumers, influencers, trade, media and any key stakeholders who participate in the activity will tell other people about the live brand experience because the engagement surprises, excites, entertains, involves, educates or benefits him or her. Inviting key influencers to preview and engage in your live brand experience is key in generating credible, unique content that comes with a seal of trusted approval, peaking the interest of those exposed to it, aligning it with those they trust and aspire to and, in turn, increasing the value of each contact.

A report commissioned by agency Good Relations found that 'Consumers are increasingly tuning in to content created by influencers to help them make purchasing decisions with one-fifth (19 per cent) of the average consumer's total media consumption now made up of influencer content.'[23] In their survey of 1,000 people over 16, they found that over half (57 per cent) have made a purchase based solely on an online influencer recommendation. This grew to 69 per cent for millennials. However, integrating the right content opportunities (ideally without the overuse of 'logo plastering'), and finding easy ways to socially create and share branded content are crucial, as is developing an appropriate and clear call to action (CTA), focusing on the right platforms for the content opportunity and your audience.

Exponential Elements: contest or game – example

If gamification forms a part of your live brand experience and you give game players a competitive incentive to invite their friends to join them in competing or playing the game and get involved themselves, you can exponentially spread the message and experience beyond the initial group like wildfire.

Exponential Elements: co-curation – example

Alternatively, say your live brand experience provides a strong co-curation or content creation opportunity. Emerging AI and other disruptive digital technology can eventually facilitate at least part of the ongoing personalized dialogue for friends and peers of those original participants, and also partake in a similar digital or mobile version of the experience, thus allowing the experience, and the story you are telling, to spread and to organically grow the positive impact and reach of the live brand experience. These 'Exponential Elements' and associated CTAs can take numerous different forms for triggering content to disseminate beyond the core participants of a live brand experience (share, snap, edit, create, compete, entertain, enjoy, etc).

R is for *Reach*

Experiential marketing is sometimes subject to faulty assumptions such as: 'experiential marketing is incapable of reaching many people'. You may have a live brand experience activation in a shopping centre that creates quality interactions with 5,000 people per day, while a YouTube video might deliver a one-way communication to 5 million people per day. In the days of the above-the-line (ATL) TV-first marketer, many were sceptical of investing in the experiential marketing landscape because the live brand experience alone often reaches significantly fewer people than mass media alone. However, we must consider the fact that each of the 5,000 people who interacted with the live brand experience has had a deeper and richer experience of the brand, and is likely to talk to a greater number of additional people about their experience. This experience will thus *Reach* a greater and greater number of people, as each will tell another, and each of those will continue to tell another. One can quickly see how the word of mouth generated from the live brand experience increases the exponential *Reach* of the experiential campaign (Figure 6.10).

Figure 6.10   *Reach* in the *BETTER* creative model

Translating live brand experience content onto the small screen

Live brand experiences have the capacity – due to their visual impact through increasingly impactful and creative production design – to provide backdrops for, and facilitate, both top-down (based on brand-generated content) or bottom-up (based on consumer-generated content).

In a Jack Morton report, 'The best of brand experience at Cannes', Caspar Mason, Senior Creative Strategist, states: 'As creators of brand experiences, we face a problem. We frequently work in a channel – real life – that technology hasn't quite caught up with yet. It is higher-res than anything you will find on a 4k display.'[24] He continues, to claim that this is 'not bound by a frame. It fully engages all five senses. The brand experiences we create are (or should be) 360-degree, immersive and multisensory. But the magic of a live moment does not always translate onto a 2D screen, which makes life difficult when creating experience-led content that travels' (Mason, 2016).

Pre, during and post; storytelling with content

The opportunity for a live brand experience to have a great *Reach* is largely dependent on how content is approached in terms of the narrative and story-telling: pre, during and post the immersive brand experience or *Two-Way Interaction*. At the final 'R' stage in the *BETTER* creative model, we look at how to maximize *Reach* and carefully craft and architect the narrative to each of our *Target Audiences*. It is here we can consider what content might be available to us prior to our live brand experience even taking place. We need to plan how to increase the impact of our event or brand experience, by promoting it in advance.

Spreading positive word of mouth about a live brand experience is crucial

Tech platforms like Eventbrite, YPlan and Design My Night are great ways to add 'paid media' into the mix to 'drive sales and reinforce key brand messages before, during and after an experiential campaign'.

Consider: 1) how else could content play a role in communicating our brand experience 'prior' to it even taking place? 2) How could this content be interesting and engaging to a far-reaching, even global, audience?

Making of/behind the scenes

One idea could be to produce videos showing time-lapsed 'making of' footage, if the brand is producing something (which is being made in advance) that is visually spectacular, for the actual experience. Examples where this could be the case include giant special builds, bespoke vehicles, artistic murals and virtual reality content.

Drone footage of Iceland For example, if a live brand experience is going to include 360-degree drone footage shot in Iceland, some short films, documenting the filming expedition itself (where the film crew go with the drones to film the content) would be an option to consider, footage could be captured and shown as a mini teaser 'coming soon' trailer/event invite to promote the live brand experience itself.

High Reach and proper relevance is key

It is important to think about which content will be most effective at reaching large numbers of people and whether it should be co-created with influencers or consumers, or manufactured with a high budget and distributed. The relevance of the content is crucial. You can capture it prior, and use it to raise awareness of a live brand experience in advance/during to showcase content while the live brand experience is taking place, and after to continue the story with legacy content, which can in turn also feed into storytelling for future live brand experiences, ideally all part of one 'branded platform' for consistent messaging.

Ensure physical real-world experiences translate well into mobile content

Tasteful and artistic brand production

Tasteful and aesthetically effective visual cues, beyond corporate 'logo plastering' are crucial, especially for millennials, Gen Z and those born after 2005. Think back to the 'E' for *Emotional Connection* stage within the *BETTER* brainstorming process, and refer to the multisensory elements that you came up with. Consider how some of these could be used to ensure that the environment is enticing for participants to capture and share, and consider how effectively the elements will translate into content with a potentially broader *Reach*.

High engagement does not always create great content

Namely, it may be very exciting for event attendees to partake in augmented reality (AR) gaming, and go through a journey of scent exploration through different areas; however, if neither of these elements translate into video or photography well, and the experience's content cannot reach a broad audience, then it could prove a costly and misplaced investment into a tiny group of people exposed. Content is crucial, and we need to get it right for both the physical attendees of a live brand experience or event, *and* ensure that the storytelling narrative is clear: pre, during and post, and translates onto mobile and the social platforms likely to be utilized by the audience.

If the live brand experience itself only reaches a handful of real-world participants, but it has a huge, impactful and relevant *Reach* to those that were merely exposed to the content second hand, that is arguably also a great success.

How will your live brand experience live on, long after the physical event has passed?

Content marketing and social media are more important than ever to integrate effectively when planning live brand experiences in the real world. We are already living our lives in parallel, in both the digital and physical world. Every hour, we upload 400 hours of content onto YouTube. Philosophers have thus theorized we are already cyborgs given our co-existence in tech space and that our digital footprint lives on even after our physical body passes! It is because of this that 90 per cent of brands intend to add content marketing to their mix, according to AOL's report at Cannes, 2016.[25]

If traditional advertising channels are still being used, such as TV, print, or outdoor media, we can look at how these – often ineffective – old styles of communication can be used more innovatively to raise awareness and facilitate interaction with our *Two-Way Interaction* concept, with a high *Reach*.

CASE STUDY

Virgin Holidays

Virgin Holidays integrated an ambitious *Two-Way Interaction* brand launch, with influencers and content as their live brand experience, which aired during a live TV ad during prime viewing of *The X-Factor*:

- The ad showcased influencers across 18 different destinations, as the company hoped to demonstrate that regular people could make these destinations a reality, not just celebrities.

- Claire Cronin, Virgin Holiday's VP of customer and marketing, told *Marketing Week* in 2016 that they wanted to move away from the unattainable celebrity perspective and bring the authenticity of real people doing realistic holiday activities back into focus.[26]

- This is a great example of how the tradition (and arguably outdated) one-way format (TV ad) was used to communicate an authentic and relevant message through a large-scale TV event, which was broadcast in real time, remotely.

- This is a very effective way to innovate and create participation with influencers and consumers through a high *Reach* brand experience.

- Sometimes integrating advertising can amplify and increase the impact of the *Two-Way Interaction* in a relevant and meaningful way.

CASE STUDY

Interactive Tostitos TV ads

In the Tostitos 2017 Superbowl ad, the brand took advantage of the high *Reach* opportunity to create an interactive experience, and they launched an anti-drink-and-drive packet that doubled up as a breathalyzer. They sampled these and ran alongside an ad, so that those who had 'overenjoyed' Superbowl festivities could get a free Uber code if they were over the limit. The simple yet effective *Two-Way Interaction* with the Tostitos pack, and the Uber app, was a success for both brands and stood out amongst a succession of lacklustre one-way advertising messages that bombarded consumers during the Superbowl.

Participation brands create intimate relationships

The *Reach* quality of one-way communications is far less likely to create a genuine relationship than that of live brand experiences. It is rare that we will see an ad in the paper or watch an ad on TV or in a movie trailer and, later on, tell anyone about the 'experience'. In contrast, participating in a live brand experience through an experiential marketing campaign is exciting and we are very likely to tell many people about it.

Integrate paid media, sponsored social and PR for maximum awareness around a brand experience

When developing an experiential marketing concept, always take into consideration both methods of increasing the initial *Reach* (the people who interact first-hand with the live brand experience) and the combined *Reach* of the experiential marketing campaign as a whole (including the amplification channels such as social media, content and PR).

Your live brand experience channel does not have to compete with the other channels, some of which can have a very high *Reach* (such as advertising). We know that other channels can be less effective when implemented traditionally, so for best results it is recommended that the live brand experience idea is connected and complemented by the other selected channels. As a result, the experiential marketing content and an authentic, personally relevant and positively connected *Two-Way Interaction* can *Reach* the highest possible volumes of your target.

How do you begin brainstorming ways to extend the Reach?

The live brand experience *Reach*

When you are in the *Reach* part of the *BETTER* creative process, first take into consideration factors that affect the initial *Reach* of the live brand experience. Consider where would be the ideal location(s) to hold your experience(s)? If we decided that the best place to hold the experience was the middle of a park, but there was no footfall in the park, then the first-hand *Reach* factor is not addressed, making the initial *Reach* of the campaign unsuccessful. On the other hand, if we researched brand-relevant events where thousands of people attended and the *Target Audience* is consistently present, then this could be a more appropriate set of venues.

The content *Reach*

Second, you should think of the role of content 'before, during and after' your live brand experiences and events, creating physical and virtual environments that reflect your brand and create an aspirational positioning that translates effectively into numerous different content formats. By curating a content-generating experiential journey for the consumer as they move through your live brand experiences' participation stages, you will ensure that the organic and paid content that your experiential marketing generates will achieve the greatest possible *Reach*. Always remember to consider the potentially exponential scope of the positive word-of-mouth *Reach* that a great brand experience can trigger.

Summary

How do you use the BETTER model?

When using the *BETTER* brainstorming model to come up with top-line concepts for experiential marketing you first complete the B, E and T stages (*Brand Personality, Emotional Connection, Target Audience*), and then combine the results as components to 'stew' in the subconscious mind before going into the main creative process, represented by the second T: the *Two-Way Interaction*. This forms the inspiration for your big idea, central to your creative. Then you build in E, an *Exponential Element*, and then the R, examining the role of content and supporting channels in trying to achieve the best possible *Reach* (a combination of the initial *Reach* of the live brand experiences, the word-of-mouth *Reach*, and the *Reach* of the amplification channels).

In summary, one must brainstorm and consider six stages when developing a top-line concept for an experiential marketing campaign. The *BETTER* brainstorm involves covering the following bases:

Brand Personality. Two or three human-like characteristics that are extracted to form the *Brand Personality.*

Emotional Connection. The brand must strive to connect on an emotional level with its *Target Audience.* This is best achieved through a combination of immersing them in multi-sensory brand environments and ensuring the experience represents the three key attributes: authentic, positively connected and personally meaningful.

Target Audience. The *Target Audience* is key when brainstorming the idea. Lots of research about the lifestyle of the *Target Audience* should be brought to the table, to ensure the right experience for the right people.

Two-Way Interaction. The live brand experience involves interaction between consumers and brands in real time (either remotely or face to face). The first three stages – *Brand Personality, Emotional Connection* and *Target Audience* – should inspire this.

Exponential Elements. The *Exponential Elements* should be designed to encourage participants to pass on their experience, spreading word of mouth both in real life and on social media.

Reach. Clearly, gaining maximum *Reach* for the experiential marketing campaign is crucial. The initial *Reach* of the live brand experience, the word-of-mouth *Reach* and the combined *Reach* of the selected amplification channels should be taken into consideration. The right amplification channels should be there mainly to expand the *Reach* of the live brand experience, thus allowing the campaign's concept to engage more people.

The total *BETTER* brainstorm process should be completed in the following way. Begin by collecting any existing research and having it handy. Start with the B stage (thinking of the *Brand Personality*, which you identify from the three main *Brand Personality* and human characteristic components), then think of how to create an *Emotional Connection* (multisensory and/or the three key attributes: authentic, positively connected and personally meaningful), then take into consideration the *Target Audience* (their likes, dislikes, lifestyle and insights) also taking into account influencers, trade and media. Combine the first three steps to create the *Two-Way Interaction*. Then build in *Exponential Elements* (taking into consideration what will trigger the conversation, and a CTA to spread that word of mouth), and think of how to maximize the *Reach* (the amplification channels as well as maximizing the initial 'first-hand' interactions with the live brand experience, and the *Reach* of the most appropriate content and influencer platforms).

Notes

1   Marranco, J (2015) [accessed 12 April 2016] The Science of Creativity, HubSpot, 31 March [Online] https://blog.hubspot.com/marketing/the-science-of-creativity#sm.000157rw9h10z0e95sdmvsculsjn0

2   Marranco, J (2015) [accessed 12 April 2016] The Science of Creativity, HubSpot, 31 March [Online] https://blog.hubspot.com/marketing/the-science-of-creativity#sm.000157rw9h10z0e95sdmvsculsjn0

3   Zaltman, G and Zaltman, L (2008) *Marketing Metaphoria: What deep metaphors reveal about the minds of consumers: what seven deep metaphors reveal about the minds of consumers*, Harvard Press, Boston

4   Cytowic, R and Eagleman, D (2011) *Wednesday is Indigo Blue: Discovering the brain of synaesthesia*, MIT Press, Cambridge, Mass.; Brang, D and Ramachandran, R (2011) [accessed 13 November 2016] 'Survival of the Synaesthesia Gene: Why Do People Hear Colors and Taste Words', Plos Biology [Online] http://dx.doi.org/10.1371/journal.pbio.1001205

5   Bradley, M M, Greenwald, M K, Petry, M C and Lang, P J (1992) Remembering pictures: pleasure and arousal in memory, Journal of Experimental Psychology: Learning, memory and cognition, 18, pp 379–907

6   AESOP (2016) [accessed 20 June 2017] Aesop 2016 Brand Storytelling Survey Results, AESOP Agency [Online] http://aesopagency.com/aesop-2016-brand-storytelling-survey-results/

7   Chahal, M (2016) [accessed 12 October 2017] Top Storytelling Brands Capitalise on Smartphone Obsessed Consumers, *Marketing Week*,

29 September [Online] https://www.marketingweek.com/2016/09/29/top-storytelling-brands-capitalise-on-consumers-smartphone-obsession/

8 Smilansky, S (2017) Excerpt from an interview with Rodolfo Aldana, Director of Tequila, Diageo

9 Gains, N (2013) *Brand esSense*, Kogan Page, London

10 Marranco, J (2014) [accessed 23 May 2016] Human-to-Human Marketing: A Trend for 2015 and Beyond, HubSpot, 17 December [Online] https://blog.hubspot.com/marketing/human-to-human-marketing#sm.000157rw9h10z0e95sdmvsculsjn0

11 Brang, D and Ramachandran, R (2011) [accessed 13 November 2016] Survival of the Synaesthesia Gene: Why Do People Hear Colors and Taste Words, Plos Biology [Online] http://dx.doi.org/10.1371/journal.pbio.1001205

12 Van den Bergh, J and Behrer, M (2013) *How Cool Brands Stay Hot: Branding to Generation Y*, Kogan Page, London

13 Van den Bergh, J and Behrer, M (2013) *How Cool Brands Stay Hot: Branding to Generation Y*, Kogan Page, London

14 Gains, N (2013) *Brand esSense*, Kogan Page, London

15 Deighton, K (2016) [accessed 20 August 2017] 'Satisfying Experiences' – Including a Bubble Wrap Carpet, The Drum [Online] http://www.thedrum.com/news/2016/04/05/satisfying-experiences-including-bubble-wrap-carpet-key-cadbury-s-latest-campaign

16 The Drum (2015) [accessed 20 August 2017] Consumer Intent: The Future of Marketing, Iotec [Online] http://www.thedrum.com/whitepaper/consumer-intent-future-marketing

17 Oracle (2016) [accessed 26 November 2016] The Programmatic Guide: For Modern Marketers, Publishers, and Media Planners [Online] http://www.thedrum.com/whitepaper/programmatic-guide

18 Van den Bergh, J and Behrer, M (2013) *How Cool Brands Stay Hot: Branding to Generation Y*, Kogan Page, London

19 Van den Bergh, J and Behrer, M (2013) *How Cool Brands Stay Hot: Branding to Generation Y*, Kogan Page, London

20 You can read more on the study here: KPMG/Nunwood (2016) Customer Experience Excellence Centre [Online] http://www.nunwood.com/customer-experience-excellence-centre-2016-uk-analysis/

21 Howell and Smilansky, S (2013) [accessed 27 August 2017] LiveBrandSocial [Online] http://www.electrifyww.com/pdf/LiveBrandSocial_survey_report.pdf

22 Smilansky, S (2017) Excerpt from an interview with Vivienne Gan, Vice President, Global Public Relations, Langham Hospitality Group (Global Luxury Hotel and Resort Brands)

23 Good Relations [accessed 27 August 2017] Influencer Content Accounts For Almost 20% of Consumer Media Consumption [Online] http://goodrelations.co.uk/2017/05/23/influencer-content-accounts-almost-20-consumer-media-consumption/

24 Jack Morton [accessed 27 August 2017] The Best of Brand Experience at Cannes [Online] http://www.jackmorton.com/wp-content/uploads/2016/07/TheBestOfBrandExperienceAtCannesLions_JackMorton.pdf

25 Jack Morton [accessed 27 August 2017] The Best of Brand Experience at Cannes [Online] http://www.jackmorton.com/wp-content/uploads/2016/07/TheBestOfBrandExperienceAtCannesLions_JackMorton.pdf

26 Gee, R (2016) [accessed 12 January 2017] Screw It, Let's Do It: Virgin Holidays on the Launch of its 'Most Ambitious Campaign' yet, *Marketing Week*, 8 September [Online] https://www.marketingweek.com/2016/09/08/screw-it-lets-do-it-virgin-holidays-on-the-launch-of-its-most-ambitious-campaign-yet/

PART TWO
SET MESSAGE

An activation framework for your experiential marketing strategy

To recap, we have gone through the *BETTER* brainstorming and creative model, created our topline ideas and shown them to the decision-making unit, boss or client. As a result, a decision has been made about which topline idea is to be developed in further detail, since a more detailed idea, strategy and plan are required prior to implementation.

This is where the *SET MESSAGE* model comes into play. *SET MESSAGE* is a more detailed planning system, which ensures that both your *Experiential Objectives* and *Experiential Strategy* are supported by systematic planning and *Evaluation*, enabling you to keep your campaign on track. These systems will allow the people responsible to assess the plans in depth prior to implementation and to *Gauge Effectiveness* during the campaign, as well as effectively evaluate it afterwards.

The *SET MESSAGE* model

The *SET MESSAGE* model stands for:

*S*ituation and Background
*E*xperiential Objectives
*T*arget Audience
*M*essage – Key Communication
*E*xperiential Strategy
*S*elected Locations and Brand Ambassadors
*S*ystems and Mechanisms for Measurement
*A*ction
*G*auging Effectiveness
*E*valuation

Figure P2.1 The *SET MESSAGE* planning system

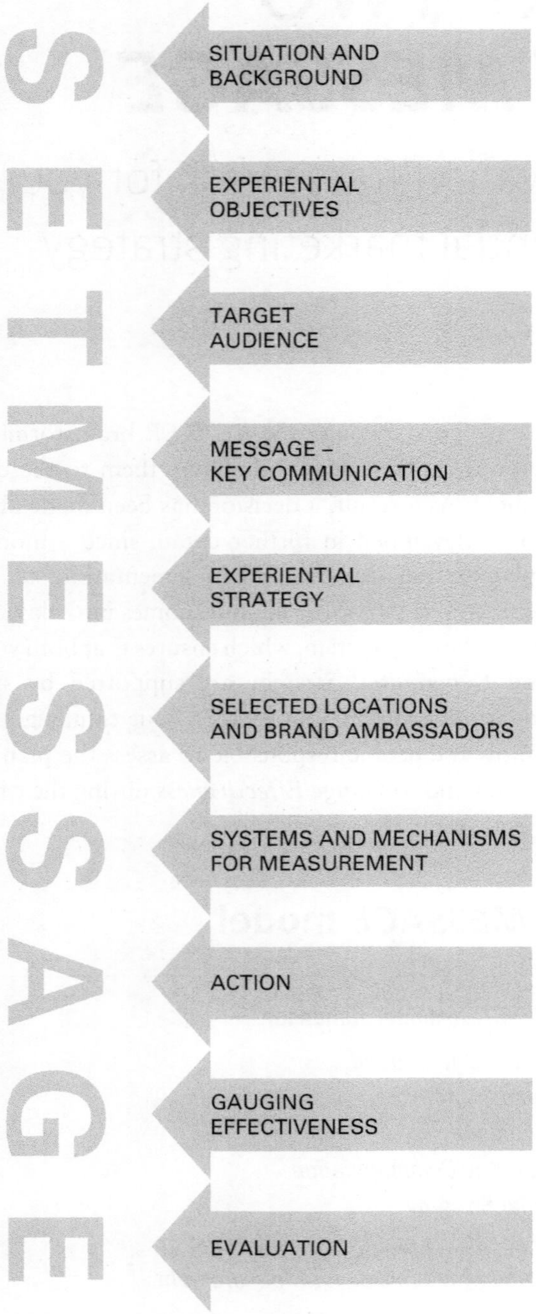
S
E
T
M
E
S
S
A
G
E
SITUATION AND BACKGROUND
EXPERIENTIAL OBJECTIVES
TARGET AUDIENCE
MESSAGE – KEY COMMUNICATION
EXPERIENTIAL STRATEGY
SELECTED LOCATIONS AND BRAND AMBASSADORS
SYSTEMS AND MECHANISMS FOR MEASUREMENT
ACTION
GAUGING EFFECTIVENESS
EVALUATION

Systematic planning

It is important to carry out a systematic planning process, so that once you have completed it you have a very straightforward framework to follow. The campaign plan becomes a blueprint for implementation success, in which delegating tasks and managing different segments of your campaign becomes simple. It has been said that 'If you fail to plan, you plan to fail.' This is certainly true for experiential marketing. The live brand experience should be at the core of the experiential marketing idea and, as with any live event, there are many more factors, both external and internal, that may lead to things going wrong.

Detailed planning

Micro planning is the only way to avoid the detrimental effects of unexpected eventualities occurring during a live brand experience. Also, by having a detailed plan that addresses every element of the campaign, you will have answers to many of the questions that will arise from those who may be sceptical about experiential marketing. Whether these inquisitive people are internal to your organization or part of a client team, it is important to show that you have covered all bases from the campaign's inception to completion.

Negative consequences

Consequences can be grave if planning is not carried out properly. As a busy individual, you will not have time to plan as you go along. If you fail to plan systematically, there are areas of your campaign that are doomed to be neglected, and sacrifices will have to be made. For example, if you do not decide in advance what the measurement metrics for your campaign are, then although your campaign may be successful, it will be impossible to prove that the benefits were a direct result of the campaign.

Planning your experiential marketing initiative

Planning measurement metrics in advance is key

Imagine that you are working in an agency. One of your clients has a website and it has given you the task of creating an experiential marketing campaign designed to promote its website. If you failed to plan, how would you track visitors to the site? There would be no way of proving the direct correlation between the increase in site visitors and the consumers who engaged in the experiential marketing campaign. There is no guarantee that your client would not claim the increase was due to the £5 million it spent on advertising. Even if you were sure that at least 60 per cent of this increase in traffic was due to the exciting and engaging experiential campaign you implemented, it is not a fact until you can prove it to your client or stakeholders.

The *Systems and Mechanisms for Measurement* part of the *SET MESSAGE* plan would have enabled you to plan how to communicate to stakeholders what portion of the increase in site traffic was due to the experiential marketing campaign. Something as simple as a promotional code or unique URL would suffice. Moreover, the client would have agreed to this form of measurement in advance and would, therefore, appreciate the significance of the results once the campaign has been implemented.

Planning for real-world experiences

Not planning a live brand experience in detail can mean staffing inappropriate *Brand Ambassadors*. No matter how promising the idea for the live brand experience is, if the wrong team of *Brand Ambassadors* interacts with the consumers, the concept behind the live brand experience could be nullified. Along with providing the right *Brand Ambassadors* (to match the *Brand Personality* and *Target Audience*), detailed project management systems, budgets and schedules are essential in attaining success. If one were to miss important deadlines and have bad project management as a result, the campaign would inevitably lead to a below-par execution. Similarly, if the amplification channels are not properly integrated in the planning stages to maximize the impact of the live brand experience, a great deal of money can be wasted on traditional media that does not contribute significantly to the overall success of the experiential marketing campaign.

Introducing the *SET MESSAGE* campaign planning system

The rest of this book is formatted according to the *SET MESSAGE* methodology, with each chapter focusing on a different letter of the planning system. By the time you finish reading, you will be able to see the importance of, and have a clear framework for, planning an experiential marketing campaign in detail.

Situation and background   07

Exploring the business context for experiential marketing

Heritage, provenance, brand story

The 'S' in *SET MESSAGE* stands for *Situation and Background*. This is the first category of your detailed experiential marketing campaign plan. The purpose of the *Situation and Background* category is to give an overview of what the company and brand have been doing up until this point, and the relevance of this background to the current experiential marketing plan. This is a great opportunity to dig deep and get under the skin of the brand, really aiming to establish its heritage, provenance, story, journey and DNA. In the plan itself this segment should set the scene for both the broader market context, trends and opportunities, as well as the compelling brand/product truths that can be expanded upon for authentic and successful communications.

It is best to begin by considering the history of the brand and how that relates to its current strategy.

Energy drink – example

For instance, there is a brand of energy drinks that targets people who play sport or live an active lifestyle. The energy drink was invented around 50 years ago and was originally targeted at sick children. However, after the realization that the drink is more effectively targeted towards people with active lifestyles, the energy drink changed its positioning. This type of information is worth considering in the *Situation and Background* part of the *SET MESSAGE* plan.

Business and market factors should be considered

In addition to the historical context, you should also explore business factors such as the size of the market and the market share currently held by the brand, its category and competitors.

It is very important to truly understand and immerse yourself in the philosophy and ethos of the brand, and determine how its mission and heritage can be encapsulated in an essence statement. For example, 'The brand is owned by a family business that operates with fair trade policies'.

Competitor insights

This stage in the planning process can also be used to identify and explore information about competitors' previous experiential marketing programmes as well as others with similar audiences or brand positioning. What experiential marketing have they done?

When you were brainstorming using the *BETTER* model and presented the concepts using the *IDEA* format, you may have looked at competitors with the same type of *Brand Personality*, product or *Target Audience*, and the experiential marketing programmes that they have created. This includes exploring how they created an *Emotional Connection*, and which sensory messages they communicated through their brand experience environment. Keep in mind: this is research that should have already been completed prior to coming up with the top-line concept, so at this stage of your plan you are simply referencing and referring to it for insight.

Previous experiential marketing campaign insights

It is also recommended that you look at the marketing initiatives and stories carried out and communicated over the last few years exploring which marketing platforms and messages were used (especially those that have been used with the most success or where there was a lack of impact on the brand performance) and what impact they had.

Research the factors that have led this brand (your organization or client) to use experiential marketing.

Denim brand – example

Jessica has been the brand manager of a denim company for the last five years:

- The majority of her marketing budget had gone into traditional advertising, with some PR and a bit of sponsorship over the last year.

- The reason that she is now thinking of placing live brand experiences at the core of the marketing communications strategy is that the live experience channel is superb at driving word of mouth and can change the perception of the brand.

- She hoped it could achieve her objective to reposition it for a 'trendy hipster' demographic.

- After exploring tools such as sponsorship, she has decided that an experiential marketing approach will give the most credibility and the live brand experience, and the content it generated, when amplified through her media and PR channels, will be most effective in attaining her objectives.

Beer brand – example

Robert is a brand manager of a beer company:

- The beer is imported from Asia and has a very different taste to other beers.

- Robert has consequently run field-marketing sampling programmes to encourage product trial, which conveyed the strength of the product in the last three years.

- The previous field marketing initiatives have successfully driven product trials, but they have not really succeeded in conveying the Asian heritage of the brand.

- Therefore, if you were Robert, at this stage in the *SET MESSAGE* method, you would examine key insights, exploring potential reasons why the field marketing campaigns may have been successful, yet have not achieved all of his objectives.

- This is why Robert now wants to try an experiential marketing approach, replacing the field marketing-style sampling with enhanced and immersive live brand experience programmes.

- He should now integrate the live brand experience content into the story of his other marketing communications such as paid media, PR and influencer marketing to form his complete experiential marketing programme.

Niche fast-moving consumer goods brand – example

Frank was Marketing Director of a condensed-milk drink brand:

- In response to a recent decision to adopt a market development strategy in which a new hard-to-reach audience of Caribbean males would be targeted, Frank decided that a traditional approach would not be appropriate.
- By using media, there would be a lot of wastage, and Frank's market research agency felt that this demographic would not be as responsive to above-the-line methods.
- Therefore, he signed a significant portion of the marketing budget to a live brand experience programme and chose PR along with radio and digital channels, to amplify it and form the complete experiential marketing campaign.
- Frank outlined this when he was preparing the *Situation and Background* part of his *SET MESSAGE* plan.

Changes and organizational climate

In the *Situation and Background*, you should also mention any important changes within the organization and any broader corporate, social or business factors that are relevant.

Sometimes an experiential marketing methodology marks the introduction of a new strategy for the complete communications mix. The reasons for this could vary.

For example, it could be:

1 a reaction to a customer and brand experience orientation developing throughout the organization;

2 that leadership have identified that real world experiences combined with a public facing CSR message will be the best way to express their missions and value;

3 that the brand propelled to success from grass-roots heritage and that its founders know nothing beats a personal recommendation.

There are so many factors as to which direction to take, so be sure to dwell on even the broadest of global or future trends if they resonate or are likely to impact your brand experience.

Summary

In summary, the *Situation and Background* part of your *SET MESSAGE* plan should provide an overview of the brand's history, its current situation or brief and what has happened in the past. We looked at why it was or was not successful when creating experiential marketing initiatives or strategies before, as well as identifying insights from other brands' brand experiences, especially with similar *Brand Personalities* or *Target Audiences*.

Experiential objectives

How to creatively define and set your goals

The second step in the *SET MESSAGE* planning methodology focuses on which *Experiential Objectives* to choose at this stage of the plan. You will already have an idea of the type of objectives you would like to achieve, because you will have decided on them as part of the broader marketing communications strategy. When you are coming up with your *Experiential Objectives*, you can often be more creative than with traditional approaches because experiential marketing facilitates meeting many objectives that can otherwise be harder to attain. As previously discussed, there are many benefits to be gained from running successful experiential marketing campaigns, and there are therefore many exciting objectives to choose from. However, you should stick with no more than three.

Keep objectives *SMART*

It is important to include all the relevant information when presenting your *Experiential Objectives*. Try presenting in a *SMART* format:

> *SMART* format
> **S**pecific
> **M**easurable
> **A**chievable
> **R**ealistic
> **T**imebound
> For example, to achieve objective X, for brand X, with target audience X, in location X, by date X. A specific example would thus be: *To increase sales for Barley Bars with 20- to 30-year-old women in France by January 2020.*

By now there should be an initial idea to develop into the plan.

Prior to embarking on the *SET MESSAGE* planning system, you will have already completed several *BETTER* brainstorms, presented the top-line creative concepts and selected an idea for detailed development. At this stage, you may need to adapt the top-line concept to ensure that it is appropriate and fits in with the *Experiential Objectives*.

> In the Eventbrite Report: The Complete Guide to Experiential Marketing, Jason Megson, Managing Director and Vice President at George P. Johnson states:
>
>> As with all marketing activity the first thing you will need to do before you even talk to a brand experience agency is to define the business problem you are trying to solve... It's as simple as always starting with the 'why?' and then continuing to reference back to this overall objective throughout the planning, delivery and post-activity.[1]

Let's look at some examples of experiential marketing campaign objectives.

Objective 1: bringing the brand personality to life

John is a marketing manager who is responsible for a breakfast bar with a **sporty** and **active** *Brand Personality* that targets healthy males and females aged 18–35. John wanted to bring the bar's *Brand Personality* to life in the United States:

- His experiential marketing agency designed a sporty live brand experience that ran for one month in each of the eight largest parks across the north-east.
- The live brand experience set featured circuit-training elements, where consumers were invited to participate in a circuit challenge across several exercise stations, such as a jogging machine, a rowing machine, a push-up bench and monkey bars.
- They were then invited to have their pulse taken and heart rate tested.
- A branded wall that showed the breakfast bar, its logo and colour scheme surrounded the circuit equipment.
- Consumers who completed the circuit challenge in under two minutes won a goody bag containing: a sample bar, a sales promotion voucher (to entice them to purchase in the future), a branded T-shirt and a branded stopwatch.

After the experience, research showed that the *Target Audience* associated this breakfast bar brand with a **sporty** and **active** lifestyle and therefore the campaign achieved this objective. It also achieved its second and third objectives of driving product trial (with the sample in the goody bag) and driving sales (with the voucher in the goody bag).

The experiential marketing agency worked on the campaign in partnership with John's media agency, which is responsible for the brand's media (creative, planning and buying). The live brand experience was filmed by the media agency and clips were edited, contributing to a digital and TV advert promoting both the product itself and the upcoming live brand experiences. The ads were broadcast during carefully allocated slots prior to major sporting events on TV.

The successful integration of the live brand experiences, sales promotion vouchers and TV adverts was a result of good communication between John's experiential marketing agency, sales promotion agency and media agency, which worked together to deliver the integrated experiential marketing campaign.

Objective 2: drive word of mouth

Mark is the brand manager for a new basketball computer game with revolutionary features. He wanted to drive word of mouth about the game among 16- to 21-year-old city-based males:

- His PR agency created a gaming experience held outside basketball courts in his target cities.
- They hired an experiential marketing agency to design branded 'chill-out zones'.
- The zones had comfortable couches, 360-degree surround-sound screens, gaming consoles and fridges containing free soft drinks (branded with the video-game imagery).
- The participants were asked to provide their contact data upon entering the 'chill-out zone', prior to playing the video game.
- High scorers (around 40 per cent of participants) were offered the opportunity to receive free (branded) business cards with their own contact details printed on them.
- Each high scorer had a special status as a 'team member' of the video-game manufacturers' 'preview team'.

- The *Exponential Element* was very strong, because the *Target Audience* used the business cards when socializing and giving out their phone number to their peers.

- Every time that they gave a business card to someone, they were likely to mention the video game and their involvement with it (especially because their membership in the preview team had become a 'cool' talking point).

The PR agency invited basketball players and sports influencers to launch the first day of the live brand experience every time it visited a new city. As a result, they succeeded in gaining a large amount of publicity and drawing large crowds.

When the same video-game manufacturer wanted to achieve its market research objectives and incubate fans in an advocacy programme, they invited the 'preview team members' to exclusive video-gaming preview sessions and gave out demo versions of the games.

This activity – by consulting and enabling audiences to participate in the brand's world – created a talking point that drove word of mouth among the *Target Audience*. As well as achieving the primary word-of-mouth objective, this experience achieved secondary objectives: gaining PR coverage, capturing data and positioning the brand as the basketball video game with the best street credentials amongst a young Gen Z *Target Audience*, who would have been less responsive to traditional channels.

Objective 3: create a memorable brand experience

Sandy owns a travel website that sells holidays to exotic locations in the Caribbean and warm places around the world. She had spent a significant amount of money with her advertising agency and had benefited from a healthy increase in web traffic when they ran print ads, but as soon as she stopped paying for ads, her site traffic would plummet. She wanted to utilize a marketing approach that would have a longer-lasting and sustainable effect.

Her main *Experiential Objective* was to **create a memorable brand experience**. She also hoped to **convey the exotic *Brand Personality*** of the travel experience company through the campaign, with the aim that after participating in the live brand experience, her *Target Audience* would think of her brand when booking their next holiday. She wanted them to **remember** her company and the positive brand experience they'd had for years to come, and she was keen to include an opportunity to **educate** them on the wondrous travel experiences offered by her company:

- She designed a live brand experience that featured a touring Caribbean beach set with *Brand Ambassadors* dressed in traditional Caribbean clothing.

- The live brand experience toured around the country during the summer and targeted families. Carefully positioned *Brand Ambassadors* invited consumers to have their photos taken while visiting the 'beaches' (which were also artificially warmed using special lamps).

- The participants entered a virtual reality (VR) beach experience, where they were transported digitally and, through multisensory triggers, were taken to a multitude of authentic local Caribbean mini experiences offered by the tour operator.

- Participants were then handed glossy, interactive augmented reality (AR) enabled brochures that both promoted the travel content and experiences while also inviting consumers to enter their contact data, after which they had the option to share content with friends and family to win once-in-a-lifetime-experience prizes.

- This live brand experience campaign created highly memorable content and brand experiences, and it also achieved secondary press coverage and data capture objectives, which ultimately led to an increase in sales.

Objective 4: bring to life product heritage, and sign up members to a club

A market-leading natural skincare brand from Asia launched in the UK. They approached an experiential agency to work on their launch, as well as ongoing live brand experience activities:

- The agency built a pop-up experiential venue that featured a cafe area where free refreshments were on offer to those who signed up to the brand's monthly beauty magazine, and pods at the rear for skincare influencer demonstrations.

- The set also had display stands that featured the beauty club magazines along with highly visible branding and signage, which reflected the brand identity and *Message – key communication*.

- The experiential pop-up toured around brand-relevant beauty shows and large-scale popular style events.

- A carefully trained team of *Brand Ambassadors* visually reflected the brand (and had relevant experience in the beauty sector) and were the interface between the brand and the guests of the shows.

- The pop-up venue had high-end, beautiful production details inspired by a Japanese Rice Village Hut that had been photographed by its team of researchers while they were meeting ingredients suppliers in remote regions.

- *Brand Ambassadors* wore tailor-made uniforms that fused Japanese and English styles, bringing to life the brand's heritage.

- By engaging consumers with the offer of complimentary skin consultations and free four-step skincare Japanese skincare rituals (along with a sample pack), the team signed up large numbers of the *Target Audience* to the brand's exclusive Beauty Advocates fan club and magazine.

- The exclusive influencer demos were filmed and the content was broadcast live on social media platforms.

- Members of the club received extra exclusive content and unlocked interactive skincare ritual tutorials, also allowing this group of super-consumers the opportunity to ask direct questions to the guest influencers remotely, via Instagram live.

The live brand experience achieved the *Experiential Objectives* of **driving product trial** amongst the *Target Audience*, as well as generating significant **organic social reach** and **signing up people for membership** to the club. The activity also resulted in an increase in direct to consumer (D2C) website **traffic and sales**, thus achieving other objectives.

Objective 5: drive personalized product trial at point of sale

When Mary, a brand manager for a popular yoghurt brand, was assigned the task of **increasing sales** and **engaging mums** with young children, she asked her sales promotion agency to come up with a creative live brand-experience concept. Her sales promotion agency worked closely with an experiential marketing agency because they knew that live brand experiences are more likely to drive purchase consideration than any other channel:

- The experiential marketing agency created a narrative around each of her fruit characters, bringing to life each of the fruits that were usually found on the yoghurt pot packaging.

- Actors who stood outside supermarkets (where the yoghurts were sold) wore the costumes and engaged passers-by in an immersive and multisensory theatre plot.
- The fruity characters engaged young children, involving them in the storyline through improvised interaction, asking them what their favourite fruits were, and surprising them with an invitation to enter a sensory fruit-pod vending booth, which used interactive tech triggers to provide them with a free sample of yoghurt (in the flavour of their chosen fruit).
- Carefully trained *Brand Ambassadors* also told the mothers about the nutritional value of the natural yoghurts, while giving them a nutritional booklet that featured scratch-and-sniff stickers (for the kids), and a discount coupon (that they could redeem inside the supermarkets).

This campaign **increased sales** by an average of 80 per cent in participating stores and created positive **brand engagement** with mums. It also achieved the secondary objectives of **driving product trial** and **delivering complex brand messages** about the nutritional value of the fruity yoghurts.

Objective 6: communicate complex brand messages

Vladimir was the entrepreneur behind a stylish, premium brand of craft vodka. He had quit his lucrative city job as a banker to re-create an old Russian family vodka formulation. He approached an experiential marketing agency with the task of taking his vodka to the next level, while communicating **complex brand messages** about the vodka both through a branded property, and **bringing the brand to life 'at retail'** for the masses:

- The vodka has a unique five-step purification process where it goes through 'hell and back' (minerals and volcano ashes) to gain its unparalleled purity.
- They created an exclusive and aspirational secret nightclub in a former bank vault, five storeys below street level.
- In the club, celebrities, taste makers, influencers and consumer super-fans would party the night away in constantly evolving immersive electronic events.
- Through the decor, venue dressing and theming, complex brand messages were brought to life symbolically across every level.

- The exclusive club brand that he created became a successful, revenue-generating 'owned branded property', and one that became ubiquitous with the luminaires of music subculture and style.

- As part of a touring retail 'mini experience', which aimed to bring a taste of the aspirational nightclub experience to the masses, consumers were invited into sensor-triggered, unbranded, black cubed-box structures.

- Here they were invited to sit on a larger-than-life luxurious 'purification chair', given merged-reality sunglasses to wear, and proceeded to be 'purified' while floating angel 'illusions' appeared in front of them.

- They also received an aromatic head and shoulder massage from a real-life 'purification angel', while at the same time virtually experiencing 360-degree immersive content from some of the most debauched nights at the club – seen through the futuristic glasses.

- Finally, each participant received a shot of vodka to complete the multi-stage 'purification process'.

- During this experience, the consumers were informed that they were going through a 'five-step purification process', just like the vodka did, bringing to life its premise of 'Be bad to be good'.

- This live brand experience successfully communicated the complex brand message, which other marketing channels would have been less able to convey with such ease and tangibility.

Objective 7: niche credibility, global appeal

Savio is the marketing and sales director of a sportswear brand that sells comfortable, sporty, jersey clothing made from organic cotton in Australia. He wanted to create a campaign platform to **position the sportswear brand as a trendy**, preferred option for comfortable streetwear with electronic music influencers to **appeal to a young and affluent emerging global club scene**.

He knew through his market research that his *Target Audience* enjoyed dance, and that the product truths resonated with the comfort and price needs of young club kids, doubled up with the insight that bold, loose, jersey prints were enjoying a comeback on the underground rave scene:

- He decided to make a bold move to invest in launching an 'owned' *Branded Property* event series to gain credibility with his audience, by holding a live brand experience platform in the form of a rave tour.

- The events were held in old sports stadiums to reflect the brand's sporty credentials, and huge sound systems were set up as stacked speaker stages for models who wore the outfits to dance above the crowds.
- The dancefloors and chill-out areas were dotted with DJs and club-kid influencers, rocking the Australian gear, while the backstage artist green room doubled as a VIP product-gifting suite, to further expand the brand's reach into additional influencers' wardrobes.
- Music and video content was streamed live on Periscope, Instagram and SoundCloud, and record numbers tuned in from far corners of the world due to the impressive dance-music DJ bill he had booked.
- This resulted in orders flooding in from many new global customer bases from countries previously unaware of the brand.
- He even created soundproof mini raves in a select few of his store changing-room cubicles so that shoppers could transport themselves momentarily into the raves, and connect with the brand more deeply.
- Gaining credibility with this niche and hard-to-reach audience was a challenge he exceeded, creating a cost-neutral, content-rich brand platform with its own value and spin-off franchise revenue streams.
- This event series was a huge success, as was the word of mouth and free publicity that the rave events and content generated.

All of this would have been impossible to achieve through traditional media channels or sponsorship alone.

Objective 8: target a new audience

When a new 'smart necklace' was launched by one of the world's most popular 'social media platforms for business', it wanted to attract a new audience to purchase the 'smart jewellery'. It had originally been targeted at the business market but the brand was keen to **attract new and broader audience segments**, busy professionals and sociable millennials.

Grace, who was responsible for the marketing of the smart necklace, wanted to create personalized interactions that tailored which of the product's many features and benefits were to be demonstrated to the wearer. She wanted to communicate that the necklace's pearlescent 'gem', which doubled up as an interactive, rectangular content screen, was ideal for organizing consumers' busy social lives:

- She hired an agency to provide carefully selected *Brand Ambassadors* (who went through intensive training to understand the product features and benefits and learn how to demonstrate the necklaces).

- During the live brand experience activity – which took the form of subtle guerrilla activity on public transport – the *Brand Ambassadors* would engage in a routine to demonstrate the features, as well as to show a tutorial on loop.

- The *Brand Ambassadors* were also positioned outside participating stores on weekends and were tasked with attracting the new consumer to participate in a tailor-made demonstration of the smart necklace's features.

- The *Brand Ambassadors* asked the consumers questions such as 'on which social platforms do you spend most time?' and 'how would you spend your dream weekend?' – to then tailor the experience to suit them.

- The answers gave the *Brand Ambassadors* an indication of which features to demonstrate. Consumers who were interested in finding out about the different styles and products available were directed to expert, stylish sales advisers in-store.

- By tailoring the demonstrations, the product's features and benefits that were showcased were specific to the needs of the consumer.

- The live brand experiences successfully achieved the main *Experiential Objective* of the campaign: **attracting a new consumer** *Target Audience* to understand and experience the novel and original smart necklace product.

Objective 9: increase customer loyalty

Marco is the owner of a family pizza chain that was undergoing rapid expansion since franchising the brand, and wanted to create a programme to **increase customer loyalty**. He had previously been offering a one-off 30 per cent discount to customers who had visited the restaurant 10 times, but his margins were tight and he soon found the promotion was not worth the investment. Mario's consumers were not overly excited by the prospect of the 30 per cent discount, and the loyalty scheme was largely unsuccessful:

- After hearing from a friend about the benefits of experiential marketing approaches, he concluded that he should start by implementing a live brand experience.

- He decided to try out the innovative approach to increase customer loyalty.

- He designed an experiential incentive of a free 'pizza-making workshop' with his well-known pizza expert Chef Tony.

- The incentive was awarded to all customers who visited the restaurant 10 times (this was monitored with stamps on a card).

- The new experiential loyalty scheme worked out well. Not only did the prize encourage customers to complete 10 visits but, also, once they had experienced a workshop they told all their friends about it with excitement.

- Marco thus achieved his primary objective **of increasing customer loyalty** while achieving his other objectives of **driving word of mouth** and **differentiating the pizza chain brand** from its competitors.

Objective 10: increase footfall in-store

Amanda is the brand manager for a popular high-street fashion retailer. The retail outlet sells inexpensive fashion garments and targets teenage girls. After an economic slump, she was tasked with **increasing footfall in-store**. After fitting new footfall detection devices into all the outlets, Amanda's bosses were keen to see an increase, fast. She had read in recent trade press that experiential marketing was delivering both instant and long-term results when it came to **driving traffic into retail** outlets, and decided to give it a go:

- She did not have a huge budget and resolved to cut funds from some of their print advertising. She decided to use her remaining print budget to run ads in a magazine that was frequently read by teenage girls.

- The ads featured a competition, inviting readers who wanted to become a 'live window model' for the day (and win a mini shopping spree) the chance to be part of the campaign.

- The readers of the magazine were extremely enthusiastic at the chance to become a model for the day, with thousands applying after seeing the ads.

- She hired an experiential marketing agency to look after the experiential marketing campaign, and had them train 100 lucky competition winners to become 'window models' (live mannequins posing in the store windows).

- All the competition entrants who missed out on the opportunity to be a 'window model' were invited to preview the new season's collections on the day before the campaign went live.

- They were excited at this privilege and the thought of previewing the collection before the public drove them to tell all their friends about their honour.

- As well as having the winners modelling in the windows, the agency also hired professional models to parade on mini catwalks that they raised outside the stores, with *Brand Ambassadors* distributing invitations for fashion consultations inside.

- Each store manager was invited to a weekend training session prior to the campaign in which they were taught how to spend time training their best internal store staff on giving fashion consultations.

- The store staff (who received good sales commissions) were attempting to consult customers on fashion advice anyway, so the training programme was well accepted.

- Amanda also got her PR agency involved, which sent members of the local press to photograph the show and add buzz to the catwalk outside.

The integrated experiential marketing campaign resulted in a consumer frenzy, with queues of teenage girls (members of the *Target Audience*) waiting to have fashion consultations, a flood of excited shoppers entering the stores, and an increase in sales because of the consultations. Everyone was happy.

There was an 80 per cent **increase on the newly installed footfall devices.** The 'window girls' and preview girls both spread word of mouth about their experiences as models and their shopping sprees. The **consumers were happy** to be treated like celebrities with personal stylists, and the store **staff were pleased** with the extra **commission** they earned.

Summary

It is of utmost importance to adapt the content of your idea to match the *Experiential Objectives.* Ultimately, the *Experiential Objectives* are the reason that you are implementing experiential marketing campaigns and live brand experiences, and therefore achieving them should always be the focus of your campaigns.

Experiential marketing can achieve many objectives, but do not overload your plan; stick to three main aims at most, and make sure that all your objectives are measurable. As we saw, experiential marketing is excellent at achieving a wide array of different objectives, including:

- bringing the *Brand Personality* to life;
- positioning or repositioning the brand;
- creating a memorable experience;
- communicating complex brand messages;
- gaining high long-term ROI (an LROI formula is given later in the book);
- increasing customer loyalty;
- gaining credibility with specific *Target Audiences*;
- driving word of mouth;
- creating brand advocacy;
- increasing sales;
- raising brand awareness;
- driving bricks or clicks traffic online or in-store.

In fact, the measurable *Experiential Objectives* are infinite. Later in the book you will learn how to build into the plan *Systems and Mechanisms for Measurement* that directly relate to each *Experiential Objective*.

Note

1   Megson (2016) [accessed 27 August 2017] Eventbrite – Complete Guide To Experiential Marketing [Online] https://www.eventbrite.co.uk/blog/experiential-marketing-guide/

Target audience 09

Gathering holistic insights
and understanding of your customers

As with all marketing, it is crucial to know your *Target Audience* in depth when planning experiential marketing campaigns. If we don't know who we are selling to, then it is impossible to tailor our campaign accordingly. It is important to clarify *Target Audiences* so that we can create the right experience for the right people.

As we discussed earlier, experiential marketing is adept at reaching large volumes of people through word of mouth and shared content. It is not simply that the live brand experience can reach a huge number of people directly, but that the impact of the communication is exponential.

Seeding influencers groups
for maximum *Reach*

In order to capitalize on this word-of-mouth process, it is important to know that the initial group reached is really the best group; best because they are the group who will influence the rest. Sometimes known as 'opinion leaders' or emerging influencers, the initial group should be people who are used to disseminating information and sharing content with their peers, and who are already seen as credible sources of information.

If this targeting is effectively achieved, the initial *Reach* and subsequent word-of-mouth *Reach* will be far greater and brand advocacy will be the heart and soul engine fuelling the campaign towards success and achieving its *Experiential Objectives*. Before continuing with the *SET MESSAGE* planning model, it is important to really think about, research and explore the customer lifestyle, or the day-in-the-life of your ideal and real consumers, as well as looking at their 'aspirational lifestyle'.

How do you conduct a day-in-the-life or an aspirational analysis?

By this, it is meant that it is advisable to identify and clarify their aspirations, who they look up to, and the lifestyles of the people that they aspire to be like, as well as the influencers they relate to. We began the thinking process about the *Target Audience* while using the *BETTER* creative model; however, during this stage it was only a top-line exploration. Now we must conduct a much more in-depth analysis to provide us with important answers for the rest of the *SET MESSAGE* model. For example, when selecting locations and *Brand Ambassadors,* we will be directly inspired by the data we will gather at this stage of the plan.

Appropriate for all audiences

Experiential marketing is especially effective at reaching specific *Target Audience*s in the real world, as well as always being the best-suited approach to communicating with consumers in their daily lives and appealing to their lifestyle aspirations. It has been proven effective for all consumer groups, including niche/mass audiences and, as discussed previously, millennials/generations X, Y and Z.

Analysing target audiences

The following examples demonstrate how we analyse particular *Target Audience*s in the context of specific scenarios and varying sectors. To begin, let's look at young British mums with kids aged 1–6, and a level of disposable income.

To carry out an experiential campaign for this audience we would have to analyse the group through market research. There are several resources that can help in providing existing in-depth research of different niche groups. Even though these reports can be costly, the information can be extremely valuable and can be key to the success of the campaign strategy. It is therefore worth investing in acquiring or creating the right data and identifying the right insights when secondary research has proved insufficient.

Affluent young mum

A day-in-the-life analysis of a young mum

- She wakes up and prepares a packed school lunch for her son. She may also ensure that he has the relevant things he needs, including his books and gym kit.
- Once the child is ready to go to school, she is likely to drive him there, possibly bringing a younger child or baby in the car with her.
- As a more affluent mother, she possibly has a childminder or someone to look after her younger child during the day.
- Once she has dropped both children off, she will probably go for a morning coffee with other young mothers in a cafe or restaurant.
- She may do some shopping during the afternoon or go to the gym, followed by lunch with another friend.
- After this, she is likely to head home prior to collecting her son from school.
- After school she may drop him off at an extracurricular activity such as a sport group, or at a friend's house.
- Once at home, she is likely to prepare dinner, and possibly watch something online before her partner returns from work.
- Once the partner is home, and their son is back from his extracurricular activity, the family may sit down together for a meal.
- Alternatively, she and her partner may go out to dinner while the children are looked after by a friend or sitter.
- When they go out for dinner, they are likely to go into town and eat somewhere more intimate or fashionable, rather than the same restaurant where they would eat as a family on the weekend.

This was a typical weekday. On the weekend…

- It is likely that the family will all go out together on a Saturday.
- They may stay at home, but she will be with her partner throughout the weekend.
- They may even all go away for the weekend, possibly to visit relatives or go to the countryside as a rest from the city.
- They may all go shopping and visit a local mall, an exhibition or show, as well as possibly going to the cinema.

- The school holidays will greatly influence this *Target Audience*, because if there is a break, the family is likely either to go on holiday or visit child-oriented attractions such as a zoo, an amusement park or the local leisure centre.

Generalized aspirations of a young, affluent mum

The in-depth analysis completed during the *SET MESSAGE* planning process at the '*Target Audience*/"T" Stage' showed that these mums are likely to look up to influencers who also have children and are able to maintain a busy lifestyle and good appearance. It also reveals that the mums aspire to have highly intelligent and creative children. Whilst it is not possible to predict the exact behaviours of individuals, by painting a picture of a typical day-in-the-life of your *Target Audience*, you will begin to understand when, where and how to engage them.

Let's look at some examples of how the analysis can influence the ideas for some brands of particular products targeted at this group:

A brand of yoghurt – example

With this background information in mind, we can focus our minds on the yoghurt brand referred to previously. This brand targeted young mums with kids aged 1–6, and used live brand experiences to increase sales at supermarkets. The brand manager, Mary, worked with her agency that utilized the *BETTER* model to devise more ideas for live brand experiences; this time with the main objective of creating a memorable experience. After presenting the ideas to the marketing director, it was narrowed down to one idea for further development using the *SET MESSAGE* model:

- The chosen idea involved having the same *Brand Ambassadors* dressed up as fruit characters, this time engaging children and inviting them to have their pictures taken together.

- However, before being able to take their photos home the *Brand Ambassadors* would give nutritional information booklets to the mothers, as well as discussing the nutritional advantages of the yoghurt.

- The booklets were reprinted with additional information and directed the mothers to a brand platform that had been specially created for the yoghurt experience.

After having looked carefully at the day-in-the-life of a young, affluent mum, Mary decided that it would be best to implement the campaign during the school holidays:

- This would be the most effective time to reach and influence large numbers of mothers and children.

- After carefully researching the footfall of the locations likely to be visited on school holidays, it was concluded that zoos and amusement parks would be the best locations for the live brand experience.

- As the primary research and in-depth analysis showed that the *Target Audience* were found to look up to other mothers who had maintained a good physical appearance, it was felt that *Brand Ambassadors* should reflect that image and personality.

- Mary decided that she would use this information when she reached the *Selected Locations and Brand Ambassadors* part of the *SET MESSAGE* planning process (this is covered in Chapter 12).

An alternative, although potentially less effective approach would have been to spend extra money on traditional adverts that promoted the yoghurt. However, this may have been less engaging and therefore would not have inspired the mums or the young child to share their experiences about the yoghurt with others. Whilst it is unlikely for someone to tell people that they saw a traditional advert on a billboard, on TV, or in a magazine, it is easy to imagine how this live brand experience could reach many people (via word of mouth and social media) for every person who interacted with the experience:

- As we already saw from the mother's lifestyle, she spends a lot of time meeting people, whether it is a friend over coffee or lunch, the people she sees every day at the gym, or the other mothers at the school.

- Her partner, inspired by his child's picture with a fruit character, may also tell his colleagues and show them on the internet.

- They may forward this picture to family and friends, especially if they also have the opportunity to use a compelling sales promotion voucher.

- The next time the mother visits the supermarket, she would probably use the voucher, found in the nutritional booklet.

- The child would also tell his or her friends at school, or at extracurricular activities, about the fruity characters.

- He or she may even forward the picture to friends, or upload it to a social networking site such as Snapchat or Instagram where the brand can encourage further engagement from digital participants who didn't see the experience IRL but can still partake using custom-branded filters and sponsored posts.

A brand of educational toys – example

When Harry was planning a campaign, promoting educational toys to young, affluent mums and their children, he came up with an idea using the *BETTER* model. After presenting it in three variations to the rest of the decision-making team, they chose one idea for the launch of a new child's toy. The toy looked similar to an easel, but had multifunctional elements, including a calculator, touch screen and special slots for different art materials:

- The idea for the live brand experience involved a design competition, where kids would have the opportunity to use the product and create pictures, which would be hung up on a gallery wall as part of the experiential sets.

- The pictures could also be scanned and shown in a slideshow on a large projected surface. Kids would also have the opportunity to use the easel's touch screen to transform their pictures into digital greeting cards for their parents and relatives.

- These greeting cards would also be available to view on social media, and share with other family members or friends of the family.

Harry concluded, based on insights identified when completing the *Target Audience* 'day-in-the-life' analysis, during the relevant stage in the *SET MESSAGE* planning process, that it would be best to target the whole family together on the weekends:

- The weekends would allow continuity. He also concluded that shopping centres would be the best locations for this campaign, partly because the research showed that the mums and their kids would visit the shopping centres, but also because the product would be available to buy there.

- He also noted from insights identified during his earlier research into these mums' aspirations (during the *BETTER* creative process) that many were focused on the intelligence of their children, and that they admired other mothers whose children showed signs of early intelligence and creativity.

- This led him to decide that the *Brand Ambassadors* would not only need to have experience working with children or have their own, but would also need to display these attributes themselves.

- Some *Brand Ambassadors* would form 'The Tech Team', which would represent intelligence, and some of the *Brand Ambassadors* would form 'The Art Team', which would showcase creativity.

Harry wondered what he would have spent the live brand experience budget on if he had not discovered this innovative new technique. He was confident, however, that the alternative option – to advertise on mum forums that targeted young, affluent mums – would not have been as effective, because these mums did not all read the same blogs. It is unlikely that the ad would have been engaging or remembered for long, or acted as a source of inspiration for a birthday or Christmas present. On the other hand, he was very excited about the current live brand experience plans and was already in talks with his full-service agency to discuss the amplification channels that would be integrated to form the complete experiential marketing campaign for the launch:

- He knew that the children would enjoy playing with the creative easel toy, as market research and focus groups had already proved that children responded remarkably well to the product.

- He knew it was likely that after the children played with the toy, they would ask their parents to buy it, possibly nagging them until their next birthday or holiday.

- He was also confident that after seeing their children engaging in an educational experience, stimulating their creativity and intelligence, the young, affluent mums would feel this toy could contribute to their aspirational lifestyle.

A brand of girls' dancewear – example

When Maggie, a marketing director, was planning a campaign to launch a new line of children's dancewear across 20 of their stores, she knew that it might be hard to achieve the desired results with a limited budget. She considered advertising, but knew that she would not be able to afford more than two months' worth.

She was not sufficiently confident that the company's old-hat marketing plan – which involved placing adverts in the magazines and local newspapers read by her *Target Audience* of parents (and their daughters) in south-east England – would have any real impact on sales. Although they might raise a certain amount of awareness about the range, it would not create a great-enough demand from the girls for them to implore their parents to buy the clothing. Maggie wanted to reach the children, but she did not know where to start, and felt underfinanced:

- A friend had told her of the successes her colleague had when using live brand experiences to launch his trendy and exclusive new restaurant. His PR agency had secured a great deal of press coverage derived from the experiences.

- They had worked with an experiential marketing agency that had created 'tasting experiences', where consumers were invited to interact with the restaurant's brand and sample canapés at various fashion shows.

The story inspired Maggie, who decided she should try an experiential strategy, and after learning about the *BETTER* model she came up with an idea to create an interactive ballet experience:

- The experience was to be positioned in local shopping centres, where the retail stores were located, with specially created ink ballet-theme experiential sets.
- The sets were to comprise a branded pink floor that featured the logo of the clothing line, along with a ballet bar and mirrors.
- She would have the clothing collection present, including leggings, leotards, legwarmers, dance cardigans and tutus.
- She planned to invite mothers to book their kids into a ballet session, while the mums could go and shop for half an hour.

The idea was simple: the young girls could learn some ballet and try on the funky new dance clothing mid-launch. She also would offer them the opportunity to receive a free goody bag, which was a drawstring backpack branded with the dancewear logo. Inside the bag would be a sales promotion voucher.

After using the *BETTER* model to generate her idea, Maggie began to plan in further detail using *SET MESSAGE*:

- After looking at the day-in-the-life of the parents, along with the primary *Target Audience*, their young female daughters, and analysing their aspirations, she found they looked up to older, pretty girls who were good at ballet.
- This is how she established the identity of the *Brand Ambassadors*. She decided to hire an experiential agency to manage the campaign.
- She briefed the agency to recruit girls in their late teens with a passion for ballet. The *Brand Ambassadors* would wear the dance clothing and teach ballet techniques.
- Her research also discovered that there were local dance competitions, so she briefed the agency to roll out the live brand experience at these events.
- Maggie decided to further reinforce the experiential concept. She hired dancers in their late teens to work in the stores.

- These dancers would preferably be the same staff who would become her *Brand Ambassadors* during the live brand experience campaign.

- This way, after the young girls learnt ballet from the older girls (and *Brand Ambassadors*) they could be invited to come back to the stores for more advice on ballet and dancewear.

- This would further strengthen the relationship between the brand and the *Target Audience*, while bringing a customer experience management outlook to the brand.

Maggie then completed the rest of the *SET MESSAGE* planning system (with the help of her agency) and found that she still had a small budget left over. She used this with her PR agency, which had an excellent relationship with a production company that made YouTube shows for young children.

The production company liked the concept of the live brand experience campaign so much that they agreed to create a reality series to broadcast the campaign as a series of branded content for the YouTube channel.

Maggie was confident that this experiential marketing campaign for the dancewear range would not only bring the *Brand Personality* to life, but would raise awareness, increase sales and gain credibility with the *Target Audience*. When she compared her campaign idea with her initial thoughts of running a relatively small-scale magazine ad campaign, which would be expensive and raise a relatively small level of awareness, she was very pleased with the increased potential of the experiential marketing campaign.

Affluent professionals

A day-in-the-life analysis of an 'affluent professional'

On weekdays:

- This demographic tends to go to work in the morning, probably during rush-hour travel by public transport or car.

- They possibly skip breakfast or grab a quick pastry snack on the way, and perhaps a cereal bar or breakfast bar when they get to work.

- They tend to be busy checking e-mails, answering and making phone calls, rushing to meetings and are often too busy to have lunch.

- They may simply grab a sandwich and bring it back to the office. Alternatively, they may go out to lunch and eat in a restaurant, possibly as a business meeting.

- They will then go back to work and, depending on how busy they are, they may leave at 6 pm. If they stay late, they might head straight home as soon as they can.
- Alternatively, they may attend a social engagement with work colleagues at a local bar. They could have a business dinner or event to go to, such as an awards ceremony.
- Sometimes they might be networking in the evening. If they do have a social engagement, they may be meeting their partner for dinner or drinks.

At the weekend:

- Affluent professionals are likely to unwind and relax from their busy week and could participate in leisure activities, which – depending on their interests – will vary greatly. These might include sports, shopping, or entertainment such as theatre, music, nightlife or concerts. In fact, interests vary greatly across the board.

When travelling:

- Affluent professionals also tend to travel, some more than others, and in business class or economy.
- When at the airport, they could have a long time to kill before the flight, during which time they could shop or perhaps sit in the business lounges available to those in business class.
- They may have nothing to do during this time and become bored.
- They could possibly use their laptop or make some last-minute calls, depending on their schedule and interests.

Aspirations of an affluent professional

Looking to whom affluent senior professionals aspire is key. Insights in the primary research might show they would look up to successful entrepreneurs and business people prominent in the media. They may look up to people who have been successful in the business world, especially in the sector in which they work.

For example, if an affluent professional works in tech, he or she could look up to Bill Gates or Elon Musk. If he or she were a marketing professional, he or she might look up to someone well known and successful in the marketing or creative industries such as the founder of a disruptive agency like Oliver (who places agency teams within client organizations).

Aspirational influencers

The aspirational influencer group for that audience might include very successful entrepreneurs whose lifestyle is one of luxury, comfort and convenience. These high-net-worth individuals aspire to travel in Tesla or Faraday Future cars and dine in Michelin-starred and innovative restaurants, live in beautiful homes and have staff at their disposal. The analysis also showed that many of these C-suite business executives look up to colleagues and acquaintances who demonstrate good business acumen, and they themselves aspire to hold conversations that demonstrate a comprehensive knowledge of successful businesses and their practices.

Adapt ideas, locations and mechanics at the detailed planning stage

The research into the life of our *Target Audience*s, in this case the affluent professional, gives us the opportunity to influence and develop existing ideas, location ideas and imagine appropriate content we would like to create through our live brand experiences while planning using *SET MESSAGE*.

Let's look at some examples of how the analysis can influence the ideas for some brands of particular products targeted at this group:

An airline brand – example

Rob was a marketing manager responsible for promoting a new and improved business-class offering for an airline brand. The organization as a whole was beginning to shape its actions around customer experience, and the philosophy lent itself particularly well to experiential marketing. Rob's boss wanted him to push the message that the new business travel experience was far more comfortable than previous offerings:

- Rob used the *BETTER* model to deliver some top-line experiential concepts, and he came up with four options.

- He narrowed them down to a favourite concept after careful deliberation with the rest of the marketing team at the airline. The concept was simple, but Rob was confident it would be effective.

- It involved setting up 'business zones', which were enclosed experiential sets. Rob decided to replicate the business section of the planes in the experiential sets.

- The zones would feature replicas of the special new 'experience chairs' installed in the airline's business-class sections.

- Rob thought it would be a great idea to integrate a gastronomic experience into the live brand experience so that he could convey the improvement in the quality of the airline menus.

- The affluent professionals could sample delicious canapés, tasting dishes and drink pairings originating from countries on the main routes of the airline, while relaxing in the 'experience chairs', which provided a special shiatsu massage.

- The trained *Brand Ambassadors* would reflect the calibre of the newly trained air stewards. Overall, the brand experience would take five minutes to complete.

- The consumer would be invited to sit in the experience chair, eat a starter, have a glass of champagne and be able to converse with one of the *Brand Ambassadors* about the new business-class offering.

- The consumers would also feel invigorated by aromatherapy-scent emissions.

Applying the insights

Even though Rob had the top-line idea approved by his team, he was still unsure of the implementation until he began his *Target Audience* analysis. When using the *SET MESSAGE* method, he looked at the day-in-the-life of his *Target Audience* as well as their aspirations.

This led him to understand that these affluent professionals **did not have a lot of time** to enjoy lunch. As they were especially busy people, they would not venture far from the office to eat during the day. He also realized that people who worked in business office parks lacked options at meal times. He therefore decided to position the live brand experiences in these types of business parks, allowing people to have a five-minute business-class lunch. This would not only add value by satisfying their hunger, but would communicate all the benefits and the *Brand Personality* of the new experience-oriented business-class service.

Aspirational insights

When he looked at the aspirational lifestyle of the *Target Audience*, he noted that they looked up to successful business people and high-profile individuals in their sectors.

- He then decided to add another aspect to the live brand experiences. He would take the 'business zone' set on tour to visit conferences and seminars, where opinion leaders, such as speakers and organizers, could also participate.

- He knew that association with these credible individuals would impress his *Target Audience*.

- He also knew that if the speakers participated in spreading word of mouth, their stamp of approval could have a great deal of influence.

After completing the plan in *SET MESSAGE* and hiring an agency to implement the campaign, Rob saw excellent results.

Following the great success of the launch of the improved business-class offering, Jake (the new CEO) was over the moon. Rob also continued to work closely with his advertising agency, which was hired to prepare more innovative adverts to go on business-related YouTube channels, promoting the opportunity to 'trial the new business travel experience'.

After the initial live brand experience campaign, he began integrating all the marketing communications channels to amplify the live brand experiences, whilst allocating a large portion of the total budget to future live brand experiences.

Since the airline adopted a customer experience management (CEM) programme and Rob pioneered the use of experiential marketing to promote the new and improved services, the brand has benefited from increased market share, and has not looked back.

A retail clothing brand – example

Francesca, an account manager at an integrated full-service agency, received a brief from one of its biggest clients. The client was a chain of successful clothing shops, providing smart, fashionable wear for young female professionals who want to stay in fashion and change their wardrobe for each season – ideal for the office and also evening entertainment. The clothing was of a reasonable quality and an affordable mid-range price. The brand collections also have a small range for men. The concept behind the clothing range is that the consumer can wear an outfit to the office, jazz it up for the evening and even wear it at weekends. The client wanted to communicate to its customers that the clothing is adaptable for many environments.

Francesca was far more familiar with coordinating advertising campaigns than live brand experiences, so when the client gave her the brief, assuming that the advertising agency could also be responsible for integrating advertising and live brand experiences to form a complete experiential marketing approach, she turned to an experiential marketing agency for specialized help.

The creative team inside the experiential agency suggested a top-line idea, which they had brainstormed using the *BETTER* model:

- The idea was for an integrated experiential campaign involving live brand experiences, billboards and bus shelter ads.
- The live brand experience channel, in the form of a roadshow vehicle, would travel around city areas, giving professional women a mini after-work makeover, ideal for after-work drinks.
- The billboards would promote the makeover roadshow while showing images of a woman quickly transforming her outfit, from office to evening wear.
- The bus shelters would feature interactive technology that allowed consumers to press a button to transform a woman from being appropriately dressed for the office to being fashionably dressed for evening drinks.

After Francesca decided on the idea, she wanted to develop the concept further in *SET MESSAGE* before presenting to the client. She completed the day-in-the-life analysis and researched the aspirational lifestyle of the *Target Audience*. She found that the experiential marketing idea was very well suited to her *Target Audience*:

- With the office women she was targeting, she found that they tended to go out in the evening, straight after work, and wanted to go out looking great without having to go home first.
- Thus, the adaptability of the clothing range was a major selling point: you could quickly **transform an outfit** from smart office chic to sophisticated city glam for the evening.
- She developed the live brand experience idea further by adding an additional element: *Brand Ambassadors* would visit offices at lunchtime, bringing branded coffee and invitations to the makeover roadshow.
- Straight after work, the roadshow bus would park outside large office blocks at a specified time.
- Makeovers were offered and women were instructed on how to go from office to evening glam with this clothing brand.

She was confident that the client would love the idea and she was right. It really brought to life the *Brand Personality* and demonstrated to the *Target Audience* what the brand was all about. This real-life context is hard to achieve with traditional media alone.

Because Francesca worked in an advertising agency, she knew she had access to something very powerful: the wide reach of advertising. She felt that the concept of the live brand experience campaign could be amplified by the traditional advertising already on her media plan, as suggested by the experiential marketing agency:

- She spoke to some of the creative and media planning teams and convinced them to run different creative on the billboard and bus shelter ads to amplify the 'big idea'.

- The content of the billboards then drove people to participate in the live brand experience.

- Even those who had not necessarily participated in the live brand experience were very excited by the thought of this brand reaching out to people just like them.

- Then content was streamed live from the brand experiences into the digital-out-of-home (DOOH) screens, creating further excitement and word of mouth.

- Influencers attended the events and they were featured alongside consumers in the co-created content for the DOOH media.

After the campaign had been implemented, Francesca's client was very pleased. Not only had the client received the desired experiential marketing campaign, but Francesca had managed to maximize the impact that each channel had by integrating them to form a unified experiential concept. The market research that the brand of clothing conducted after the campaign showed that the *Target Audience*'s perceptions of the brand changed significantly after the campaign, because consumers could understand its proposition from a completely different perspective.

The campaign was tailored around the busy lifestyles of female professionals, and by feeling that the brand had catered to them, they developed a real bond with it. The experiential campaign implied that the clothing brand understands and appreciates their daily lives and connected them with the identity of the glamorous businesswomen whose lifestyles they aspired to live.

A gambling website – example

Owing to changes in advertising regulations, an online gambling company wanted to reach out to its *Target Audience* of affluent British males, without using advertising. Short of ideas, it contacted its PR firm with a brief to generate press coverage:

- The client suggested generating some compelling headlines via a consumer survey as a method of achieving its objectives. Unfortunately, the PR agency was less than enthusiastic.

- They said it would be difficult to get any coverage at all because of the negative perceptions of gambling in the media.

- The client was really keen, however, as there had been a recent change in regulations and the client was nervous about a potential loss in revenue.

- The PR agency was worried that promoting gambling could attract negative attention from the media and they did not want to risk generating unwanted coverage. They said that no matter how much the client spent implementing a research project or an elaborate stunt, it would be hard to control the coverage and it could potentially become a wasted effort.

The PR agency bosses passed on the brief to Larissa, an account executive who had come from an events background. She recommended that the gambling company drive people to its website and app, driving member registrations using live brand experiences. Larissa then approached an experiential marketing agency with whom she had an existing relationship. Together, Larissa and the experiential marketing agency brainstormed to come up with a creative idea. The *Brand Personality* and message of the online gambling website (which originated from the Far East) was about **transforming luck** and **bringing good fortune** to others. The word 'fortune', which was central to the *Brand Personality*, and was usually represented by **oriental** imagery in advertising, became the focal point of the live brand experience campaign.

- Using the *BETTER* brainstorm, they came up with an idea to target businesspeople with an authentic oriental-style experience.

- The *Two-Way Interaction* was designed to target affluent businesspeople and involved a guessing game about Fortune 500 businesses.

After completing the *BETTER* brainstorm, the concept was still not fully developed, but everyone was keen to present a proposal to the board as soon as possible. There was increasing concern within the PR firm about losing the account, which knew its client would struggle to maintain its market share without a good campaign. It worried that the client may go elsewhere if Larissa did not propose something promising.

Larissa and the experiential marketing agency then continued to plan the idea in further detail using *SET MESSAGE*:

- When they got to the *Target Audience* section of the planning stage, they identified a few key points.

- After completing a day-in-the-life analysis and identifying insights and key aspirations of the *Target Audience* they discovered that affluent professionals spent a large proportion of their time travelling and waiting for flights.

- It was identified that waiting and boredom were negative factors that businesspeople associated with catching flights, and that they would be potentially open to engaging during that time.

- In addition, because the client was targeting the more senior C-suite end of the demographic, the professionals would often travel business class. This insight was essential in inspiring the ideal location for the idea: business lounges in major airports.

Building on these insights and developing the 'fortune' *Brand Personality* a little further, Larissa decided to develop the idea:

- They would hire small sections of the business lounges for the duration of the campaign and theme them with authentic oriental decor, subtle branding, and showcase the gambling website's homepage on giant interactive gesture walls and touch-tables.

- Attentive *Brand Ambassadors*, dressed in authentic oriental attire, would greet the business travellers who were waiting for their flights.

- The *Brand Ambassadors* would give the business traveller fortune cookies containing promotional codes that enabled participants to play with varying amounts of 'free money' when gambling on the site within the interactive area of the lounge.

- To create a buzz and inspire participation from others waiting in the lounges, *Brand Ambassadors* would then invite the *Target Audience* to participate in a Fortune 500 quiz game, with the aim of entertaining those waiting for their flights in the business lounges.

- The game would also provide the *Target Audience* with the opportunity to showcase their business knowledge, which was a process identified earlier as being enjoyable to them.

The live brand experience would simultaneously drive sign-ups to the gambling site, and authentically and relevantly engage the *Target Audience* with the *Brand Personality* while they had disposable time on their hands. The PR agency completed the *SET MESSAGE* plan and presented it to the client, and received a delighted response to the proposal. The client did, however, state that it still wanted the PR agency to amplify the live brand experience and gain media coverage for the gambling site, because that was the original objective.

The PR agency, inspired by their new concept, was now looking at the campaign very differently to when it had first received the brief.

Broader editorial coverage Colette, a senior member of Larissa's team, was now involved and had a good contact: the editor of a leading airline's in-flight magazine. Colette resolved to wine-and-dine the editor, convincing him to write an article reviewing her experiences, referring to them as 'the most up-to-date, revolutionary business lounges, ever'. Once the client signed off the activity, and the brand experience went live, Colette and the editor visited one of the business lounges that featured the live brand experience.

The editor was so enthused with the activity and the immersive stylish environment that the gambling brand had created that, in addition to a double-length feature, a stunning photo of the interactive wall projection from the experience made it onto the front cover of the in-flight magazine.

Driving business results This achievement amplified the reach of the live brand experience and generated huge interest and app downloads from the *Target Audience*, while also impressing senior company stakeholders, who had seen the coverage while on their own business travels.

The number of new members that signed up to the gambling website as a direct result of the experiential marketing campaign was record breaking. It far exceeded the numbers the client had previously received from running traditional print advertising campaigns; interestingly there was greater retention and use of referral codes from those who had signed up as a result of the experience, in contrast to retention figures from affiliate-generated sign-ups.

The CEO of the gambling website decided it had been a 'blessing in disguise' that the advertising regulations had changed, because otherwise he would never have considered such an innovative approach – experiential, which has been central to their marketing communications strategy ever since.

Targeting different audiences

We started by conducting a day-in-the-life analysis of a young, affluent mum and saw how by completing this process during *SET MESSAGE*, different brands from different sectors could develop their top-line concepts, improving them with insights about these mums' lifestyles and aspirations. We have also looked at how conducting a day-in-the-life analysis of an affluent professional can influence the plans of three very different companies. It must be noted that those mentioned above are not the only potential *Target Audience*s. In fact, it has been known that live brand experiences generate a good response from *Target Audience*s across the board. The *Target Audience* stage of SET MESSAGE can be an extremely useful process, no matter who the campaign is targeting.

A day-in-the-life analysis of a Gen Z

Live brand experiences can be particularly effective at targeting demographics born after 1982, namely millennials and generations X, Y and Z. With 60 per cent of Gen Y consumers saying live brand experiences are very influential in their brand perception, millennials and Gen Z tend to prefer organic, grass-roots tactics and conscious brands, and they often shun any marketing that does not benefit them, their community or the planet in some way, unless it has aspirational relevance to their lifestyle.

Let's look at some examples of how the analysis can influence the ideas for some brands of particular products targeted at younger age groups:

A vodka brand – example

When Dan, the marketing manager at a vodka brand, was tasked with launching a new canned, ready-mixed-cocktail version of the product targeting trendy youth, he immediately conducted a brainstorm with the creative team at his full-service agency to generate ideas:

- It wanted to position a live brand experience at the core of an integrated experiential marketing campaign.

- This direction for the launch was decided collectively amongst the team members, because of research showing that this *Target Audience* would respond exceptionally well to experiential marketing.

- The brainstorm generated a favourite idea that was well liked, but needed further development in the *SET MESSAGE* methodology.

- The idea involved driving product trial of the cocktail version of the canned drink, which was already popular with the *Target Audience*.

- Inspired by the fact that the drink comes in three different cocktail flavours, the creatives wanted to communicate the *Message – Key Communication*: 'What's your flava?' throughout a live brand experience event platform, and all the relevant amplification channels.

- They wanted to play on the slang word 'flava' and its double meaning; insinuating both a statement about style and culture, as well as a preference for specific tastes. The concept involved encouraging people to participate in a mood test that would determine their particular flavour.

- The mood test would involve a colour-sensitive drinks bar, which consumers could touch, and it would change colour according to their mood (in actuality this was in response to the heat of their body, which has been known to be associated to mood).

- They would then be served a sample of the drink in the 'flava' that corresponded to their mood (the colour that the bar changed into when it was touched).

This experiential concept was interactive and fun, and Dan was confident that the young audience would buy into it. He thought they would enjoy the free samples and that the added interactivity would further strengthen the relationship with the product and brand.

It would show them that the brand was taking their preferences and state of mind into consideration. In other words, it would subliminally say 'We care how you feel' and 'We understand'. The core concept was originally developed during the *Emotional Connection* stage of the *BETTER* brainstorm.

Further development

After deciding to use *SET MESSAGE* to develop the idea further, Dan and his market research agency conducted a day-in-the-life analysis of the *Target Audience*. The integrated agency also consulted several of its own real-life sources to discover more about the lifestyle of trendy youths.

They kept stumbling upon the same insights: music festivals were very popular, influential to people's tastes, and brought large numbers together in one place. In addition, the aspirational analysis revealed that many of the two main groups of people the consumers aspired to – DJs and fashionable peers – would be present at festivals. The festivals would allow the brand a scenario where it could reach both. At the same time, Dan was confident that the word-of-mouth effects and social media content reach would be high, because the live brand experience would target the right people in the right places.

Dan and the agency team developed the idea further using the key insights:

- Just having a sponsor-hosted bar/and pouring rights would no longer be enough to achieve cut-through in a cluttered environment.

- They decided to build branded and immersive 'Flava Tents', themed around music and festival fashion, and position them at selected music festivals.

- By having its own event areas, the brand would have more control over curating the *Target Audience*'s experience.

- For example, the bars would be completely interactive and the only drink served would be the new vodka cocktail in its several different 'flavas'.

- Additionally, the live brand experience would feature nightly festival fashion shows (from up-and-coming avant-garde festival-fashion brands), as well as popular dance music DJs and live music performances (from underground talent).

- The other marketing communication channels that would be used to amplify the live brand experience were advertising (in the festival guides and selected online ticket platforms), and social media/PR (targeted at relevant festival-fashion, dance-music social-media influencers, blogs and websites).

- The digital ads would link to live stream broadcasts from the 'Flava Tents', the ads would promote the opportunity to win tickets to the festivals where the 'Flava Tents' would be situated, and the social/PR activity leveraged the reach of the social channels belonging to the DJs, fashion brands and musicians who would be performing at the 'Flava Tents'.

The launch plan was completed and Dan's boss loved it, signing it off immediately. The integrated experiential marketing strategy was a big hit, and though the integrated agency outsourced some of the campaign to an experiential marketing specialist agency, it did a fantastic job of ensuring consistency across all the selected channels and leveraging the live brand experience content for maximum organic exposure.

The *Target Audience* element of the *SET MESSAGE* planning process facilitated a better understanding of how to develop the initial concept into a complete, relevant plan, and proved to be a crucial step in the development of this exciting campaign. Dan was very pleased with the outcome of his initiative when comparing this engaging campaign to some of the possible alternatives, including the launch campaigns of some of the vodka-cocktail brand's competitors, such as field marketing (basic on-trade sampling, point of sale (POS) and sales promotion) and traditional outdoor advertising.

A microwave meal brand – example

Craig is the marketing manager at a healthy microwave-meal manufacturer. He was briefed to plan and implement a face-to-face campaign that would target students. He knew that it was of great importance to come up with an idea that related to the lifestyle of this niche audience. As a former student himself, he was already aware of some of the habits of this demographic.

After he came up with a few ideas using the *BETTER* creative process, he showed them to his boss in an IDEA-formatted presentation for input and feedback. One of the ideas stood out and he suggested developing it further using the *SET MESSAGE* methodology. He had completed the S (*Situation and Background*) and E (*Experiential Objectives*) stages, and was pleased with the plan thus far, but knew that it was still missing a certain relevance to the *Target Audience*:

- The concept involved giving out free microwave meals to students in return for them filling in a questionnaire.

- This questionnaire would obtain valuable insights into their eating habits, which could be beneficial for the product development team, who had contributed some of the budget for the experiential activity.

When Craig began planning using *SET MESSAGE* and got to the *Target Audience* section, he carefully looked through several sources of secondary data about students and their eating habits. He also conducted primary research by arranging focus groups.

He acquired enough data to allow him to prepare a day-in-the-life analysis, as well as identifying the aspirations of the *Target Audience*. He realized that student lifestyles did not tend to involve cooking, and that students – who were often supported by their parents – preferred to spend their spare money on entertainment and socializing rather than 'proper meals'. They often bought unhealthy and cheap takeaways or canned goods because they did not usually know how to cook the meals they were familiar with from home.

The analysis also showed that the students had a desire to eat healthier food, cook for themselves and looked up to peers who were good at cooking, but their lack of expertise was the main barrier to the attainment of these culinary aspirations. He found that they sometimes missed the nourishing home environments that they knew before they went away to university.

This information inspired Craig to develop the idea further:

- Instead of simply giving away the healthy microwave meals, he would hire a specialist agency to create a home-themed live brand experience pop-up at the universities.

- There would be small house-shaped sets with 1950s-style decor cues, representative of a traditional family kitchen.

- The students would book into dining slots after being invited to visit the 'homes' and enjoy home-style meals, which were then revealed to be easy-to-make microwave meals.

- This would show the students that they could still experience home-style cooking, simply by pressing a button on the microwave.

- While the students would wait for their meals to be prepared, they could fill in the questionnaires on tablet devices or mobile surveys.

- Therefore, in the setting of the comforting environment and with the promise of a delicious meal arriving, the questionnaire would not seem like such a chore, and the experience would be relevant to their lifestyles.

- After completing the remaining planning stages, Craig was confident that the healthy microwave meal brand would benefit greatly from the live brand experience strategy, which resonated with the students and their needs.

Summary

A 'day-in-the-life' and aspirational analysis

We have now explored how to conduct a 'day-in-the-life analysis', and explain the insights generated in the *Target Audience* part of the *SET MESSAGE* planning process. The process is simple. During the *Target Audience* stage of the *SET MESSAGE* planning methodology, you carefully research the *Target Audience*'s lifestyle and aspirational lifestyle, then analyse the data to extract core insights. Later in the planning process, these insights will allow you to double-check that the experiential strategy has all three key attributes – ie: it is authentic, positively connected and personally meaningful – and to adapt it if needed.

Live brand experiences that are customer-centric should form the core of your campaign

Overall, experiential marketing is most successful when it features a live brand experience at its core, creating the right experience for the right people. In other words, this stage of the planning process will help you to ensure that the experience matches the *Target Audience*'s lifestyle and aspirations.

Aim high, and don't forget influencers for credibility and word of mouth

Careful targeting is very important, especially when 10 per cent of a *Target Audience* (opinion leaders) usually shape the opinions and purchases of the other 90 per cent (opinion followers).[1] This is why it can be highly beneficial to target influencers of your *Target Audience* group, who will proceed to influence the remainder of that population, spreading word of mouth via social media or peer-to-peer, expanding the reach of the campaign. By applying the techniques covered in this chapter, your plan will remain relevant to the consumers with whom it wishes to engage, bringing you a step closer to building strong relationships between your *Target Audience* and brand, with the aim of generating and maintaining brand advocacy and customer loyalty.

Note

1 Weimann, G (2003) *The Influentials: People who influence people*, University of New York Press, New York; and Keller, E and Berry, J (2003) *The Influentials: One American in ten tells the other nine how to vote, where to eat, and what to buy*, Simon and Schuster, New York

Message 10

Key communication of your brand message using experiential marketing

This chapter strives to improve the ways in which you communicate with your *Target Audiences*, providing a planning framework that facilitates a superior level of consumer engagement through experiential marketing campaigns. In this part of *SET MESSAGE* we will look at the importance of your campaign *Message – Key Communication*. We will cover the process of integrating components of your brand message into your experiential marketing campaign, starting with the live brand experience. It is then recommended that you utilize the other marketing communication channels to amplify the live brand experience, which in itself becomes content for the broader campaign message.

The message can extend far beyond the core live participants of a brand experience

The purpose of the *Message – Key Communication* section of your plan is to provide you with a systematic approach to ensuring that participants interpret your live brand experiences as intended. Subsequently, when the other marketing communication channels are integrated to form the complete experiential marketing campaign, the *Message – Key Communication* of those channels will be led by the live brand experience. When members of your *Target Audience* see or hear of your live brand experience, even if they themselves are not participants, they will still identify that your brand is reaching out to them, trying to benefit their lives. The feeling that the brand cares for them, enough to go out of its way to create a positive experience that is catered to them, will be enough to plant the brand and this positive message into their consciousness.

It may be that you have already planned your brand's *Message – Key Communication*, as these messages are usually already integrated across all your marketing and advertising. If you already have a brand *Message – Key Communication*, then this is the time to bring it into the planning process.

Combining emotional and rational messaging

Verbal messages – or 'strap lines' – and key communications are essential to every type of campaign. Marketing materials and adverts translate the *Message – Key Communication*s of the brands they are promoting into emotional messages, rational messages or a combination of both. Emotional messages tend to relate to the aspirational lifestyle of the *Target Audience* as well as aiming to generate moods and feelings, and are therefore customer-focused. Rational messages tend to focus on conveying the features and benefits of a product or service, and are therefore product-focused. This choice between a rational or emotional message often relates to whether the product or service is a low-involvement or high-involvement purchase. Often successful communications combine both emotional and rational messages.

Encode the message into your experience

Whichever approach you take, you will need to encode the message that you wish to convey into the *Two-Way Interaction* (the live brand experience). The message should be authentic, consistent and clear enough that the participants properly decode it during their experience. While the consumer is participating in the *Two-Way Interaction*, the message will need to be successfully conveyed to them both mentally (how they feel and think) and physically (through their senses and the environment). Live brand experiences provide excellent opportunities for bringing to life the different components that form your brand's *Message – Key Communication* (Figure 10.1).

At this stage, you need to dissect your generic messages to extract their very essence. By breaking generic messages into various essential components, then encoding those components into your live brand experience's interaction and environment, you will increase the likelihood that the participants' experience will embody the message that you aim to communicate. If the live brand experience succeeds in this respect, then you heighten the chances that participants will proceed to disseminate the desired key communication to their peers.

Figure 10.1   *Message – Key Communication*: brand messages encoded into participant experiences

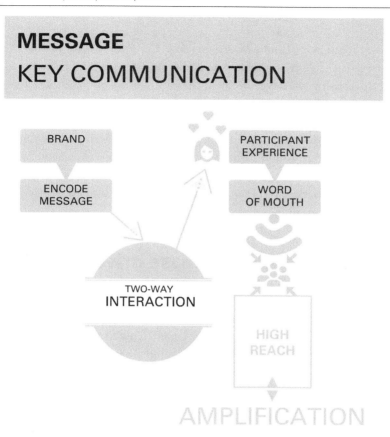

Distilling the message to its very essence

Ask yourself the following question: what is it that we want our *Target Audience* to understand, believe or identify with about our brand? Once you have your answer, you can identify and focus on these elements and integrate them into the live brand experience. You need to refine your live brand experience to ensure that the brand message is communicated effectively and concisely, in a way that will be correctly interpreted by its participants. The message must also be relevant to the activity they are engaging in, though this should not be an issue because the activity itself should reflect the *Brand Personality*. The message should represent the identifying nature of what you want the consumer to know, act on and believe in.

Tailoring to real-time formats or platforms and localizing messaging

You can adapt your brand *Message – Key Communication* to suit the live brand experience environment. The communication can be different to that of an advertising message, because the message forms part of a two-way dialogue, and allows immediate feedback and input from consumers. It is always important to adopt a coordinated approach. The message used in the live brand experience channel should be consistent with the messages used in the rest of your communication channels. To keep messages consistent across all channels, it is recommended to first adapt the message to suit the live brand experience, and then amplify the message and content across the other selected communication channels.

Emotions are key purchase drivers

The authentic, genuine part of your brand's personality should become the sources of inspiration for many elements throughout the live brand experience. If you understand what your brand truly stands for and believes in, you are on track to reflecting that philosophy through the messages communicated across your campaign. Emotions are pivotal drivers of our buying behaviour. YouTube is loaded with vloggers and consumers unpacking their newly bought game console or gadget in an excited fashion. Whenever gaming brands launch a new sought-after game, hundreds of people often happily spend more than 12 hours camping in front of the stores to be among the first in line to get one. And you don't have to be a fanatic to get emotional about the things you buy. Just take a look at the products that are present around you. Now think back to why you bought these products. For some of them you might find a very reasonable explanation. For a large group, however, we're sure you cannot bring the exact purpose back to mind. You might remember the occasion or context in which you bought the product. Undoubtedly, you will recall how you felt at that moment. Rational buying is increasingly replaced by emotional shopping.

Bringing the message to life

A brand of flavoured water – example

A naturally flavoured water brand's message is 'Quench your soul':

- Breaking down this message into its essence, these good-for-the-soul components were discovered: rehydration, vitamins, natural extracts, a good body, natural relaxation and invigorating effects.

- The brand wanted to communicate its message effectively while also promoting three different varieties: relax, invigorate and refresh.

- When this brand created a series of live brand experiences at fairs and festivals, it brought to life the brand message components of each of its products through the atmospheres and interactions of each experience.

- One experience featured a 'relaxation zone', where guests could enjoy a relaxing massage, smell a wild lavender aroma, and be exposed to relaxing ambient mood lighting and music.

- At the same time, they would enjoy a sample of the 'relax' variety of the water.

- There was also an 'invigoration zone', where consumers had the opportunity to bounce on a branded trampoline to energizing music, while smelling the invigorating aroma of citrus and rosemary essential oils, prior to receiving a sample of the 'invigorate' variety of water.

- As well as the 'relaxation' and 'invigoration' zones, the brand also had a 'refreshing zone' where consumers were invited to have a mini aromatic-cleanse facial, before being given a cool-gel eye mask to wear.

- While they engaged in the facial, refreshing smells of freshly chopped grass would fill the moist room (the moisture was emitted from a humidifier).

- After having their refreshing mini aromatic-cleanse facial, they received a sample of the 'refresh' variety of water.

- While festival-goers waited their turn, the brand's video content (featuring interviews with homeopathic experts, exploring the beneficial properties of plants and flowers as they picked fresh herbs in the wild, and communicating the key communication 'Quench your soul') was projected onto framed flat surfaces integrated into the live brand experience structures.

- The projection frames were adorned with the natural ingredients, as displayed in the video content.

- In addition, *Brand Ambassadors* wearing yoga-style clothing were inviting festival guests to enter the immersive areas and 'Quench their souls' while giving out branded gifts such as aromatherapy cleansing wipes (refresh), stress balls (relax) and smart skipping ropes (invigorate), all featuring the 'Quench your soul' branded message.

The overall effect was completely immersive, bringing to life all of the components and elements that formed the *Message – Key Communication* of the innovative water brand. This all ensured that when the live brand experience's participants spread word of mouth and shared social content, they would pass on a message that reflects the brand's essence.

A brand of washing powder – example

An example of a brand that effectively integrates rational messages into its communication is a washing powder with strong environmental credentials. Its message 'Get Clean, Be Green' is designed to communicate that the washing powder combines superior cleaning performance with environmentally friendly ingredients and packaging. The *Message – Key Communication* aims to relate to two of the key aspects that are important to its *Target Audience*, the first aspect being that it can succeed in cleaning their clothes effectively; the second that it can make them feel that they are doing something positive for the environment.

- The washing-powder brand's campaign involved converting hundreds of previously coin-operated launderettes into immersive live brand experience sets as themed pop-ups, where consumers were invited to come along and have their washing done for them. The message's components were brought to life through the special design of the set and added-value service provided at the launderettes.

- First, the brand gave the launderettes a design makeover by branding every surface with messaging and iconography, ensuring that the visual decor matched the brand identity.

- Then, they emblazoned the *Message – Key Communication* 'Get Clean, Be Green' on every washing machine and dryer.

- By using recycled materials and reclaimed wood to construct the waiting benches, and minimizing wastage (by encouraging consumers to bring their own bags to carry their laundry home), they succeeded in conveying their environmental credentials.

- They even installed new, environmentally efficient washing machines, courtesy of a leading white-goods manufacturer with whom the brand had formed a partnership.

- Aside from the green component of the message, the clean component of the message was also vital to communicate.

- Therefore, the brand invested in ensuring that the launderettes were immaculately clean and featured a fabulous clean laundry fragrance that they then released as a limited-edition fragrance for PR and social coverage.

The *Brand Ambassadors,* who were responsible for washing and drying the participants' laundry and engaging them in relevant dialogue, had experience working with environmental charities. They were carefully selected and trained to produce perfectly clean clothing and maintain their uniforms' pristine appearance:

- After completing the laundry, the *Brand Ambassadors* would give the neatly folded 'Clean and Green' laundry back to the consumers, with a free sample of the washing powder and a sales promotion voucher.

- The voucher offered a discount against future purchase of the product and a promise that a percentage of sales would be donated to an environmental charity. Those who did not bring their own bags to collect the laundry were gifted with a branded eco laundry bag in return for a donation to their chosen environmental charity.

- In addition to the makeover it provided to the local launderettes, the brand also gave the launderette owners training on the environmentally friendly washing systems it had installed, as well as recycling and energy-saving practices. It helped set up permanent donation boxes, allowing their customers to continue contributing to the environmental causes. The relationships that the brand formed with the launderettes and their customers continued, and by helping the small businesses to adopt the brand's 'Clean and Green' message and philosophy, they strengthened the impact of their *Message – Key Communication.*

The participants of the experience had previously been used to manually operating the machines themselves and waiting while they completed their cycles. The immersive environmentally themed locations, combined with clean ready-to-collect laundry, were very enthusiastically welcomed. After the initial set-up costs, the ongoing live brand experience proved to pay for itself, with word of mouth and social media mentions (the PR amplification channel generated huge coverage) helping to increase sales for the brand by over 50 per cent.

A skincare brand – example

There is a skincare brand whose *Message – Key Communication* is 'Beauty Secrets from Japan'. The message was created with the aim of conveying important components that form the brand identity: elegance, beauty and Japanese tradition. The message also implies that beauty secrets are passed on in the form of coveted personal recommendations. The inspiration for this process is the brand's holistic philosophy. Product sampling to achieve product trial is in fact one of the main marketing communications objectives. Distributing samples is important to this brand because they found that when people try the product they are astonished with the results, buy into the brand story and in turn feel they discovered 'beauty secrets' and then tell those 'secrets' to their friends in the form of personal recommendations.

This brand places great emphasis on the live brand experience channel, because it facilitates the tangible communication of beauty secrets (through product sampling) and provides a great platform for bringing the *Message – Key Communication* to life.

The core elements of the message are integrated, both physically and mentally, into every aspect of the live brand experience's communication – from its *Brand Ambassadors*, their uniforms and the packaging of its samples, to its literature, verbal dialogue and physical environment, every touchpoint is designed to embody and bring to life this *Message – Key Communication*.

Summary

When you are at the *Message – Key Communication* stage in *SET MESSAGE,* it is time to refer to your organizational philosophy, heritage, provenance and story, as well as existing messaging through 'strap lines' and content. You should decode/break down the chosen messages into their most important components and then recode those components into the live brand experience. The live brand experience itself, and its content, can then become the message for amplification across selected channels, with call to action and skews adjusted and varying depending on the medium, channel and platform. What you want the participants of your live brand experience to know, believe and do about your brand, should be at the heart of the *Two-Way Interaction*, in order for them to communicate your message effectively through word of mouth.

It can be special and unique to recode your message into an experience because your *Target Audience* will have the opportunity to interact personally and viscerally with your key messages. The messages will be deeply internalized by your *Target Audiences* through real-life experiences and remembered due to the impact of their multisensory touchpoints, which they are far more likely to appreciate and pass on than the one-way, bombarding messages they receive from many media channels.

Immersive environments and emotional cues are paramount for encoding brand messaging effectively

To achieve this desired response, we need to integrate multisensory, emotional elements (inspired by the brand message and key communications) into activation concepts to create a genuine link between the sensory motor, feelings and thoughts. These three areas, in harmonious interaction, generate lasting impressions in the mind of the participant, which lead to action. This is because they align four of the key areas of the whole person: feeling, thinking, being and doing. The first principle that stems from the psychodynamic theory is that all action that has been triggered by communication is a result of the emotional translation of the brand's message because it is perceived, not consciously but subconsciously, through the filtering of the participants' 'inner world'.[1]

Note

1 Isaacs, S (1952) *The Nature and Function of Phantasy*, in *Developments in Psycho-analysis*, ed M Klein, Haygarth, London

Experiential strategy 11

How to develop live brand experience strategies and frameworks

Strategy is essential to any plan. It is at the core of achieving your *Experiential Objectives*. This is the part of the plan where you outline your experiential intentions and the campaign's main guiding principles and executional concepts. It is the answer to the questions 'How will we achieve our *Experiential Objectives*? and 'What is the big idea?' This book recommends that the big idea for the experiential marketing campaign is based on a *Two-Way Interaction* between the consumer and the brand, in real time. In other words, a live brand experience.

Several common components in any *Experiential Strategy*

Almost all experiential marketing strategies include two or more of the 10 STRATEGIES: 'Experiential Elements'. These elements can be mixed in any combination to create the *Experiential Strategy* framework. At this point in the planning process, you should at least have a rough idea of the kind of thing you want to do in your experiential marketing campaign, because you will have already brainstormed creative ideas for your *Two-Way Interaction* and amplification strategies if you have utilized the *BETTER* creative model. In *SET MESSAGE*, you have already covered the *Situation and Background*, the *Experiential Objectives*, the *Target Audience* and the *Message – Key Communication* stages. In the process, you will have planned your aims; decided on the components of your message that you will encode and integrate into the live brand experience; and carefully analysed your *Target Audience*'s lifestyle and aspirations.

STRATEGIES is an acronym that allows you to pick your chosen 'Experiential Elements' and combine them to formulate your *Experiential Strategy* framework:

STRATEGIES
Service
Theatre
Research
Adverts
Televised or Broadcast
Entertainment and Culture
Game (or Competition)
Interactive Technologies
Educational
Set

S is for Service

Service is something that you can provide as an added-value element for the *Target Audience*. *Service* can mean many things: for example, a laundry provision, car washing, transport, delivery, pampering or a makeover. In this context, anything that human beings (or in some cases, bot and new technologies) do as a process that adds value can count as a *Service*. By using the *Service* element in your *Experiential Strategy*, you can bring to life the *Brand Personality* and benefit consumers. *Service* can facilitate a *Two-Way Interaction*.

T is for Theatre

Theatre is clearly an important element, and there have been many examples of how brand *Theatre* has been used to creatively deliver storytelling and immerse consumers into an alternative world where they become deeply engaged participants in the live brand experience narrative. *Theatre* is a key element of many *Experiential Strategies*, and can be integrated with other elements, adding an exciting and immersive engagement component.

R is for Research

Experiential marketing lends itself perfectly to providing both qualitative and quantitative **Research** as part of a campaign. *Research* strategies can be integrated easily into the interaction in a way that is unobtrusive to consumers, yet still manages to uncover significantly valuable information. Beyond benefiting the organization with new insights, involving consumers in influencing and shaping the future of a brand or campaign, by giving their input, is the most effective way to create brand advocacy and stimulate a passionate response. In fact, the *Research* element is very popular because it makes the most of an interaction with the *Target Audience*. Brands and marketing agencies alike are finding that the experiential marketing campaigns that they run give them insights into the thoughts, feelings, lifestyles and purchasing behaviour of their consumers, and that by involving them and seeking their input, consumers are mobilized into brand evangelists who 'do the marketing for you' through personal recommendations, word of mouth and the creation of social media content and sharing. It is simple to build in simple mechanics to gather valuable data in the form of consumer conversation and surveys, because there is always direct contact with consumers at a live brand experience, and many live brand experiences involve face-to-face interaction allowing for a real-time *Two-Way Interaction* and dialogue.

A is for Adverts

In this context, the **Adverts** element is representative of one of several elements that combine to form the *Experiential Strategy*. Just as an advert can amplify a live brand experience, a live brand experience can bring to life an advertising campaign creative or content. First, the live brand experience can reinforce advertising that the *Target Audience* may have already been exposed to, and second, it gives consumers the feeling that they are closer to the brand, and that the brand is a real and important part of their everyday lives.

Live brand experiences can be used to communicate the content of an advert in situations where it is unlikely that the *Target Audience* will otherwise see the *Adverts*. For example, if there are no billboard sites in a target area or event, then a live brand experience, which reflects the theme and content of the ad, is the perfect alternative. If a sporting event is held and sponsorship is out of budget, sometimes it is more cost-effective (and more interesting) to bring to life the advertising campaign with an experiential element. Also, using an *Experiential Strategy* to convey your advertising message can be an effective way to make the campaign more memorable and allow the consumer to interact with the brand, resulting in a deeper relationship that stimulates word of mouth, generates unique yet brand-relevant content and broadens social media *Reach*.

T *is for* Televised *or* Broadcast

Imagine how much you can expand the reach of your live brand experience by having it *Televised* or *Broadcast*. This could be by forming a media partnership, broadcasting it on television, radio, digital or social media channels. You can thereby create a far-reaching live event, accessible to view and interact with far and wide. A media partnership that informs consumers about a live brand experience prior to it taking place, and then broadcasts the experience live – increasing its reach beyond those who can physically attend in person, can be very successful in enforcing the brand's position as one that cares about all its customers. This perception can be achieved with those who do not participate in the live brand experience (but simply saw/heard about it) as well as those who do have a chance to interact and participate first-hand.

E *is for* Entertainment *and* Culture

Entertainment and *Culture* can inspire elements of your *Experiential Strategy* that can be valuable in terms of adding interest, providing an opportunity to align the brand with an interest that resonates deeply with your audience, tapping into their passion points, often gathering large numbers of people to a live brand experience, and positioning the brand in a particular way. In fact, many companies create their own brand-relevant music festivals, sporting events, family events, art shows, concerts or dining experiences as core elements in their experiential strategies in order to generate valuable content and consumer engagement. In this context, the *Entertainment and Culture* element can represent music, fashion, sports, arts, food or culture-based activities. Creating your own branded event-property-brand extension can provide an excellent alternative to pricey and restricting sponsorship, while opening up new revenue streams and brand franchise opportunities. *Entertainment and Culture* can provide fabulous triggers for word of mouth, shareable content and positive social currency, while tapping into customers' personal interests to forge deep relationships between brands and their *Target Audience*s.

G *is for* Games *or* Competitions

Games or *Competitions* are great ways to create brand-relevant, *Two-Way Interactions* between consumers and brands. For game-based products, creating a ludic experience is a fairly straightforward option. But that does not mean that this element should be limited to gaming or toy brands alone. In fact, gamification can be used to bring even an intelligent and strategic *Brand Personality* to life (think giant/interactive chess, sudoku, or jenga).

Explore existing games for inspiration

If you would like to use games as an element in your *Experiential Strategy*, look to existing games, sports, board games and gameshows for inspiration and make sure that you select and adapt components into brand-relevant and engaging mechanics for engaging your *Target Audience*. There is a huge variety of games from which to draw inspiration for your specific purpose. Consider *Research*ing TV gameshows, quiz games, board games, traditional playground games, sports-team matches, arcade games and simple logic games such as crosswords, sudoku and rock-paper-scissors. It is also worth *Research*ing the wide range of games from the online gaming and app world, which are hugely successful in engaging consumers and tapping into their competitive streak.

Gamification is great for creating buzz

Gamification can provide inspiration for effective mechanics for driving mass-reaching word of mouth, as explored in the *Exponential Elements* stage of the *BETTER* creative process. Using 'leader-board' style mechanics that incentivize the spreading of content can be a great method of driving social media *Reach*.

The best thing about taking inspiration from classic games within the experiential marketing context is that you can take something we already know to be fun or enriching, and personalize it to the brand, the objectives and the audience, making it larger than life. Even when a **Game** element is not wholly relevant or appropriate in an immersive, participatory or interactive sense where it might be central to the *Two-Way Interaction*, you can still effectively build-in a **Competition** mechanism, where the prize itself is an experience that in turn provides a means of bringing your *Brand Personality* to life and generating further content. By integrating a simple but effective **Game** or **Competition** component into your *Experiential Strategy*, you can create a memorable and fun experience for the participants that taps into human nature's competitive spirit to achieve high engagement and social sharing.

I is for Interactive Technology

By studying the *BETTER* model, you already understand the importance of *Two-Way Interaction* in experiential marketing, and the value that can be generated from participation in brand-relevant activity such as *Interactive Technology* for your *Target Audience*. We live in the digital age, one of rapidly accelerating advancements in technology and constant innovation into its possible applications. Each day it becomes increasingly cost-effective to customize technology to better serve customer needs and desires. The personal connections we have with digital apps has fostered a deep level of interactivity through our mobile devices. Smart products, appliances and wearables are providing data and facilitating the innovation of customer experiences in unique and previously stagnant areas. Even in more analogue interactions, think of visiting a museum or art installation and participating in an interactive display, lifting flaps, pressing buttons, pulling levers and enjoying the discovery process, presented in a creative way: interaction is key.

Trigger, set, go

Trigger-reaction technology such as motion sensors, pressure sensors and buttons can facilitate an amazing range of both face-to-face and remote *Two-Way Interactions*. When integrated into your *Experiential Strategy*, *Interactive Technology* can be a great catalyst to interact deeply with your *Target Audience*s, whether it is used to gather data, educate, demonstrate or provoke reaction. Even (and especially) when your product is in a non-technology-based sector, the *Interactive Technology* element can be formulated in an innovative way that is relevant through engagement that is fun, *Educational* or inspiring – and conveys complex brand messages.

E is for Education

Experiential marketing is a fabulous way to educate consumers about your product or *Service*. In addition, you can create an experience designed around **Education**. A chance to educate your audience about something seemingly separate, which brings your brand to life, thereby aligning with it and creating a thematic association. The education element can be integrated to communicate your product's heritage, its features and benefits, or subjects that reflect its *Brand Personality* and show relevance to your *Target Audience*'s aspirational lifestyle. Education-based experiential marketing strategies have been historically popular with government bodies, wishing to educate stakeholders on issues such as voting, health and crime. But likewise, if your campaign is for a car brand that is superior to other cars in its class, one of your main objectives might be to educate your consumers about its technology, in which case education is likely to be a key element of your *Experiential Strategy*. This element can be especially beneficial when conveying rational messages, and can be an integral part of your strategy, regardless of sector.

S is for Set

The *Set* element of the *Experiential Strategy* represents a purpose-built/ designed environment of the live brand experience, and this applies for both face-to-face and virtual *Set*tings. The *Set* can also form part or all of a retail environment or pop-up. It could be housed within an unusual environment such as a converted vehicle (think boat, bus, truck or plane) or a purpose-built themed environment such as a garden, beach, raft etc. Takeovers of existing locations that are unexpected often work well, such as a penthouse apartment, abandoned school, car park or office block. The *Set* is any environment that becomes the stage and location for the live brand experience. It should be designed with all the elements of your *Message – Key Communication* in mind, and should reflect the visual identity of your brand as well as its personality. Taking inspiration from the multisensory elements brainstormed during the emotional connection stage of the *BETTER* creative process is a great starting point when beginning the process of exploring an appropriate *Set*.

Immersive, experientially – transportation environments that evoke feelings and transcend moods

The *Set*s of most live brand experiences attract a lot of interest because they are enticing to the *Target Audience*. A *Set* that is unusual is one of the best drivers for consumers to capture and share their own social media content. A good *Set*, designed as an immersive sensory environment, might be remembered by the participants for years to come. Some experiential marketing agencies outsource the production of purpose-built *Sets* that are used for face-to-face live brand experiences to companies that traditionally make props and stages for television, film and *Theatre*, or immersive theatrical experiences. These particularly are on the rise, with Secret Cinema, You Me Bum Bum Train, Punch Drunk Theatre and a range of live, immersive zombie experiences taking London, New York, Paris and other cities by storm, gaining large amounts of revenue and an impressive reputation. Following suit, some experiential marketing agencies outsource the production of *Sets* that are used for remote/virtual live brand experiences to digital content production agencies, programmers and TV production companies in order to allow consumers to interact with an experience, remotely from their mobile or device.

Remote or virtual live brand experience *Sets*

Some social media platforms and entertainment companies offer remote or virtual live brand experiences via interactive streaming events. This is another reason why, when appointing an experiential marketing agency, it is good to *Research* their speciality, project history and understand how they began and evolved, because this will give you an idea of which areas within experiential marketing are their forte, helping to establish if they are the best partner for finding or creating your ultimate *Set*, should this component be integral to your *Experiential Strategy*.

It is advisable, where relevant, to integrate the *Interactive Technology* element with the *Set* element into your *Experiential Strategy*, because the more innovative and interactive your *Set* is, the more engaging your live brand experience will be.

Integrating the selected elements from the *STRATEGIES* acronym

It is important to remember that your selected elements from the *STRATEGIES* acronym need to be integrated to form your *Experiential Strategy*, which will be a combination of two or more of these elements. The *Experiential Strategy* provides a structural framework for your idea(s), as well as a clear direction for your plan. When you pick your combination of *Experiential Elements* to create the *Experiential Strategy*, keep in mind your original ideas generated from the *BETTER* creative process, and the steps that you have taken thus far to develop and refine it.

The original concept that was formulated using the *BETTER* model we have already explored in Chapter 6:

- *Brand Personality.*

- *Emotional Connection*, with three multisensory brand values that sum up the brand's human-like characteristics: authentic, positively connected and personally meaningful.

- *Target Audience* (their daily lifestyles and aspirations).

- *Two-Way Interaction* (the participatory big idea in the form of a live brand experience).

- *Exponential Elements* (the word-of-mouth stimulant and triggers).

- *Reach* (expanding how many people are exposed to the experience, taking into account both the *Two-Way Interaction Reach*, the word-of-mouth *Reach*, and the *Reach* of the chosen amplification channels such as PR, social media and broadcast).

Since you began mapping out the plan in *SET MESSAGE* format, you have refined the idea further, carefully considering the *Situation and Background, Experiential Objectives, Target Audience* and *Message – Key Communication.*

As well as ensuring that the *Experiential Strategy* elements you select encompass your idea, it is also very important to remain open to new approaches and executions, regardless of whether you have already seen similar examples from your sector of any preconceptions that may exist concerning the tastes and preferences of your *Target Audience.*

The STRATEGIES acronym works across all sectors and target audiences

Whether your consumers are affluent executives, over 50s, influencers or shoppers, or your product is a fast-moving consumer good (FMCG) (such as a chocolate bar or toothpaste), or a high-involvement luxury purchase (such as a Rolls-Royce or a holiday apartment on a secluded Ibizan resort), *Experiential Strategy* elements can be combined successfully. As long as they are relevant and have been formulated in line with the stages identified during the *BETTER* process, they are likely to resonate and feel on-brand. By selecting elements that stay true to your *Brand Personality*, creating an *Emotional Connection* with the participants, and always keeping your *Target Audience*, their lifestyle and aspirations at the forefront of your mind, you can develop an *Experiential Strategy* that delivers on the ultimate goal, creating the right experience for the right people.

You should pick two or more of the most appropriate *Experiential Elements* from the *STRATEGIES* acronym, then integrate them to form your *Experiential Strategy*. Below are sample combinations that mix three or four elements, illustrating how you could go about mixing the selected elements to formulate an *Experiential Strategy*, thereby informing your creative and providing it with a structured framework for your ideas.

Example scenarios

Educational + Service + Research + Set When Sophie – the marketing director of a popular brand of margarine – wanted to show the brand's *Target Audience* how the margarine could be used to lower cholesterol, as well as bring the active, health-conscious and medical *Brand Personality* to life:

- She designed an *Experiential Strategy* involving a cholesterol-testing experience in a 40-foot branded trailer. First, doctors and leading experts gave talks to participants about the negative effects and risks of high cholesterol, with video content versions overlaid with compelling stats projected onto the walls (*Educational*), and second, they provided guests with free cholesterol and heart-rate tests (*Service*) in a medical-themed branded environment (*Set*).

- Sophie received a contribution from the market *Research* budget towards this campaign and wanted to gather data from the participants to facilitate tailoring of marketing and distribution to customer needs.

- She wanted to know which supermarkets the *Target Audience* members shopped with most regularly, how frequently they purchased butter or margarine, which brands they preferred, and why.

- The *Brand Ambassadors*, who were assisting the consumers through the cholesterol and heart-rate testing, asked consumers a few quick questions (*Research*) prior to receiving a pass onto the vehicle and taking their cholesterol or heart-rate test.

  In return for answering the questions, the consumers were given the chance to partake in an on-the-spot cholesterol and heart-rate test (*Service*) and those that purchased were given a free heart-rate monitoring smart bracelet that they could keep to monitor their progress.

The campaign successfully achieved Sophie's *Experiential Objectives*: it gathered insightful *Research*, drove sales and brought to life the healthy *Brand*

Personality. The selected *Experiential Strategy* elements educated consumers about the product's benefits, differentiating it from its competitors, and provided a free relevant *Service* to its participants in a memorable way.

Theatre + Advert + Game   Mark, the creative director at a leading advertising agency, was informed that a brand of small pocket mints wanted to bring to life its existing advertising campaign with a live brand experience. The unique selling point of the product (and a key focus in the *Message – Key Communication*) was that the mints had a special frosty cooling effect.

- The live brand experience channel was intended to reinforce the creativity from the *Adverts* that Mark's team had developed.

- Mark wanted to bring the mint's *Brand Personality* to life so he carefully analysed the creative, looking for inspiration on how to do so.

- The *Advert* featured hundreds of life-size mint characters that visually symbolized 'cooling agents', so he decided that these would become the inspiration for the experience.

- The *Experiential Strategy* incorporated **Theatre**, a **Game** and the **Advert**.

- Professional actors dressed up as the cooling agents in costumes that were identical to the ones worn in the TV *Advert*.

- The actors, reincarnated as mints or 'cooling agents', participated in an immersive plot and gave out samples of the cooling mints while they engaged participants in a *Theatrical Game*, where they were tasked with spotting hidden ice blocks as part of a plot that was centred around the need to cool the planet.

- Those who participated in the *Game* and engaged with the actors were given branded cooler bags and had a chance to win a skiing holiday, which reinforced the cooling USP.

The *Experiential Strategy* neatly and relevantly integrated elements of the *Advert*, with added components of *Theatre* and a brand relevant *Game*, which in combination succeeded in bringing to life the advertising campaign and achieving broader brand objectives.

Service + Set   Jaleel, the marketing manager for a brand of paint ranges for the home, ran live brand experiences to position the brand as a colour-matching expert with the *Target Audience* of affluent women aged 25+. His *Experiential Strategy* was designed to convey the colour-matching expertise of the brand, which had launched a new app that enabled users to scan any object and in turn purchase that exact shade of paint as well as view recommendations for complementary colours.

Jaleel was keen to show off this capability and promote its three best-selling paint ranges named Pure, Cirque and Revolution. The first, 'Pure', was a range of neutral paints; the second, 'Cirque', a range of bold paints; and the third, 'Revolution', a range of metallic and iridescent paints.

- He combined what he felt were the most appropriate combination of experiential elements to formulate the *Experiential Strategy*: **Service** (to benefit and relate to his *Target Audience*'s lives), and **Set** (to demonstrate the stunning appearance of the paint ranges on real walls and surrounded by real objects in complementary shades that consumers would be able to scan).

- He had already come up with a concept and completed the first four stages of *SET MESSAGE* during which he carefully *Researched* his *Target Audience* through focus groups.

He discovered that the demographic aspired to having beautiful homes decorated by professional interior designers and that they aspired to own unique objects and artefacts.

The women also spent a proportion of time discussing their personal appearances, and aspirations to look as fashionable and stylish as some influencers they followed online. These insights inspired Jaleel's *Experiential Strategy*.

- He created a live brand experience involving a *Set* that toured the central atriums of major shopping centres where the paint was on sale in participating stores.

- The *Set* represented three adjoining rooms of a beautiful home, and each room was decorated by interior designers to reflect one of the brand's three paint ranges: Pure, Cirque and Revolution.

- The rooms featured complementary colours from their respective paint ranges, alongside unique objects sourced by social media influencers demonstrating the brand's expertise in colour-matching.

- The mini house-style *Set* had nail technician *Brand Ambassadors* positioned in each of the rooms, fully trained on the style principles of the three paint ranges and on the brand's colour-matching techniques and app.

- The *Brand Ambassadors*, who were seated at branded counters, invited consumers to have their nails painted in shades that matched their outfits, and to watch a demonstration of the colour-matching app while they waited for their nails to be completed.

- The women were invited to pick one of three different themes to reflect the neutral, bold and metallic ranges offered by the brand.

- This process closely replicated the process that the brand and store advisers used to intelligently match paint ranges and individual colour choices with consumers' style and home furnishings.

- The influencers who picked the objects and artefacts also came to the *Set* to check out their selections in situ, and were inspired to capture and share pictures, which they posted onto their high-reaching social media channels.

- This *Experiential Strategy* successfully combined two elements: *Service* (colour matching and painting nails) and *Set* (a beautiful home environment) to achieve Jaleel's *Experiential Objectives*.

Research + Entertainment + Advert + Game (or Competition) James, a brand manager at a well-known banking brand, was tasked with generating leads for a new unsecured loan that offered a reasonable interest rate and targeted lower-income families who would not typically qualify. The brand's advertising agency created a YouTube ad that showed staff from the bank's branches dancing and singing about the new loan product (in the style of a Broadway musical) about an unsecured loan product that the bank had launched.

James decided to reinforce the ad campaign with experiential marketing.

- He hired an experiential marketing agency to produce a series of live brand experiences that would replicate the advert as a live performance, thus bringing to life the advert's creative.

During the *Target Audience* stage of *SET MESSAGE*, James referred to data that indicated that the demographic was most susceptible to applying for loans during the period that preceded school holidays, because these periods were most popular for expensive holidays abroad.

- Taking this insight into consideration, he decided that the performance should be presented as a five-minute live replica of the advert, performed as a stunt during the commercials at cinemas during school holidays.

- A host manned the microphone and introduced the musical performance. Before the performance began, he encouraged the families to complete a quick 'dream holiday survey', facilitated on their website while *Brand Ambassadors* asked them about their ideal holiday destinations and activities.

- In return for completing the online survey on the spot, the kids received free popcorn (in a branded container) and the families were entered into a competition to win their dream holiday.

This successful and simple live brand experience was performed many times a day during the winter and summer holidays at over 20 cinemas, entertaining families that might not have been able to afford to go away on holiday. The *Experiential Strategy* combined the three chosen experiential elements; *Advert, Entertainment, Game* (or *Competition*) and *Research* to achieve the brand's *Experiential Objective* of lead generation, whilst also reinforcing the impact of the advertising campaign through a memorable experience that was captured by the consumers and shared online, thereby generating social currency and fantastic *Reach*.

Game + Televised/Broadcast Andrew is the sales and marketing director at a drinks company. He was planning the launch of a new brand of Caribbean rum. The brand had a pirate-themed *Brand Personality,* and Andrew was keen to launch it with an integrated experiential marketing campaign. The *Experiential Objectives* were to bring to life the Caribbean and pirate-themed *Brand Personality*, drive product trial and generate word of mouth and social-media *Reach*. After carefully developing a concept he was keen to identify which strategy elements it combined; he decided on the *Televised/Broadcast* and *Game* elements for his *Experiential Strategy*.

- Following a *BETTER* brainstorm session with his creative team, he selected a pirate-themed one-hour 'Treasure Hunt Challenge' experience with prizes of cases of rum and Caribbean cruises provided by a trendy cruise brand aimed at millennials.

- The campaign ran six 'Treasure Hunt Challenges' simultaneously, one in each of his six main markets. Each city was re-created as a map and transformed into its own branded treasure-hunt map, with key points identified as locations to pick up clues.

- Andrew's PR agency secured PR coverage, blog posts and social media mentions in advance, and his media agency ran targeted social media ads promoting the Treasure Hunt Challenge, ensuring a high level of participation in the live brand experience.

- The articles instructed those interested to form teams of five with their friends before meeting at the start points in each city, where they could download the app and run around hunting virtual treasure.

- On arrival at the meeting points, participants were greeted by *Brand Ambassadors* (wearing pirate hats, fake parrots and eye patches) who registered them for the game and gave them their kits containing treasure maps, rum samples and branded T-shirts.

- Participants raced around the cities to hunt for clues – within the allotted hour – in the hope of finding the virtual treasure and carefully planted real chests that contained prize tickets.

- Andrew secured a media partnership and the nationwide 'Treasure Hunt Challenge' was broadcast live online in a one-hour slot that gained enormous reach, showing the teams running around each town hunting for clues and treasure chests.

- A 30-minute content special was broadcast the following month showing the winners dressed as pirates and enjoying their rum cases and Caribbean cruises.

In addition to the 10,000 registered consumers that participated in the actual challenge, another 70 million people were exposed to the live brand experience via the broader content and PR *Reach*.

The *Game* element enabled a high level of *Two-Way Interaction* between the brand and participants, while the *Televised/Broadcast* element enabled the live brand experience to achieve a massive *Reach*. The *Experiential Strategy* brought to life the rum's Caribbean and pirate-themed *Brand Personality*, created original content and generated massive word of mouth and social media *Reach* at the same time.

Educational + Interactive Technology + Set   Adriana was responsible for launching an innovative notepad that had a built-in, high-quality video camera. It also had a revolutionary function that allowed consumers to edit and decorate their videos on their notepad using the pens provided, which functioned uniquely, activating colour grading and effects. The smart product was the first of its kind, and Adriana wanted to create an experiential marketing campaign that would educate consumers on its special features.

- Her *Target Audience* – fun-loving Gen Z's – inspired Adriana to hire an experiential agency and create an innovative live brand experience on global beaches.

- They created a giant *Set*, a 'Smart Zone' shaped like the notepad and pen *Set* itself, and positioned it on beaches that attracted the young, fun Gen Z demographic.

- *Brand Ambassadors* were trained and armed with the smart notepad and pen *Sets*.

- They approached groups of friends who were sunbathing on the beach or playing sports such as volleyball, and invited them to be filmed by the *Brand Ambassador* holding the smart notepad.

- The groups of friends were excited at the thought of making and decorating their own mini beach movies, and were keen to oblige and participate.

- Beachgoers were then encouraged to enter the 'Smart Zone' to watch a demonstration and tutorial that educated them about the video-editing features of the notepad and magic pen *Set*.

- *Brand Ambassadors* taught the participants how to use the features to create magnificent results and encouraged them to participate in editing the movie clips in which they starred. Life-sized projections on the *Set*s walls showcased the content already generated during the experience from other countries.

- Thousands of excited consumers from beaches around the globe filmed their own content on the notepads and edited fun colours and Special FX into their movie clips, which could be voted on by participants at the other beaches around the world. The participants had the opportunity to post direct to YouTube, Snapchat or Instagram from the notepads.

- As well as being given a chance to win free smart notepads, every participant received branded beach balls and fake tattoos, which had high visibility and raised brand awareness to other beachgoers.

Adriana's *Experiential Strategy* featured **Educational** and **Interactive Technology** elements built into a brand-relevant and visually exciting *Set* (passers-by were excited by the visual spectacle of people queuing to enter the enormous larger-than-life smart notepad *Set*s). The live brand experience content achieved enormous organic *Reach* and was also amplified with digital ads driving traffic to the content, showing some of the video highlights.

The experiential marketing campaign achieved its *Experiential Objective* of educating consumers about the smart pad's video-editing features. The memorable and fun *Two-Way Interaction* also succeeded in generating brand advocacy, driving word of mouth and generating tons of unique content amongst the young, fun, *Target Audience*.

Make the experience memorable and ongoing

Keep in mind that even without any additional actions or triggers, a live brand experience is by its nature more memorable than any other form of marketing, and the live brand experience should be at the core of the experiential marketing campaign.

Memories themselves do not merely exist across time, linking the past, present and future, nor are they only alive within the individual's consciousness. Memories exist at the very heart of 'lived experience', whether collective or individual.[1] To ensure that the *Experiential Strategy* creates an experience that will be remembered for the maximum possible length of time, you can create external aids that reinforce the memories of the people that it reached, which can then gain longevity and posterity on social media platforms.

Visual evidence lives on

A great option when the live brand experience is executed face-to-face in real life (IRL) is to provide participants with prized visual evidence such as professionally captured photo or video montages that stitch together several highlights of their experience. In addition, the provision of a physical object or souvenir anchors their memory of the experience, aligning it with the positive emotions experienced at the time and keeping those feelings accessible far beyond the initial moment of participation.

For example, you can take the consumers' photos while they are in or on the *Set* and then print their photos onto objects that they will use or see day-to-day such as mugs/magnets/stickers/lunchboxes/placemats etc. Visual evidence in the form of a physical souvenir is a great way to trigger positive emotions in the memories of the participants by reminding them of how much they enjoyed the experience (the souvenir may also become sentimental and lead them to romanticize their experience). When provided in a digital format, the visual evidence can incorporate an *Exponential Element* (as discussed in the *BETTER* creative process) such as an incentive like 'share and get five friends to participate, to increase your chances of winning' (a competition).

Memory triggers last for years and create deep bonds

Relevant branded gifts are another great way to trigger memories. The gift then acts as an external aid, and an 'important reason for why external aids facilitate memory is that the physical presence of an object usually stimulates memory more than imagining or thinking'.[2] They can either be given in person (when the live brand experience is face-to-face IRL) or by inviting consumers to digitally order their free gift themselves (when the live brand experience is remote). By providing the participants with a call to action prior to receiving their gift, therefore making it necessary that they actively request the gift, you stimulate their intention to remember the experience.

They will need a memory anchor and trigger mechanism

It is recommended that you provide participants of the live brand experience with a trigger mechanism that makes it easy for them to pass on their experience, and then support that system with an incentive for doing so. A scheme to encourage participants to share their experiences, or a link to the product on social media, with the incentive of receiving a gift, or entry into a competition, can yield substantial increases in *Reach*.

Pass it on

This forms an IRL *Exponential Element* for the campaign. When the incentive involves asking live brand experience participants to give a gift (to those not there), the recipients of the participant's gift should also have the opportunity to give gifts, as should those who heard about the live brand experience from an amplification channel, thereby ensuring the *Reach* of the live brand experience is uncapped and can grow exponentially. Even though the individuals in these groups did not all participate in the original experience themselves, they have the opportunity to receive something, and still participate with the gift. This symbolizes the positive sentiments created by the experience that they heard about from a peer or amplification channel. In this way, the external aid does not only serve as a tangible reinforcement of the participant's memory, it also provides the recipient of the message with the opportunity to engage further with the brand and form their own personal connection with it.

Interview excerpt: creating a lasting emotional connection through memorabilia

Max Abbott, National Brand Advocate Manager, Cellar Trends (global drinks brand portfolio)

When people go on a night out, they are out to have fun. If you as a brand can do something fun or provide them with something that they are going to carry around for the rest of the night, that is important and hopefully they will wake up with that little item or whatever you have given them, and they will remember why they've got it.

I still think there is something quite nice about that. What I am still interested in understanding is how you then get that consumer to share their experience again, and make it last just that little bit more for the brand.

I still think I've got pinned up on my corkboard two strips of photos from a night out that I went on two years ago and I still remember the whole night from looking at those two simple things. I still have a keyring from a night out too and that must have been five years ago.

Those nostalgic triggers create an *Emotional Connection*, they are really great but it is how you link them together that counts. The things that consumers really hang on to are the moments and the 'things' – such as pictures or 'bits and bobs' – that they can take away, savour and keep that will remind them of that night.[3]

Make it live on

By creating further interaction between the brand and both the participants and the recipients, the relationship continues beyond the initial campaign. Ongoing positive interaction is key to establishing long-term customer advocacy, this being the ultimate aim of experiential marketing. By capturing the contact data of the participants of your experience and the recipients of the experience message, and then contacting them with (perhaps private) invitations to future experiences (to be delivered either as real-world events or remote events on social media platforms) you can convert recipients of a *second-hand* message about a live brand experience into *participants* of a live brand experience.

Forming golden bonds

By *continuing* the ongoing experiential marketing communication platform with a live brand experience at its core, you can build coveted golden bonds with your *Target Audience* and strengthen the understanding that your brand is truly customer-centric and wants to add value to their lives. As a result, the consumers will remember that the relationship that they have with you is long-term and two-way, and that it does not end when the first experience or purchase does.

The other phenomenon that can occur as a result of inviting consumers (participants and recipients) to future live brand experiences and into ongoing dialogue, is that bonds will form between the individuals in the groups of those invited, and the memory of the group realizes itself in individual memories.[4] This long-term view should be considered when formulating your long-term *Experiential Strategy*, which when coupled with a customer-experience orientation within your organization will build the foundations for brand advocacy and long-standing customer relationships.

Summary

In summary, there are 10 basic elements in the *STRATEGIES* acronym:

STRATEGIES
*S*ervice
*T*heatre
*R*esearch
*A*dverts
*T*elevised or Broadcast
*E*ntertainment and Culture
*G*ame (or Competition)
*I*nteractive Technologies
*E*ducational
*S*et

You should take your existing experiential concepts as developed using the *BETTER* model (explained in earlier chapters) and explore the *Experiential Elements* from the *STRATEGIES* acronym that best define it, then develop the framework and ideas further by combining two or more of those *Experiential Strategy* elements.

All *Experiential Strategies* should:

- bring the *Brand Personality* to life;

- aim to create an *Emotional Connection* (via multisensory elements and the three key attributes: authentic, positively connected and personally meaningful) with participants;

- be relevant to the *Target Audience*'s lifestyle and aspirations.

You should always have an *Exponential Element* or a talking point that:

- inspires word of mouth;
- encourages the creation and sharing of content;
- strives to attain maximum *Reach*.

This should combine the initial *Reach* of the live brand experience and the word-of-mouth *Reach* and the *Reach* of amplification channels (such as social media, influencers and PR) whilst maintaining quality engagement. The *Experiential Strategy* should be fitting to the *Experiential Objectives*, and should integrate the brand's *Message – Key Communication*. Use the BETTER model as your checklist to ensure your *Experiential Strategy* is as effective as possible.

Notes

1 Middleton, D and Brown, S D (2005) *The Social Psychology of Experience: Studies in remembering and forgetting*, Sage, London

2 Gruneberg, M and Morris, P (1992) *Aspects of Memory: The practical aspects*, vol 1, Routledge, London, p 154

3 Smilansky, S (2017) Excerpt from an interview with Max Abbott, National Brand Advocate Manager, Cellar Trends (Global Drinks Brand Portfolio)

4 Halbwachs, M and Coser, L A (1992) *On Collective Memory*, University of Chicago Press, Chicago, p 40

Selected locations and brand ambassadors for your experiential marketing strategy

12

You have probably heard many times the popular sayings 'Location, location, location!' and 'People buy people!'. These two statements may be most frequently used in retail, property and sales environments, but they apply to every touchpoint that a consumer has with an organization or brand during his or her journey with it. This journey includes the marketing communication that the individuals participate in. As previously outlined, it is suggested that the big idea in your experiential marketing campaign is based on a *Two-Way Interaction*, in real time.

Synergy between locations and people is crucial

This live brand experience needs to be positively managed and interfaced by people, and whether they are your employees, part-time representatives or influencers, they should fulfil the role of *Brand Ambassadors*. The synergy between participants, locations and *Brand Ambassadors* is very important. To be successful in experiential marketing you must strive to create the right experiences for the right people, and those experiences need to happen at the right place, at the right time.

When you completed the *Target Audience* part of the *SET MESSAGE* plan, you completed the day-in-the-life analysis, also looking at the aspirational lifestyle of your *Target Audiences*, taking time out to truly consider where to find them and how best to appeal to their desires. Therefore, finding the ideal locations for the experience (whether face-to-face and in real life (IRL) or remote and facilitated through tech or social media platforms) and setting it up effectively is key.

A live representation of your brand

There are many factors to be taken into consideration when deciding on your *Selected Locations* and *Brand Ambassadors* for live brand experiences, which is why this entire segment of the *SET MESSAGE* planning system is designed to facilitate that process. This chapter will give you an in-depth understanding of what needs to be considered at this stage in your experiential plan, and how the choice of locations and people will ultimately make or break an experience.

The *Brand Ambassadors*, of ultimate importance, are the key facet of this chapter. During the live brand experience, they must embody the identity of the brand – they are the only human interface between the *Brand Personality* and the consumer. They are the people who have the potential to appeal to the desires of the participants and build or strengthen their relationship with the brand.

You can spend all the time in the world planning your live brand experience and ensuring that the production is magical and everything is logistically perfect, but if a *Brand Ambassador* is not carefully trained or not properly matched to the brand and the *Target Audience*, then the live brand experience will not be successful.

Select the best locations

To help you to avoid wasted efforts, this stage in the *SET MESSAGE* planning system looks at how to plan and carefully select the right locations for live brand experiences, how to choose the right *Brand Ambassadors* and how to train them, aiming for flawless and problem-free delivery.

In the 2017 AdAge Marketing Fact Pack, Lucinda Martinez, SVP, from Multicultural & International Marketing, HBO, states: 'Recognizing a more diverse marketplace is also essential. Marketing to multicultural, millennial and mobile audiences requires finding the suitable brand ambassador with the right messaging that communicates content to them in a truly meaningful way.' This echoes the one-on-one communication style and authentic transparency that modern consumers expect from brand. Martinez continues, 'If you have done that well, they will feel compelled to evangelize on your brand's behalf. And to be clear, this is not as easy as it sounds – authenticity is everything here.'[1]

Heineken believes the Heineken Experience attraction has allowed it to create loyal internal *Brand Ambassadors*. It currently has almost 160 students working at the attraction. They can only stay for four years, after which a new batch of students takes their place. This provides 'fresh blood and energy', according to the Heineken Experience's managing director Dirk Lubbers, quoted in *Marketing Week*.[2]

In *Living the Brand: How to transform every member of your organization into a brand champion*, Ind states: 'The goal of the concept of living the brand: to inspire individuals to identify and internalize the brand; to become committed to delivering value so that customers and consumers can enjoy a seemingly seamless experience that lives up to (and exceeds) their expectations.' He continues by proposing that 'companies that do the best job of living up to their values and developing ethical employees, including managers, recognize that the real cause of success – or failure – is always the people, not the words'.[3]

Influencer recommendations

The Drum wrote a striking opener headline paragraph in January 2016: 'Consumers are increasingly tuning in to content created by influencers to help them make purchasing decisions, with one-fifth (19 per cent) of the average consumer's total media consumption now made up of influencer content.'[4]

The article continues, explaining that Good Relations, a PR and content agency, surveyed 1,000 people over the age of 16, finding that more than half (57 per cent) have made a purchase based solely on an online influencer recommendation, increasing to 69 per cent for millennials.[5]

Selecting locations

There are five key factors to consider when evaluating possible locations for your live brand experience, when executed face-to-face IRL:

The five key factors for choosing *Selected Locations*

1 **Demographics** (of the location's visitors).

2 The **state of mind** (of the location's visitors):
   - Are they seeking to purchase/socialize/be entertained/learn?
   - How much dwell time do they have available? Are they in a rush, or in leisure mode?
   - If they are with others, who are they with (and what are the implications?)

3 **Footfall** (or number of visitors).

4 **Practical** and logistical considerations.

5 **Cost** (which should be related to the spaces, footfall, ambience, attributes and positioning).

Demographics – key factor #1

Since different locations are frequented by people of mixed demographics, it can be challenging to know exactly where to place your live brand experience. Some places, such as business districts, tend to have an affluent population. This could suit a live brand experience for a credit-card brand, if it wished to reach a *Target Audience* of affluent professionals. Areas with large universities nearby will have a strong student demographic, and could therefore be ideal for a brand that wanted to create brand experiences for students, hipsters or Gen Z's. Likewise, some regional areas are predominantly suburban and could be ideal for targeting family demographics.

No matter who your primary *Target Audience* group is, there are locations (whether face-to-face or remote) such as venues, events, institutions or digital/social platforms that are perfect for reaching them in their natural environment. This applies to every population, no matter how niche or mass-market they may be.

When identifying and choosing your *Selected Locations* for your live brand experience, it is of vital importance to ensure that the core demographics of the location's visitors match those of your *Target Audience.*

At this stage in the plan you have already analysed or conducted market research into the *Target Audience*'s lives, and you should now be referring to that data to identify key insights and findings to extrapolate the perfect settings for your live brand experience. The day-in-the-life analysis completed at the *Target Audience* stage of the *SET MESSAGE* planning system should be referred to at this stage. If you are working with an agency, this process could be part of their remit, but you as the client should still be checking that they have made the optimal choices for your *Selected Locations.*

State of mind – key factor #2

The second factor to be considered when choosing your live brand experience's *Selected Locations* is the state of mind that the *Target Audience* is in while they are visiting and frequenting that space. In this instance, the 'state of mind' refers to three facets:

A What they are **seeking** (to purchase, socialize, be entertained, get to work or learn, for example)?

B The **dwell time** that they have available (whether they are in a rush or in leisure mode).

C Whether they are alone or, if not, **who they are with**.

If it takes five minutes to engage with the experiential interaction, then it is important that the participants have at least five minutes to spare in the *Selected Locations*. For example, people at airports or on planes tend to have lots of dwell time, and therefore their state of mind could be more available. They can often be bored while waiting for a flight or while on a plane, and it is most likely that they would welcome an interactive added-value experience.

However, in contrast, commuter points, rail stations and transport hubs (though having clear appeal as they are high-footfall locations) will not always succeed in capturing a consumer's attention due to a distracted state of mind. Twenty seconds of captive interest may be the maximum here, and it is crucially important not to be a nuisance to participants by attempting to keep their attention for longer than they desire.

A denim brand's music-festival activation – example

Young music lovers at an outdoor music festival are likely to have lots of dwell time available and to be open to interactive experiences, especially ones that address an immediate desire or need in what they are seeking and clearly relate to their state of mind.

- Imagine you have been camping at a festival for three days with no laundry or cleaning facilities, and a *Brand Ambassador* representing a denim brand approaches you, offering to wash and return your (muddy, sodden, crusty or damp) jeans to your tent.

- This is an added-value experience that relates to the state of mind of the festival-going *Target Audience*, there and then.

- It is easy to imagine this person returning to find the laundered denim, putting on the crisp, freshly washed jeans and telling all his or her peers about the excellent and surprising experience he or she just had with the denim brand.

- This peer-to-peer recommendation would be facilitated especially well if each (washed) pair of jeans returned included a card for the happy festival-goer to give to a friend, so they can text their tent's location to request their dirty denim is laundered and have the same experience as their friend.

- The experience and its *Selected Location* takes into account the complete state of mind of the participants – what the audience is seeking, their available dwell time and who they are with.

A strong word-of-mouth marketing dynamic cannot be effectively created if the experience is positioned in the wrong location or the mechanic does not take the audience's state of mind into account.

The research that you or your team analysed earlier, in the *Target Audience* section of the *SET MESSAGE* planning system, will be crucial now. By understanding the state of mind of your *Target Audience* while they are in their natural locations (the ones you noted while doing the day-in-the-life analysis), you will be able to ensure that you pick the most appropriate *Selected Locations* for your live brand experience and that they are relevant, appropriate and welcomed.

Footfall – key factor #3

The third, and vital, factor to take into consideration is footfall (or visitor numbers). The *Reach* of your live brand experience is crucial, as discussed and addressed during the *BETTER* creative process. The number of people reached directly (first-hand participants) in your live brand experience will largely depend on the number of people that visit the *Selected Locations*.

Busier, heavily populated locations tend to be better choices for live brand experiences as they allow a larger number of interactions, and therefore both the initial and the word-of-mouth reaches will be higher. Some live brand experiences that target niche audiences might have to compromise on volume of first-hand participants and use locations with a high concentration of the target demographic, but which sacrifice high footfall. Either way, footfall or visitor numbers should be taken into consideration, as it ultimately affects the ROI and long-term ROI (LROI) of the live brand experience.

If a live brand experience is situated in a fairly quiet location or is designed for small volumes of direct, first-hand participants, then it is of extra importance to compensate with other components designed to increase the *Reach*. There are many methods of extending the *Reach* beyond primary interactions, such as choosing influencers as your *Brand Ambassadors* (who can co-create content and share it with high impact and *Reach*), and strategically integrating amplification channels like PR and paid content distribution.

Practical or logistical – key factor #4

The fourth essential aspect to consider when choosing your *Selected Locations* is the practical or logistical factors.

There are plenty of permission-oriented, health and safety as well as legal implications to consider when setting up a live brand experience IRL and, depending on who owns the rights to space, permission will need to be granted, hire fees may need to be paid, insurance will need to be in place and all health and safety, and risk-assessment paperwork, will need to be completed. When the experience is delivered face to face, weather is also a serious consideration, especially when deciding whether to position the live brand experience inside or outside.

Sometimes the space may not be practical for the set that you have in mind (this should have been provisionally considered when looking at ideas for your set in the *Experiential Strategies* segment of the *SET MESSAGE* planning system). If you planned to create a luxury experience located in a park or public garden, for example, then underplanning for rain and mud could potentially ruin the event, especially with a discerning audience.

Space hire, permits or rights

If you are thinking of hiring an external floor space in a shopping mall, *that* ideal spot located just outside the store that sells the product in question – which would showcase your product in its best light – may already be contracted to someone else. These are examples of practical considerations that impact the feasibility of achieving your ultimate location choice.

If you wanted your live brand experience to be executed remotely, as a digital event for people around the world to engage with, and you chose for it to be held on your brand's website homepage but the streaming environment takes up more visual space or bandwidth than is available, then a micro-site may have been a better choice.

If you need to set up your live brand experiences within a short timescale and with minimum planning resource, but you want the experience to be positioned at airports, then it may need to be reconsidered in light of the bureaucracy and time required to process the permit applications, not to mention countless security checks and logistical implications prior to and during the live brand experience.

If you want to target families and young children face to face, then the *Selected Locations* must always be child friendly, safe and appropriate, with a set made of soft, non-harmful materials, without intrusive or flammable surfaces, and the *Brand Ambassadors* will need clearance from the Criminal Records Bureau (CRB check) and need to have experience working with children.

Keep in mind that the set (its materials, size, look, capacity and purpose), whether it is a physical or virtual set, must be appropriate for the *Selected Locations* and their surrounding environments, whether face to face (IRL) or remote (digital/virtual).

Cost – key factor #5

Aside from the many practical and logistical factors to be taken into consideration when choosing locations for a live brand experience, there is the pressing fifth factor: cost. Space hire and permits can vary from free to extremely expensive, and can be the make-or-break factor when it comes to the ROI and LROI from a live brand experience. The cost should reflect with the location's demographics, footfall (or visitor traffic), ambience, physical space and positioning.

A high-footfall location, for example, might cost more to hire than a low-footfall location, but if you compare the cost per thousand (CPT) people visiting both locations, then you may find that the space with the lower price is far more expensive when it is related back to the volume of interaction opportunities that it provides.

In this respect, looking at the cost of hiring live brand experience space is similar to looking at the cost of hiring media space. Placing an experience in the right physical or virtual space is similar to scheduling an advert in the right media space.

Some media owners (MOs) are aware that their space is perceived well by visitors and is therefore (due to the value of association) valuable from an ambience or brand-positioning perspective, and the MO might take advantage of this by charging high rates (compared to locations with similar footfall) to those who wish to hire space. Other MOs (from event promoters to property tycoons and website entrepreneurs) will not have taken into consideration the potentially highly lucrative financial opportunity of hiring space for live brand experiences.

When this is the case, they will usually be willing to provide good rates, partnerships or contra deals, so sometimes it is good to be creative and think 'out of the box' when brainstorming, location scouting or on recce (reconnaissance). Think of places that other brands may not have used for this purpose (live brand experiences) in the past, in order to maximize the value of the space you can get in return for your investment.

The planning work completed should inspire the Selected Locations *and* Brand Ambassadors

Every element that has been covered thus far in the *SET MESSAGE* planning system will come into play when choosing your *Selected Locations* for the live brand experience. Therefore, when considering the location options that you have available you should keep in mind the stages you have completed by this point in the planning process: *Situation and Background*, the *Experiential Objectives*, the *Target Audience*, the *Message – Key Communication*, and the *Experiential Strategy*.

Unusual spaces can be anywhere. Bear in mind that any location with people in (or on) could be a potential location for a live brand experience. For example, cinemas; shopping malls; empty petrol station forecourts; car parks; apartment buildings; offices; music festivals; gyms; libraries; museums; sporting events; concert halls; art galleries; digital, social and television channels; as well as emerging social 'virtual worlds' such as Sansar (brought to us by the creators of Second Life). Below are some examples of *Selected Locations* that have been used for live brand experiences.

Examples showing a variety of live brand experiences at a range of Selected Locations

An in-store live brand experience

Harry is a marketing manager for a market-leading brand of laptops and home printers. When his experiential marketing agency was tasked with the brief of increasing sales and bringing to life the stylish *Brand Personality* of an expensive new 'social art' printer brand his company was launching, the agency decided that the right locations would be in-store.

The printer, which has a premium price point and a primary target of affluent males aged 35+, required a simple experience that both added value to the participant and drove sales:

- The experiential marketing agency designed an experience held in the stores where the printers were sold.

- The experience – that was held in the run-up to Mother's Day – invited participants (mostly dads with their kids) to use the printer's unique functionality, combined with instant social-media content feeds, to create beautiful art to give as a greeting card (celebrating Mother's Day).

- Those who chose to buy the printer that day also received a high-quality, sterling silver frame to display their greeting art.

- The strong sales promotion mechanic, and the ability to both trial and buy the product on the spot, demonstrates how the 'in-store' environment can be a great choice, especially when complex product functionality is at play (as it was with this unique 'social art' printer).

Live brand experiences, pop-ups and events

Events-based live brand experiences can be partly organized by brands, when activating sponsorship rights or hiring an experiential 'pitch'. That said, many brands are taking the plunge, truly embracing an experiential approach and creating wholly owned events, where the event is in itself an 'owned' revenue creating branded property or creating 'brand takeover pop-ups' for a test-and-learn approach.

Revenue-generating experiences

Creating your own branded event, pop-up or permanent brand engagement space from scratch is a big investment, but one that can also bring in large revenue streams. Owning your own brand experience space can provide the opportunity to create an entirely bespoke and carefully curated environment with plenty of chances to add value to the customer, showcase products in a relevant way, and bring the *Brand Personality* to life. Given how easy it is for consumers to purchase online, physical bricks and mortar stores are rapidly being transformed into permanent live brand experience hubs, playing host to various events and plenty benefiting the communities they serve.

Large-scale events are resource-intensive to organize entirely

Even though it can be successful to organize your own large-scale event, this can be an enormous commitment of resources and, often, tapping into existing events is more practical and can provide fantastic settings for activating your live brand experiences to existing captive audiences with a great state of mind for brand engagement. They can be especially effective for achieving *Experiential Objectives* such as 'position the brand as X' or 'gain credibility with Y'. By positioning a live brand experience at an existing event, you can affiliate the brand with the event's established values and in many cases align your brand with the aspirational lifestyle the event brand represents for its guests, in much the same way as sponsoring such an event.

The visitors' perceptions of the event brand instantly 'rub off' onto their perceptions of the brand, and vice versa. Though live brand experiences enable deep and relevant *Two-Way Interactions* that sponsorship cannot achieve alone, the branding opportunities that sponsorship deals provide can be complementary to the live brand experience, reinforcing awareness and strengthening the impact of the live brand experience channel.

Sometimes, cost-effective package deals that include both live brand experience space and sponsorship branding can be negotiated at events.

A guerrilla-style live brand experience near a sports match/game

The founder of a casino website wanted to bring to life the brand's 'Living the Dream' *Message – Key Communication* while driving membership sign-ups:

- The experience he designed with his experiential marketing agency involved a branded stretch Hummer limousine with external screens.

- The Hummer parked (guerrilla-style) outside transport hubs near popular sporting events and a team of Las Vegas-style *Brand Ambassadors*, the 'Dream Girls', exited the Hummer, which had a casino-themed interior, and they invited the sports fans to enter the limo and partake in some classic casino games such as roulette, where they had the chance to redeem five times their winnings as gambling credit online.

- Video content of the glamorous spectacle was filmed and shown on social media. When the sports fans enjoyed the Hummer's casino interior, sitting alongside the 'Dream Girls' (*Brand Ambassadors*), they felt like they were 'Living the Dream'.

- The team of glamorous *Brand Ambassadors* distributed scratch cards to passers-by, encouraging them to scratch off the printed casino design and win '5x free money' (online gambling credit).

- The videos were uploaded to Facebook and Instagram, and the sports fans were entered into a competition to win prizes such as trips to Las Vegas, and a VIP night out with the 'Dream Girls'.

A live brand experience at an exhibition

A brand of premium gin from Iceland that targets fashionable females aged 18–35 wanted to create a live brand experience that brought its Eskimo-themed brand to life, and drove product trial. They also hoped to capture participant data from those who appeared especially engaged, in order to incubate a small group of brand fans into advocates and ultimately evangelists. The data would enable continued communication with the participants, allowing the brand to invite them to exclusive gin events for advocates and influencers that they planned to organize in the future, as well as consult the consumer brand advocates on flavours, marketing ideas and other innovations to give them a chance to input and, in turn, entice passion and brand love.

Sandy, the marketing director for the brand, hired an experiential marketing agency to deliver the live brand experience on a test basis, prior to shifting more resources and investing in rolling out the ongoing live brand experience programme globally and launching the incubator club/advocates group:

- For the trial, the agency hired space at a fashion exhibition that was a spin-off from London Fashion Week, knowing that the *Target Audience* was the primary demographic of the exhibition's guests. It also identified that it would be the only gin brand to exhibit at this show, which would be saturated by clothing and cosmetics brands, enabling it to achieve stand-out and align with their customers' passion point: fashion.

- The set was an extremely cold igloo-style stand, clad with real ice and convincingly real-looking snow. The participants were invited to put on branded Eskimo coats and go into the two-degree igloo, enter a competition to win a fashion-filled party holiday to Iceland and receive a complimentary shot of flavoured gin.

- The *Brand Ambassadors* (influencers) were carefully recruited from social media, many were themselves fashion models with their own emerging fashion brands, and were dressed in creative garments from Icelandic designers.

- The team engaged the participants and appealed to their aspirational lifestyle (to become an influencer on Instagram, a model or a fashion designer) as identified during the *Target Audience* stage of the *SET MESSAGE* planning system.

- By positioning the brand experience at a fashion exhibition, the gin brand gained credibility with a hard-to-impress audience, and the experience became 'the talk of the show', while organic content captured by the event participants was shared like wildfire.

- The influencer *Brand Ambassadors* themselves felt deeply engaged and shared tons of their own content onto their high-reaching social channels, captivating the attention of their global fans and helping set the scene for the forthcoming international roll-out.

By capturing data through the competition entries, the brand succeeded in building a database of super-engaged participants who would soon become brand evangelists and spread word of mouth – especially after being invited to exclusive invite-only fashion events and consulted on flavours and innovations.

An online live brand experience

Live brand experiences are not only suitable for face-to-face locations; you can deliver a great live brand experience online or in any remote environment that facilitates *Two-Way Interactions* in real time. In recent years, a well-known global brand of iced tea wanted to reach large numbers, bringing to life its creative messaging and theme:

- The iced-tea brand had a summer-loving, sexy and fresh *Brand Personality*, and the *Experiential Objective* of the live brand experience was to create far-reaching social engagement.

- The brand worked with a digital agency to develop a 24-hour contest, hosted via a bespoke Snapchat filter.

- The filter featured elements found in a beach setting and showed lots of animated 3D objects that could be found when sunbathing, surfing, strolling the beach and playing volleyball.

- Entries were shown on a leader board and live-voted-on for a chance to win a trip to beaches around the world.

- The brand released the filter for a limited time period and challenged users to create their own beach-themed content before they 'became dehydrated' (a timer showed the ice-tea bottle emptying, which signalled time was running out and the filter would disappear), and to share their entries – encouraging others to vote for them.

The brand worked with emerging influencers from each market, who creatively used the filters and extended the reach of the contest by organically sharing their content to increase their votes.

A live brand experience outside a pop-up

A marketing manager at a smartphone manufacturer launched a new handset claiming to function as your own 'personal assistant':

- It created a series of immersive theatre pop-ups with one-hour events that were themed around organizing a hectic day, and wanted to drive footfall into the pop-ups while communicating some of the more practical functionalities of the product's features.

- She designed a simple live brand experience held on the street outside the pop-ups. The experience involved a team of tech-enthusiast *Brand Ambassadors*.

- The phones carried by the team were connected to projections that appeared on the exterior frontage of the pop-ups, and the *Brand Ambassadors* demonstrated the unique features of the phone to passers-by in a live, giant, interactive projection display.

- During this time they were able to communicate the *Message – Key Communication*, and ask participants about how they organize themselves, demonstrating how the phone's personal assistant-like features could facilitate a smooth day, eliminating chaos.

- This interactive demo succeeded in driving footfall into the pop-ups, and communicating some of the more rational product messages that were somewhat missed within the theatrical and immersive environment of the pop-up events.

A live brand experience in shopping malls

A high-end and innovative clothing club app that targets busy women aged 35–55 has a fashionable and relaxing *Brand Personality*. The *Message – Key Communication* was that, with the brand, busy women can shop easily and conveniently from their phone without the stress of shopping malls and that they did not pay for the clothing unless they kept it. The delivery team could be booked directly from the app to pick up returns for free after the women had tried on the garments, hassle free.

Its brand manager wanted to encourage consumers who were in shopping malls to relax and shop from home or on the go, using the app and club. Her *Experiential Objectives* were to promote the app's offering, bring to life the fashionable and relaxing *Brand Personality*, and sign up people for one month's trial to the app's service:

- She worked with an experiential marketing agency who helped her to book temporary retail units that had been sitting empty in high-footfall malls, and created a live brand experience pop-up that toured malls (with a high percentage of the *Target Audience*), popping up for a few weeks in each mall.

- The experience invited visitors to enter the branded environment and sit in a set designed like a runway show, with the only difference being that they donned virtual-reality gear transporting them to the front row at the brand's fashion show, while a team of reflexologists from a brand partnership were on hand to pamper them. They were offered a relaxing foot massage, relieving their tired 'shopping feet'.

- While they waited to enjoy this treat in a separate area of the pop-up, they were given a demonstration of the app and were informed about the unique benefits of joining the club, by *Brand Ambassadors*, who were themselves all customers.

- The team encouraged the pop-up's visitors to sign up to a free trial of the club's services and explore the fashion collections on offer.

The brand manager succeeded in driving club subscriptions by making subscription to the trial a prerequisite for participating in the full live brand experience (the front-row VR and pamper experience).

A live brand experience in offices

An upmarket credit-card brand that targets affluent professionals and allows them to accumulate air miles for every purchase wanted to communicate its

Message – Key Communication that it goes 'the extra mile' for consumers and has a helpful, attentive, concierge-style *Brand Personality*.

- The credit-card brand gained permission for its *Brand Ambassadors* (who were former concierges recruited from hotel desk) to enter the office blocks of large, successful organizations and offer executives the chance to have their suit jackets dry-cleaned and returned by the end of the day.

- The *Brand Ambassadors* returned the pristinely dry-cleaned blazers in a protective branded wrap and gave each office a hamper, courtesy of the airline with which it had partnered.

- They communicated the message that when the professionals signed up with the card they could call and ask for advice on anything, from dry-cleaning services and hard-to-find sports tickets, to restaurant reservations and movies, while accumulating air miles as they shopped.

- This office-based live brand experience succeeded in engaging the right, hard-to-reach demographic while communicating the brand's message and bringing to life the credit card's concierge-style *Brand Personality* in a relevant way that added value to its participants, resulting in a large increase in credit-card sign-ups, and tons of social media and PR coverage.

A live brand experience on the beach

The owner of a restaurant chain located in tourist resorts, targets families during their holidays. The restaurant chain's *Brand Personality* was 'fun', 'summery' and 'kid friendly'. Greg had not seen a good ROI from his previous marketing and advertising campaigns and wanted to try an experiential marketing approach with live brand experience at its core. He hired an experiential marketing manager and gave them their first responsibility – to develop and organize an interactive live brand experience programme that would run for one year plus, targeting families at the beaches near his restaurants around the world:

- Jackie, his new employee, carefully followed the *SET MESSAGE* planning system and designed a live brand experience that invited beach-going kids to enter the 'Sandcastle Challenge', a global sandcastle-making competition.

- She asked kids from families who already ate at the restaurants to use the crayons provided and draw pictures of themselves on the beach, making sandcastles.

- The best drawings were adapted to form adverts promoting the 'Sandcastle Challenge'. The ads served as an amplification channel and were also featured in printed local tourist guides, shown as digital ads on resort and tourist sites and apps, and even used to make⎸ere displayed in branded dispensers at reception desks in lo⎸ as inserts within in-flight magazines.

- She appointed local talent agencies in each market who ⎸ned engaging children's entertainers, forming teams of chil⎸*and Ambassadors*.

- The teams were deployed at beaches and hotel lobbi⎸ out competition kits, which contained sandcastle moulds, t⎸that featured the restaurant chain's branding.

- The *Brand Ambassadors* encouraged kids to participate ⎸pres-sive sandcastles in the hope of winning a free meal for t⎸mily.

- All participating children received branded caps to w⎸king their sandcastles, while the mums and dads received f⎸g the restaurant's menu and a buy-one-get-one-free offer.

- On the selected beaches, the 'Sandcastle Challenge' ⎸e the chain of restaurants) became the main topic of conv⎸every family with kids.

Jackie also used PR as an amplification channel by givir⎸paper editors free dining passes in return for them featuring p⎸mpe-tition winners on the front pages of their publications. ⎸e kids making the sandcastles were uploaded by happy parent⎸tured on a hall-of-fame board inside the restaurants, further e⎸estau-rant's fun and kid-friendly *Brand Personality*.

Live brand experiences are like theatre p⎸

A live brand experience is like a theatre production⎸*Brand Ambassadors* can require as much training and rehe⎸s on a stage. The cast, the lighting, the rigging and the audienc⎸factors in the smooth delivery of a successful performance. This⎸hat the *Brand Ambassadors* should not believe what they are ⎸would be far from ideal. In fact, a vital factor in the success o⎸experi-ence is that the *Brand Ambassadors* are authentically ⎸have an opportunity to experience the product themselves, li⎸method actors who truly feel that they are the character they ⎸Ideally, they are already fans or influencers, and they tap int⎸*Target Audience* aspirations while effectively representing ⎸*ssage – Key Communication*. Existing employees of a bran⎸those in customer-facing roles, can often become its best B⎸*ados* if correctly engaged with and managed to become so.

rand Ambassadors are given the opportunity to trial the product
prior to the live brand experience going 'live', they will always
speak from the position of a genuine personal recommendation
municating with participants. The personal recommendation and
10uth, as previously discussed, are the ultimate marketing tools
the golden bonds between consumers and brands.

he right people is critical

it is important to draw a parallel between actors and *Brand*
rs is that they need to be carefully trained on and immersed in
the product, its aspirational or fantasy world and *Experiential*
Most importantly, they must truly believe in the brand – in the
1 which actors must get into their role, fully rehearse their lines
1ents, and truly believe in/and are the character they embody
role.

d Ambassadors should be as rehearsed and feel as authentic
luct-knowledge dialogue as actors to a script, and the cast and
ve brand experience need to work together as a team, just like
atre production. There must be a strict schedule, highly organ-
ion managers and contingencies in place across every element
; of production, because, as with theatre, live brand experiences
in real time. As with theatre, and unlike film, these actors have
:hallenge of all, as there is no scope for post-production.

ibassador selection

lon of *Brand Ambassadors* is of ultimate importance to the
ᶳe brand experiences. When your agency is selecting *Brand*
₄, there are 'three key considerations' to be taken into account:

---

y considerations

the *Brand Ambassadors* to the *Target Audience* and/or their
ᵢal lifestyle.

Brand Ambassadors who are suited to the brand's *Message* –
ᵢunication and the *Experiential Objectives*.

ntingencies into place when hiring *Brand Ambassadors*.

Key consideration #1

Matching the Brand Ambassadors *to the target audience and/or their aspirational lifestyle*

The first key factor is deciding when it is appropriate to match the *Brand Ambassadors* with the *Target Audience* themselves (so that participants can *relate* to the *Brand Ambassadors*), versus when it is preferential to match the *Brand Ambassadors* to individuals who reflect the *Target Audience*'s aspirational lifestyle or are themselves influencers (so that the participants look up to the *Brand Ambassadors*).

A nappy brand – example

A popular brand of nappies uses an integrated experiential marketing strategy and places live brand experiences at the core of its campaigns. If it hired glamorous young models to become its *Brand Ambassadors* while promoting its brand of nappies to parents (primarily mothers) at supermarkets, it is unlikely that the mums would be able to relate to the *Brand Ambassadors*, or that a genuine relationship between the two groups would form with any authenticity or credibility. Young *Brand Ambassadors* of this type are unlikely to be running a family of their own, and therefore would not be able to relate to the concerns and considerations that the mothers have when they are purchasing nappies.

The nappy brand knows that it is best to match its *Brand Ambassadors* to the *Target Audience*, which is why when briefing its promotional staffing agency it clearly specifies that its highest priority in *Brand Ambassador* selection is that the *Brand Ambassadors* are themselves mothers with young children, and it is compulsory that they receive nappies to trial before they are able to work on the live brand experience, so that they can communicate with the consumers from an authentic perspective and give a genuine personal recommendation (thus creating the golden bond).

A tanning product – example

In contrast, a brand of tanning products targets suburban women who aspire to be glamorous and sun-kissed, and it is correct (in contrast to the aforementioned nappy brand) in encouraging its agency to select the glamorous variety of model-like *Brand Ambassadors*. The brand knows (from its *Target Audience* research) that its customers purchase tanning products because using them makes them feel closer to achieving their aspirational lifestyle.

During its last campaign, tanned and beautiful *Brand Ambassadors* engaged women and encouraged them to participate in the tanning product's live brand experience. As a result, the participants made the connection between the beautiful *Brand Ambassadors* and the tanning product, which led them to associate the outcome of using the product with their desired physical appearance. Therefore, in this brand's live brand experience programme it was more appropriate that the *Brand Ambassadors* matched the aspirational lifestyle of the *Target Audience*, rather than if they had been selected to match the *Target Audience* themselves.

A nicotine patch – example

When a brand of patches that help people quit smoking designed a live brand experience to promote the patch, it ensured that the *Brand Ambassadors* were non-smokers who at some point in their lives had smoked but succeeded in quitting. The reason for this choice was that during the *Target Audience* part of *SET MESSAGE*, Tom, the patch's brand manager, had identified a key insight while he studied the *Target Audience*'s aspirational lifestyle (smokers who want to quit). He found that the *Target Audience* aspired to be like people they knew who had previously smoked and succeeded in quitting. The *Brand Ambassadors* were able to encourage many of the live brand experience's participants to try the patch because they had inspired them with their stories of having previously achieved quitting smoking themselves.

Just imagine the consequences if the brand had not taken any precautions, and *Brand Ambassadors* wearing anti-smoking T-shirts were seen smoking cigarettes on their lunch breaks!

A life insurance brand – example

Recently, a financial services company launched a live brand experience that targeted one of its life insurance products at men and women aged 55 to 80. The *Selected Locations* were bingo halls and golf clubs frequented by the *Target Audience*. The day-in-the-life analysis and aspirational lifestyle research conducted by the company's experiential marketing agency showed that the 55- to 80-year-olds considered their 40s to have been the time of their lives that were most enjoyable, and they often aspired to recapture the way they looked and felt during that time. Some additional supporting research also provided an important insight: the *Target Audience* did not consider young people to be credible sources for information on important financial matters such as life insurance.

The agency had an in-house staffing division and strategically selected *Brand Ambassadors* who were mainly in their 40s because they were old enough for the *Target Audience* to relate to, while still young enough to represent the *Target Audience*'s aspirational lifestyle. As a result, the *Brand Ambassadors* were able to successfully connect with the participants, strengthening the relationship between the brand and its *Target Audience* whilst selling the life insurance product to a record percentage of participants.

Key consideration #2

Selecting Brand Ambassadors *who are suited to the* brand's Message – Key Communication *and the* Experiential Objectives

It is important that the *Brand Ambassadors* are reflective of the *Brand Personality* and messaging and are suited to the campaign's *Experiential Objectives*. Some *Brand Ambassadors* are good at driving sales; they have the qualities required, including persistence, charm and stamina. *Brand Ambassadors* need to be carefully selected to reflect the *Brand Personality* and bring it to life. If a *Brand Personality* is sophisticated, its *Brand Ambassadors* must be the epitome of sophistication. On the other hand, if a *Brand Personality* is fun and comical, so must be the *Brand Ambassadors*.

A streetwear brand – example

A brand of hooded sweatshirts, hats and jackets had the *Experiential Objective* of positioning itself as a preferred choice of funky streetwear, and gaining credibility with a funky youth audience. The brand manager, Laura, hired a promotional staffing agency to provide *Brand Ambassadors* who were skateboarders and graffiti artists with progressive looks, such as visible tattoos and piercings. The skateboarders and graffiti artists who were selected locally were well known on the streets in their areas, and once they interacted with the *Target Audience* through the brand's live brand experience, a street art competition, the results were exceptional.

The experience invited the *Target Audience* to participate in spray-painting the purpose-built walls surrounding the stores, as well as the skateboarding ramp inside the store, giving them a chance to win concert tickets and other youth-oriented prizes. The brand benefited from gaining the respect and credibility of the skateboarders and graffiti artists involved in the project, who were themselves local influencers.

Key consideration #3

Contingencies need to be put in place when hiring Brand Ambassadors

The third and most important factor to remember when you or your agency are selecting *Brand Ambassadors* to represent you as the human interface with the customer during a live brand experience is that many of them (especially when part-time) have other commitments that they may see as a higher priority than being your *Brand Ambassador*.

Other priorities

Historically many *Brand Ambassadors* are actors, models, singers or dancers who are well suited to live brand experiences because of their gregarious, performance-oriented nature and attractive appearances and warm personalities. Though these types of people can be very good choices on many ad hoc occasions, and the work suits them because they need to maintain flexible employment to enable them to go to castings, auditions and performances when necessary, they may be liable to cancel at the last minute due to 'call-backs', or bookings for their 'real careers'.

Some *Brand Ambassadors* are parents with small children, or students who again have other important commitments such as families or degrees, which they are likely to see as higher priorities than your campaign, and if they need to attend to their existing commitments due to an unexpected occurrence, they are liable to let you down. Many of the 'promotional staff' variety will also be freelancers, with schedules likely to change at short notice.

If social media influencers are chosen, they might require hefty fees and, despite a strong consumer influence, they will not necessarily have the experience interfacing directly with members of the public en masse and IRL.

Calamity

Additionally, there are also many genuine reasons (and genuine-sounding excuses) why *Brand Ambassadors* might let down their agencies and their agencies' clients. They might pull out at the last minute due to sickness, car breakdowns, deaths of relatives, along with a multitude of other unpredictable emergencies, or excuses.

These apparently devastating and unavoidable occurrences need not jeopardize the success of the live brand experience. If *Brand Ambassador* contingencies are adequately planned and prepared, and a 'problem-solving in advance' approach is employed, then these types of cancellations will not cause major problems.

No matter how friendly, well-meaning or committed your *Brand Ambassadors* are, difficult things will happen and in a live real-world environment there needs to be a Plan B for every scenario. By having additional *Brand Ambassadors* trained and on standby, or present during the live brand experience as 'reserves', a full team headcount can usually be achieved.

Reserve *Brand Ambassadors* are crucial to the success of the live brand experience. Most good experiential marketing agencies have an in-house staffing division, because the agency will know the importance of the *Brand Ambassadors* to the success of the live brand experience (especially when it is executed face to face).

Resource-intensive and specialized expertise

It can be highly detrimental to attempt to book, train and manage *Brand Ambassadors* yourself if you do not have the proper resources to do so. This is a full-time activity and requires a lot of patience, skill and experience. Therefore, it is best for clients not to attempt to manage *Brand Ambassadors* but to leave this task to a specialist agency (or an agency that will effectively outsource to one).

The extensive experience that is required for this type of problem solving and troubleshooting strengthens the argument for not attempting to bring staffing in-house. It must also be remembered that experiential marketing agencies or staffing agencies often provide their *Brand Ambassadors* with regular work, and they maintain a certain level of loyalty as a result. The relationship between an agency and its *Brand Ambassadors* (other casually employed personnel and event managers) is extremely valuable, and its importance should not be underestimated.

Recruiting Brand Ambassadors

It is good to try to gain an understanding of your experiential marketing agency's recruitment strategies and policies, because its approach to recruitment can make a difference to the performance and success of the *Brand Ambassadors* in your live brand experience.

There are typically two different approaches to recruiting *Brand Ambassadors:* either they are recruited specifically and exclusively for a one-off live brand experience (such as carefully chosen influencers or those with specialized attributes), or they work frequently as *Brand Ambassadors* for numerous brands and are recruited to join a general database where they can be booked for lots of jobs, and then selected from that database for specific live brand experiences. *Brand Ambassadors* can be headhunted and reached out to specifically – usually the case with influencers or those with specialized talents – or recruited more broadly. Recruitment ads can be placed online on relevant websites, forums and social media groups, or offline, for example posters in independent shops or scouted face to face at events or in the street.

Introduction to *Brand Ambassadors* via personal networks

Word of mouth is also a common recruitment driver. Once an agency gives lots of enjoyable work to its *Brand Ambassadors*, they often tell their friends, peers and colleagues about that agency and many *Brand Ambassadors* start applying to join their books. Word-of-mouth recruitment can be encouraged by the use of 'refer-a-friend' schemes, where *Brand Ambassadors* are incentivized to recommend others to join the agency's books. There can be downsides to such schemes. For example, if a team of friends are booked to work together as *Brand Ambassadors*, and one cancels, the others are more likely to cancel too. A social attitude to work can develop that is unprofessional; it can create a situation where *Brand Ambassadors* spend too much time socializing and not enough time engaging with participants.

That said, there are some advantages. Small or remote geographic areas can be hard to recruit in, and in these cases 'refer-a-friend' schemes can be successful as long as relevant precautions are taken, such as not booking friends to work together and ensuring that only experienced *Brand Ambassadors* are able to work. In addition, good *Brand Ambassadors* who have worked in live brand experiences for years tend to know other good *Brand Ambassadors* from past live brand experiences. This is a definite advantage and can mean that when *Brand Ambassadors* try to join an agency's books, another member of staff can vouch for them. The *Brand Ambassador* who vouches for them is unlikely to put his or her own reputation on the line to get work for a friend, so this can usually be trusted.

Important points that an experiential marketing agency's staffing division should review when selecting and recruiting *Brand Ambassadors* are as follows.

Three key considerations

1 The *Target Audience* and their aspirational lifestyle.

2 The *Brand Personality* and the *Experiential Objectives*.

3 Contingency *Brand Ambassadors*.

Additional factors:

- the communication skills of the individual;
- their willingness to learn;
- their experience;
- their interests, and passion points;
- their appearance;
- access;
- their willingness to travel;
- references from other agencies;
- their availability;
- whether they drive or own a vehicle;
- how easy they are to reach;
- their skills and abilities in producing content;
- any existing legal factors such as other contracts and rights deals;
- their own social media channels and reach.

Briefing Brand Ambassadors

The agency should always send a briefing manual or document to the *Brand Ambassadors* prior to their attending or participating in a more immersive training experience. The briefing manual should cover all key points about their role and the campaign, but must have some minimum requisite components, as outlined in the following list:

- legal considerations;
- code of conduct;
- background information on the brand;

- the live brand experience's objectives;
- a description of their role and what is expected from them;
- the elements of the *Message – Key Communication*'s they should say (with thorough scripting);
- the *Target Audience*;
- practical information such as times, dates, locations, routes or transport schedules;
- their rate of pay and payment-processing information;
- a summary of any bonus scheme or fines;
- the agency's terms and conditions;
- rules prohibiting *Brand Ambassadors* from poor conduct or last-minute cancellations;
- contact information;
- a confidentiality agreement (to ensure that information about a launch or live brand experience does not leak to the public prior to the intended date).

Training Brand Ambassadors

It is necessary to train *Brand Ambassadors* and event managers prior to a live brand experience. In some cases, face-to-face training is not feasible due to budgetary or geographic restrictions. Though this is not ideal, in this instance it is highly recommended to deliver intensive remote training. Remote training should include online webinars, video conferences and one-to-one phone training, supported by an automated digital quiz. It is important to remember to train (and budget for) the reserves and back-ups as well as the main team, so that if someone cancels, the replacement is of an equivalent standard.

Must have tried and enjoyed the product in order to build genuine bonds with the audience

A key part of training is that the *Brand Ambassadors* have the opportunity to trial the product or service sufficiently. This ensures that their positive attitude towards a brand is genuine, and participants will be able to 'buy into' the real enthusiasm that the *Brand Ambassadors* have for the product, and that the communication takes a natural and authentic tone of personal recommendation, thus creating the coveted golden bond.

When holding a face-to-face training session, below is a sample format that has proved highly successful. It should be conducted only after the *Brand Ambassadors* have received and had a chance to study their briefing manuals (as recently described within this chapter). The face-to-face training format should include elements such as those outlined in this sample training agenda.

Outline for face-to-face training agenda

1 **Brand overview**, information and tonality.

2 **Demonstration** of the product or service/product trial if relevant.

3 *Message – Key Communication* training by a representative of the agency.

4 **Role play**: the *Brand Ambassadors* are split into small groups, some taking on the role of the consumer and others taking on their actual role as *Brand Ambassadors*. This should be supported by constructive feedback provided by at least one agency representative.

5 A **mini-performance** from each of the small teams to the larger group. The team should swap so that everyone has a chance to perform as a consumer and as a *Brand Ambassador*.

6 A **quiz** game with a prize for the highest-scoring *Brand Ambassador*.

7 A **question-and-answer** session where a member of the client team and a member of the agency team address any queries from the *Brand Ambassadors*.

8 A **fitting**: the trying on of **clothing/uniforms** to ensure good fit.

9 A brief **code of conduct** lecture from the agency member and clarity on their required grooming or physical appearance.

Managing Brand Ambassadors

When a live brand experience is active and involved, *Brand Ambassadors* will need an experienced event manager to oversee them. The role of the event manager can be varied but usually includes:

- rating *Brand Ambassadors'* performance;
- giving constructive feedback and on-location coaching;

- positioning the team members strategically in high-footfall positions, and away from each other to prevent chatter;
- managing the budget and expenses;
- giving a briefing and pep-talk prior to each shift;
- managing the uniforms and stock control;
- monitoring distribution data and data capture;
- managing social media platform activity, the *Brand Ambassadors*;
- noting results, consumer feedback and qualitative surveys;
- taking photos and video footage;
- filling in reports and feedback forms;
- driving vehicles and overseeing the on-site production team when rigging a set.

Remuneration

Event managers are usually paid around double the rate of the *Brand Ambassadors*, unless influencers are used – in which case rates of pay can vary drastically. Team leaders, who are like senior *Brand Ambassadors*, are a good idea for most live brand experiences. They support the event manager and act as motivators for team spirit and positive morale, and they usually get paid approximately 50 per cent more than the *Brand Ambassadors*.

Loyalty

A loyalty scheme on each live brand experience, to incentivize successful individuals, is a big motivator. Points should be given to reliable, punctual and high-performing *Brand Ambassadors*, team leaders and event managers. This can be very effective at encouraging loyalty among a live brand experience team. Inside an agency, the bonuses of its staff bookers and staffing managers can also be linked to the positive performance of the *Brand Ambassadors*.

Summary

In summary, *Brand Ambassadors* are like the face or identity of the brand during the live brand experience, especially when it is executed face to face. Their attitude, communication, appearance and morals represent your brand to your *Target Audience*. Adequate selection, product trial, briefing, training and management are all important phases in ensuring the right human touch for your live brand experience.

Brand Ambassador expertise is very important when selecting an agency, whose approach to this matter should be a major consideration in whether they are appointed to look after this area on behalf of your brand. By applying the best practice guidelines detailed in this chapter, you will be doing everything possible towards achieving the ultimate goal: that the *Brand Ambassadors* speak from a perspective of personal recommendation; form a genuine connection and golden bond with your *Target Audience*, inspiring the live brand experience's participants sufficiently that they themselves become brand advocates who spread positive word-of-mouth; create and share content on your brand's behalf.

As well as providing an exceptional face for your live brand experiences, this part of your *SET MESSAGE* plan will ensure that the *Selected Locations* (whether face to face or remote) are ideal in regard to the *Target Audience*, their state of mind, practical considerations, and maximize the reach of your live brand experience. This chapter should have guided you in planning a live brand experience that achieves 'the right experience, for the right people'.

Notes

1 Neustar (2017) [accessed 21 February 2017] Advertising Age Marketing Fact Pack [Online] http://adage.com/d/resources/resources/whitepaper/2017-edition-marketing-fact-pack

2 Roderick, L (2016) [accessed 5 January 2017] Heineken: Creating Brand Ambassadors starts internally, *Marketing Week*, 23 December [Online] https://www.marketingweek.com/2016/12/23/heineken-creating-brand-ambassadors/

3 Ind, N (2007) *Living the Brand: How to transform every member of your organization into a brand champion*, Kogan Page, London

4 Mortimer, N (2017) [accessed 30 January 2017] Influencer Content Accounts For Almost 20% of Consumer Media Consumption, The Drum, 25 January [Online] http://www.thedrum.com/news/2017/01/25/influencer-content-accounts-almost-20-consumer-media-consumption

5 To read more from Good Relations on this, see: http://goodrelations.co.uk/2017/05/23/influencer-content-accounts-almost-20-consumer-media-consumption

Systems and mechanisms for measurement for experiential marketing planning

13

Benchmarking across marketing channels

Live brand experiences are becoming an increasingly dominant marketing discipline yet traditionally have been the subject of heavy criticism regarding the metrics used to measure their success. Traditional marketing channels tend to have metrics, which can be applied to benchmark and cross-reference campaigns against each other. Because these industry-wide metrics are generic, they provide a standard way to gather and compare results.

In fact, live brand experiences lend themselves perfectly to cost-effective, qualitative and quantitative measurement of success regarding their capacity to meet their *Experiential Objectives*. This is because of the interactive nature of the discipline. While a brand is interacting with consumers during an experience, the consumer is usually benefiting and receiving to one degree or another, and is therefore very likely and willing to give back. This can take the form of answering questions, on-the-spot reactions, or agreeing to future communication.

An important stage in the planning process

This chapter is designed to demonstrate how to go about integrating systems and mechanisms that allow one to measure how successfully a campaign has achieved, or is achieving, its *Experiential Objectives*, into your plan. Because each live brand experience can differ greatly from the next, it is important to tailor these *Systems and Mechanisms for Measurement* to the activity itself (the location, the time, the people) and ensure that from a practical perspective it is feasible to implement these systems with the resources allocated to the live brand experience.

In earlier chapters we looked at different options for *Experiential Objectives*. At this stage in the *SET MESSAGE* planning system you will be building into the plan several *Systems and Mechanisms for Measurement* that are specific to the *Experiential Objectives* as defined earlier in your plan.

This stage of your plan is not to be confused with the *Evaluation* stage, which will look at evaluating every aspect of your live brand experience, focusing on creating an *Evaluation* scorecard and exploring how to quantify the true impact of your experience. This chapter and part of your plan purely concerns creating a tailored measurement strategy that is bespoke to your live brand experience's own mix of *Experiential Objectives*, and the results will contribute to the data used in the overall *Evaluation* stage of the experiential marketing campaign as a whole (which will consist of the live brand experience channel and other amplification channels). The amplification channels should still be measured using the standard metrics of each channel respectively.

Investment into measurement

Different live brand experiences require and justify different degrees of and investments into research. Some situations require an in-depth level of insight and analysis, such as cases when a live brand experience is a pilot that has the possibility of a large-scale roll-out. In this instance, anything that can be learnt from the successes and failures of the live brand experience will be valuable for a test-and-learn approach to be utilized when planning the larger-scale roll-out. This in-depth analysis looks at why each specific element worked or did not, and creates insights into what can be changed or expanded. In this case, it is worth investing more significantly in good *Systems and Mechanisms for Measurement*. When a multimillion budget is being invested in the larger-scale activity there is little margin for error. Therefore, the pilot should serve as a learning experience that helps perfect the broader plan.

There are varying degrees of resources that can be applied to the *Systems and Mechanisms for Measurement*, and depending on how high *Evaluation* is on your list of priorities, you will spend a relative amount. The good thing about the nature of live brand experiences is that successful and valuable *Systems and Mechanisms for Measurement* can often be implemented without any significant or additional investment to your existing budget.

Many of the *Systems and Mechanisms for Measurement* detailed in this chapter can be built into the *SET MESSAGE* plan without any financial implications.

Qualitative and quantitative data

Qualitative data

Qualitative data cannot be expressed as a number. Data that represents opinions, perceptions or factors such as gender, economic status or religious preferences are examples of data sets that are considered to be qualitative data. Qualitative data can be gathered by *Brand Ambassadors* or additional event staff easily, while they are engaging with and talking to participating members of the *Target Audience*.

Qualitative data can help to analyse why you got the results that you did, as well as achieving market research objectives during the live brand experience.

Quantitative data

Quantitative data sets are anything that can be expressed as a number, or quantified.

Quantitative data can include hard numbers that are figures-based and can be calculated. It can also include the number of specific and similar responses to qualitative survey questions, and quantitative data can be a combination of survey results, numbers, and the quantification of qualitative responses. Quantitative data gives hard facts and numbers, which are always valuable because they enable easy comparison.

Best of both

You need to have a combination of both quantitative 'counting' mechanisms (eg how long people stayed in a shop; how many items were sold; how many products were trialled; and how many people interacted with the experience) and qualitative open question-type mechanisms (eg what does brand X represent to you?). Then, by grouping and analysing qualitative 'open question' responses, and correlating answers for similarities, you can extract hard numbers and data from apparently 'woolly/fluffy' questions, therefore enabling factual measurement of 'fluffy' objectives, and the conversion of qualitative data into quantitative data. This method is outlined throughout the chapter.

Create your own bespoke research process

Table 13.1 shows many common *Experiential Objectives* and then aligns *Systems and Mechanisms for Measurement* that quantify whether (and to what degree) these specific goals and aims have been achieved. Each *System and Mechanism for Measurement* should be:

- tailored to the live brand experience;
- tailored to its available resources and technology;
- built in seamlessly without interrupting the natural flow of the live brand experience.

Table 13.1 *Systems and Mechanisms for Measurement*

Code	Experiential objective	System or mechanism for measurement
A	Conduct market research (eg, gain understanding of consumer opinions about the brand and product, and competitive brands and products)	1 Note relevant consumer feedback, questions, etc 2 Administer surveys with participants, with relevant questions (qualitative and quantitative)
B	Drive word of mouth	Number of interactions (Y)
C	Raise awareness	1 OTS 2 Distribution data
D	Drive product trial	Number of product trials
E	Demonstrate a product's features and benefits	Number of product demonstrations
F	Capture data	Number of data entries captured
G	Drive word of mouth	1 Word-of-mouth reach (Y × 17) + Y based on 'Y' being the brand experience participants, and '17' people being an estimated number reached from hearing about it. 2 Monitor number of referrals from any 'refer-a-friend' schemes initiated by the experiential live brand experience

(*Continued*)

Table 13.1 *(Continued)*

Code	Experiential objective	System or mechanism for measurement
H	Drive traffic to website	1 Number of hits to website (compare to previous hits)
		2 Number of hits to micro-site, and from micro-site to main site
I	Drive word of mouth online	1 Number of people sharing the online content/experiential element with a friend
		2 Number of sales promotion vouchers/ codes redeemed
J	Increase footfall into store	Compare activity with footfall into store during and after activity
K	Increase customer loyalty/strengthen brand relationships with target audience	1 Monitor consumer behaviour long-term through loyalty schemes
		2 Contact participants subsequently
L	Create a long-lasting, memorable experience	1 Monitor consumer behaviour long-term through loyalty schemes
		2 Contact participants subsequently
M	Bring the brand personality to life	Survey non-participants and compare results with participants
N	Communicate complex brand messages	Survey non-participants and compare results with participants
O	Gain credibility with target audience X	1 Survey non-participants and compare results with participants
		2 Analyse customer demographics prior to live brand experiences activity and then at specific intervals during and after ongoing activity, and note a shift in customer demographic long-term
P	Position the brand as X	Survey non-participants and compare results with participants

When you arrive at this stage in the *SET MESSAGE* planning system, you can:

1 Cross-reference your *Experiential Objectives* against those examples provided in Table 13.2.

2 Assign and tailor the most relevant systems.

3 Once you have allocated the chosen *Systems and Mechanisms for Measurement*, you can create your own table that demonstrates in more detail what your method will be, exactly which questions you will ask, or exactly what data you aim to capture.

For example, if your *Experiential Objectives* for a live brand experience are to increase sales, drive footfall into store and bring your *Brand Personality* to life, your *Experiential Objectives* and *Systems and Mechanisms for Measurement* might look similar to the example shown (based on a campaign promoting a drink outside 50 of the stores that retail it) in Table 13.2.

Table 13.2 Example 1 of *Systems and Mechanisms for Measurement*

Experiential objective	System or mechanism for measurement
Increase sales across the 50 main stores during live brand experience	We will ask the store managers to provide data that shows the sales of this product in each of the 50 participating stores for one month prior to the experiential live brand experience.
	We will then ask the store managers to provide the same data and monitor sales volumes of the product in the same participating stores during the experiential live brand experience. By comparing these results, we will measure any direct increase in sales that the experiential live brand experience made while it was live. Note: If sales-tracking technology is not built into a store's cashier system, then the above data will also be collected by the *Brand Ambassadors*. They will count stock at the beginning and end of every day, noting the percentage of stock that was sold.
We will also want to gauge whether the increase in sales volume is temporary or has longevity	To do this, we will monitor the product sales at the stores that participated, for one month after the live brand experience is finished.
	We will then compare these sales volumes with those of the same stores in the one month prior to the live brand experience going live.

(Continued)

Table 13.2   *(Continued)*

Experiential objective	System or mechanism for measurement
Drive footfall into store	We will note the data on the stores' electronic footfall tracker prior to the live brand experience.
	This data will be compared to the data on the electronic footfall tracker during the live brand experience.
	Any increase in footfall will be noted as a percentage (when comparing, ensure that factors such as days of the week are kept consistent between control data and live brand experience data).
Bring the energetic brand personality to life	We will create a brief survey application to be loaded onto the *Brand Ambassadors'* reporting apps.
	At the beginning of each live brand experience, they will come in 30 minutes early, and without wearing their uniform or being in close proximity of the set, they will ask passers-by a brief question about the brand.
	The question will be: what do you think of when you think of brand X?
	a) being energized;
	b) being relaxed;
	c) being happy;
	d) being trendy.
	The *Brand Ambassadors* will ask the same question of consumers during their participation in the brand experience.
	An increase in the target audience choosing the correct answer (a) will be measured as a percentage increase in recognition and understanding of the brand personality.

Table 13.3 Example 2 of *Systems and Mechanisms for Measurement*

Experiential objective	System or mechanism for measurement
Drive traffic to website	We will compare the number of hits we are getting to the website (and their geographic location) prior to the live brand experience against the number of hits (and their geographic location) we are getting during and after the live brand experience.
	The increase will be noted as a percentage, which will allow us to benchmark the success the live brand experience's channel had in achieving this objective against the percentage increase we had in web traffic from previously implemented forms of marketing communications.
Spread word of mouth online	When (as per the *Experiential Strategy*) consumers download the photos (which are loaded into a gallery on the site) of themselves participating in the live brand experience, they have the opportunity to forward their photo (which arrives in a branded e-mail) to 10 friends and receive a free T-shirt.
	To measure word of mouth driven as a direct result of this strategy, we will monitor the number of times this offer form is completed, and with each time counting for 10 recipients of the key communication message, we will easily be able to quantify the word of mouth online.

Consider how to tailor the way you measure against your specific *Experiential Objectives*

Whichever *Experiential Objectives* you have chosen, you will be able to plan how to measure them by thinking carefully, creatively and with agility about how you will go about building the *Systems and Mechanisms for Measurement* that are recommended for your *Experiential Objectives* into your live brand experience.

The example shown in Table 13.3 demonstrates that this approach works with any combination of *Experiential Objectives*. The example shown is based on a live brand experience promoting an online retailer at shopping malls, where the *Experiential Objectives* are to drive traffic to the website, spread word of mouth and social content reach and capture data for future marketing purposes.

Summary

The level of investment you wish to put into understanding how the experiential marketing campaign, and specifically the live brand experience channel, are impacting the *Target Audience*'s behaviour and opinions is a decision that you will need to make in advance while planning. Experiential marketing can include simple, cost-effective *Systems and Mechanisms for Measurement*, which when built into the live brand experience channel during the planning stages will enable you to evaluate the success of the live brand experience (as well as the amplification channels) and gauge whether it has achieved its predefined *Experiential Objectives*.

Don't fall into the classic trap of forgetting to tailor your measurement plan! In many instances, marketers and agencies overlook this crucial stage of experiential marketing planning. As a result, live brand experiences have been subjected to the criticism that it is 'difficult to measure whether a live brand experience has done the job it set out to do'.

Many people will argue that when you know how to achieve something, it is no longer difficult (like a dish that appears hard to cook, but which is easy once the recipe is followed step by step). It is not a particularly time-consuming process to build in *Systems and Mechanisms for Measurement*, compared to the value gained in doing so.

By integrating the guidelines in this chapter into your *SET MESSAGE* plan and campaign implementation, your live brand experiences can be fully accounted for, you will be able to evaluate their long-term return on investment (LROI) and make it easier to demonstrate the results of your overall experiential marketing programme to key stakeholders and those 'pulling the purse-strings'.

Action

14

How to deliver and project manage live brand experiences

It is now time to integrate all aspects of project management and planning the *delivery* of your live brand experience. This *Action* part of the *SET MESSAGE* planning system is of utmost importance. You, or your agencies, can develop the most innovative and ground-breaking concepts and strategies, but if your campaign activation and project management are flawed, then it can be a waste of time and money. The execution of a successful experiential marketing campaign, especially the live brand experience, is not an easy task, and should be regarded as being as involved as the production of live TV, live theatre and live immersive events.

Choosing the right expertise for activation in the live environment

It is important to press the recommendation that a specialist experiential marketing agency is employed for the execution of your campaign. Some experiential marketing agencies have a stronger background in strategy, while others are more experienced in activation. This is an important distinction to make when choosing an agency to activate your campaign. In fact, some experiential marketing agencies outsource the *Action* part to other more action-oriented experiential marketing agencies. The ideal situation is to work with a fully integrated experiential marketing agency that has: 1) expert strategy/planning/creative; 2) activation/logistics/staffing in-house.

The reason is that communication between planners and activators needs to be clear, with great attention to detail. Without this communication, what is promised to a client may be very different to what is delivered. In addition, the more attention to detail and experienced thinking that goes into the *Action* plans, the higher the chances that those following it will succeed.

This chapter should prove useful whether you are a traditional agency that is outsourcing to an experiential marketing agency, or a client working directly with the experiential marketing agency. From a client perspective, this chapter can provide a guide that will help when discerning between a good, detailed activation plan and a poor one. Obviously, different agencies may be inclined to proactively involve their clients in the finer details of the *Action* plan to a greater or lesser degree. However, most will aim to accommodate a client's desire to see at least some of the activation planning, on request. Even if you are an experiential marketing practitioner yourself, this chapter will provide an outline for best practice for the *Action* part of your *SET MESSAGE* campaign plan.

Contents of the *Action* plan

The action part of your *SET MESSAGE* plan should include the following sections:

---

1 **Recipe** (how the experience will actually happen from a consumer perspective).

2 **Budgets**.

3 **Project management** (WBS, Gantt chart, critical path analysis, schedules, risk analysis, checklists and external analysis).

4 **Communication** and collaboration.

5 **Suppliers** and third parties.

6 **Approvals** schedule.

The recipe

Every live brand experience has behind-the-scenes activity and requires a great deal of careful coordination, and it is important not to lose sight of the customer journey from the consumer perspective. The *Target Audience*, and participants' experience, is extremely important. The *Action* plan starts with a breakdown of what happens if you are looking at it from the perspective of the *Target Audience*. This part comes first in *Action* planning because it will keep the rest of the plan grounded; it is a blueprint summary of what will happen 'live'.

The best way to write the 'recipe' is to think of it as similar to a good cake recipe. It should start with a paragraph stating the ingredients (including quantities) that will be in place, and specifying where the experience will be positioned (whilst naming the set, the live brand experience components and the *Brand Ambassador* team). This introductory paragraph creates a still photographic image in the mind of the reader of your plan.

Recipe: intro paragraph example

The *106.9 Radio Experience* is positioned outside a surfing festival and includes: the Radio Experience Zone (one giant radio set, two branded DJ hummers, two sampling trolleys, one branded reception counter, lots of branded tables and chairs), and the '106.9 Team' (a team of 10 *Brand Ambassadors*, one DJ and one event manager).

This intro paragraph sets the scene of the recipe segment of the *Action* plan in the mind of the reader, because it allows him or her to correctly visualize the physical elements that will be in place. This is a vital step, as it provides clarity to both the clients/people who are funding the campaign, and the people who are executing it.

After the intro paragraph, the recipe continues with a step-by-step process in a similar manner to a recipe for baking a cake, by breaking down the customer journey, systematically outlining what actions are involved in the experience itself.

This should be formatted as a simplified numbered list of summarized steps.

Recipe: example of a step-by-step consumer journey

1 The DJ is playing funky music and hosting on the microphone.
2 The 106.9 *Brand Ambassadors* approach the *Target Audience* and invite them to participate in the experience.
3 The *Target Audience* signs in at the front counter.
4 The *Target Audience* is greeted by *Brand Ambassadors* that bring them into the radio zone.
5 Once inside the radio zone, consumers can make their own compilation CDs.
6 As the consumers leave the zone, they receive branded goody bags containing branded headphones, free concert tickets and stickers.

As you can see, this numbered list allows a moving image to be visualized in the mind of the reader, or executor, which is key in creating a framework and story for the experience.

Estimating the length of time it takes to complete the customer journey

This recipe step should also facilitate an estimation of the duration of the experience, as well as the maximum number of participants at any one time. This is highly important because it will then allow you to calculate how many consumers can potentially participate in the experience per day and location. By multiplying these figures by the number of live days and locations, you will get the number of interactions. This, as previously mentioned, is a crucial common metric when measuring live brand experiences and justifying the cost, because the number of interactions will enable a prediction of the word-of-mouth reach and the LROI.

Finally, to finish off the recipe, you should write a paragraph that summarizes what the outcome of these steps will be.

Recipe: example of a closing summary paragraph

By participating in the *106.9 Radio Experience*, the *Target Audience* of alternative music fans will feel satisfied after enjoying the process of compiling their own customized playlists. They will be pleased to receive the goody bag, the contents of which will act as memorabilia for their positive brand experience.

This summary stage of your recipe is equivalent to answering questions such as: 1) 'Why is this happening, again?' 2) 'Remind me, what will this achieve?' Your response is the same as it would have been when answering such questions, except for the fact that you are still wearing a consumer hat (as per the consumer journey), rather than a marketing hat. By placing yourself in the position of the consumer, you maintain an objective outlook, with your number-one priority being the participant experience. With this approach, you will be more likely to spot any flaws in the *Action* plan or story.

When you think of a cake recipe, it starts with the ingredients, then it lists the method, then it clarifies the desired outcome. By following the recipe formula as outlined above and integrating it into the first stage of the *Action* part of your *SET MESSAGE* plan, you will crystallize the experience *story*, ensuring ultimate clarity from a customer-centric perspective.

Budgets

The next part of the plan is the all-important budget. There will always be two budgets: one is the internal (agency) budget and the other is the external (client) budget. The internal budget should state the maximum amount that everything should cost the agency. This will be used for agency purposes only, and will allow the project management, or activation team, to adhere to clear guidelines on how much they can spend. This part may also elaborate on certain internal costs that are not to be passed on to the client (to provide added value), such as staff incentives or any anticipated increase in overheads (such as large calling volumes, etc).

The client budget will be presented to the client and should already include agency mark-ups, margins and fees. If a traditional agency is outsourcing to an experiential marketing agency, then partner agency commissions will need to be built in (by either party, depending on their policies). There are certain broad, generic cost categories that can be looked to for structure when considering all possible costs of experiential marketing. Some sample, broad categories for a live brand experience budget include: production, staffing, face-to-face training, remote training, logistics and transport, stock control, space hire, expenses and amplification channels.

Sample budget categories

- Production:
  - set/branded roadshow vehicles/audio and lighting or other equipment and wiring;
  - merchandise (goodies, gifts, vouchers, giveaways, flyers, etc);
  - uniforms.
- Staffing:
  - front-of-house team;
  - brand ambassadors;
  - speciality staff;
  - event managers;
  - team leader.

- Behind-the-scenes crew:
  - riggers and production crew;
  - photographers/videographers;
  - driver.
- Face-to-face training:
  - venue hire;
  - staff (payment for their time and expenses for attending);
  - refreshments and snacks;
  - equipment (PA/projector, etc);
  - training-session administrators (may be agency staff);
  - assistants (meet and greet, registration, etc);
  - campaign manuals/other printing or documentation.
- Remote training:
  - webinars or video conferencing;
  - conference calls;
  - staff (payment for participation – less than face to face);
  - automated quizzes and surveys.
- Logistics and transport:
  - vehicle hire;
  - petrol (calculate as cost-per-mile x estimated mileage);
  - parking;
  - travel time (calculate by mileage).
- Stock control:
  - storage/warehousing (calculated by space, keeping in mind that storage will be required for promotional merchandise, sample stock, sets, vehicles, and uniforms – possibly in several locations sometimes for sustained or intermittent periods);
  - couriers (to deliver stock to the team and crew, either hired directly by the experiential marketing agency or outsourced to a courier company such as UPS);
  - temperature control (refrigeration or freezing when and if the campaign involves samples of food, drink, ice cream, etc).

- Space hire:
  - venue/space-owner/location hire fees;
  - intermediary fees if applicable (if space is booked through a specialist broker or agent);
  - administration, for the time and service of the completion of space hire-related paperwork (such as set maps and dimensions, risk assessments, portable appliance testing, fire safety documents, method statements, hire forms, contracts, health and safety certificates, criminal-record bureau checks, public liability insurance, etc).
- Expenses:
  - travel fares/petrol;
  - travel time;
  - phone (for event managers and other managerial activation team members);
  - hotel (when travelling);
  - food (when travelling);
  - parking (for team and crew members).
- The amplification channels.

The cost sections below can vary greatly depending on whether they are implemented by the experiential marketing agency, outsourced to third parties, or executed in collaboration with the client's existing agencies:

- ads (used before or during experience to drive participants and generate awareness);
- broadcast media slots, live or recorded (to expand the reach of the experience);
- PR prior to live date (to drive participants and generate awareness);
- PR at or post-campaign (to expand the reach of the experience and create interest);
- digital and social media (to generate pre, during and post-campaign interest or to broadcast the experience, live or otherwise);
- buzz, word of mouth, seeding and influencers (either online or offline), designed to create an interest prior to the experience, and drive traffic.

Agency fees and management

This cost category is usually presented as one item and calculated as a percentage of totals, or by the estimate of time that will be spent by different agency personnel, plus expenses (unless itemized separately):

- research and idea testing;
- creative and strategic planning;
- activation planning and project management;
- evaluation.

Reporting

- technology (surveys, tablets, etc);
- campaign audit (an audit, either internal or by an external research agency, to measure outputs using the *Systems and Mechanisms for Measurement*);
- administration (reporting app/online client access pages, data entry, etc);
- visual reports (post-production on visual evidence such as photography, video footage and preparing presentations).

Table 14.1 shows an example budget for additional extras.

Contingency planning

Built-in contingencies should equal around 5–10 per cent of the campaign total, and agency commissions should usually equal 10–25 per cent (beyond fees that cover time) depending on the number of partner agencies. The budget should be broken down to include unit costs, descriptions, quantities, duration of time and totals. This budget should relate specifically to the costs of booking additional elements (staff and extra venues) as an add-on to an existing live brand experience for a juice brand.

It is widely accepted that some of the categories listed are not applicable across every experiential marketing campaign, and there will undoubtedly be unaccountable elements that will arise in specific situations. The most important thing when budgeting is to include contingencies and to remember to think about each and every cost, however small. Sometimes, clients who are used to planning only media campaigns, or more predictable forms of marketing, will find it hard to accept that their experiential marketing agency is billing them for contingencies. Therefore, it is not uncommon for

Table 14.1   Additional items budget

Additional budget 'Juice April 2'					
Staff costs					
Item	**Description**	**Unit cost**	**#**	**Days**	**Total**
Brand ambassador	Will activate the interactive juice game + engage consumers	£119	4	12	£5,712
Event manager	Will manage team, take photos, and feed back data	£213	1	7	£1,491
Event manager (on travelling days)	Will manage team, take photos, and feed back data	£213	1	5	£1,065
				Total	£8,268

Transport					
Item	**Description**	**Unit cost**	**#**	**Days**	**Total**
Travel expenses when travelling	Plane ticket return to Town x	£80	1	1	£80
Travel expenses when inside local area	To and from event 1	£20	1	5	£26
Parking	Parking budget for van to park outside locations for the day	£20	1	12	£240
Food	Food budget per day for event manager	£30	1	7	£210
Hotel	Hotel for event manager	£80	1	7	£560
				Total	£1,116

Space hire					
Item	**Description**	**Unit cost**	**#**	**Days**	**Total**
Event 1 space hire	Space hire 4m × 4m	£5,550	1	7	£5,500
Event 2 space hire	Space hire 4m × 3m + additional branding	£5,940	1	5	£5,940
				Total	£11,440

Client totals	
Subtotal	£20,824
10% mgmt fee	£2,082.40
Grant total	£22,906.40

experiential marketing agencies to build a contingency margin of around 5 per cent into all the unit costs rather than itemizing it as an independent cost category.

Whichever way a contingency is built into a campaign budget, it is crucial that it is not neglected, because to successfully and flawlessly activate an experiential marketing campaign – including a live brand experience, an attitude of predicting potential problems and preparing contingency solutions in advance – is vital. An 'It'll be alright on the night' attitude is the worst approach to this stage in your planning.

Payment schedules

At the end of the budget, a proposed payment schedule should be detailed. This would usually require several upfront costs to be paid to the agency in advance, with ongoing or running costs paid at regular intervals or immediately after the campaign. Sometimes, clients buying experiential marketing services for the first time may have unrealistic expectations about payment terms, such as a desire to receive 100 per cent credit until up to 30–45 days after the campaign ends. This is not because they wish to exploit their agency, but they simply require some additional knowledge and understanding. This is why it is important for their agency to explain to them that there are many upfront set-up costs involved in activating live brand experiences, which is something that can usually be appreciated across the board. Clearly no client would expect their experiential marketing agency to become an interest-free bank, and provide them with a loan, which is exactly what they would be doing if they agreed to payment terms akin to those that are commonplace when buying other traditional media.

Project plans

The project plans should include a combination of both the top line and detailed blueprints that will guide the project management team in their step-by-step preparation and implementation of the campaign. Remember, 'If you fail to plan, you plan to fail.' This could not be closer to the truth in the case of detailed live brand experience project plans.

When there is a short timescale involved, some say they do not have time to plan carefully, but in this case, it may not be worth taking on the project. If you are a client considering live brand experiences, keep in mind that though an agency may accept a short lead time, the more time that you allow them for careful project planning, the better the execution and the results will be.

The project-plan section should include the following elements (or equivalents): work breakdown structure (WBS), a Gantt chart, a critical path analysis, a schedule, a risk analysis, checklists (for staffing, production and logistics) and an external analysis (PESTEL 'problem and solution' table).

The work breakdown structure

Start by creating a work breakdown structure (WBS) for the project. A WBS is an important element that you will need in order to develop your *Action* plan. It lists all of the categories and sub-elements that you will use to achieve and deliver the project. A tree structure of sticky notes can be a great help in developing your WBS.

Gantt chart

The Gantt chart is a table that shows the amount of work done or production completed in certain periods of time in relation to the amount planned for those periods (Figure 14.1). The first column features task categories with each individual small-detailed task appearing in the rows under each category header. These will be extracted straight from the WBS. The Gantt chart organizes the items on the work breakdown structure against a timeline. The titles across each column are dates, months or weeks. After creating this table, the next step is colour coding each person who is part of the project activation team. Then, simply highlight each square of the table in a colour that is affiliated with the individual due to complete it, as well as the number of hours required for its completion.

Project scoping is crucial

According to the PMBOK Guide,[1] it is absolutely crucial that you include '100 per cent of the work defined by the project scope and capture all deliverables – internal, external and interim – in terms of the work to be completed, including project management'. The best way to define tasks is to state the deliverable outcome or result, rather than the actions required to achieve that outcome, ensuring that defined outcomes are bite-sized, and not too broad. It is also important to remember not to allow any overlap between tasks, as this causes confusion and potentially repeated work.

The total number of hours in each colour will indicate the estimated workload of each member of the project team. This will allow the manager to assess whether the tasks they have allocated to each individual on the

Figure 14.1   The Gantt chart

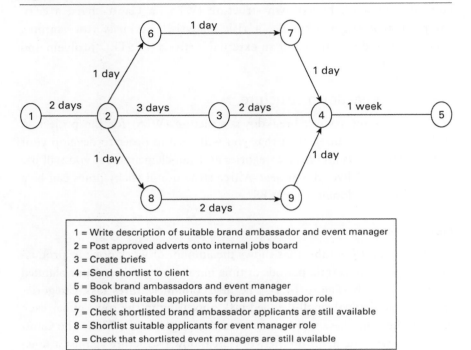

1 = Write description of suitable brand ambassador and event manager
2 = Post approved adverts onto internal jobs board
3 = Create briefs
4 = Send shortlist to client
5 = Book brand ambassadors and event manager
6 = Shortlist suitable applicants for brand ambassador role
7 = Check shortlisted brand ambassador applicants are still available
8 = Shortlist suitable applicants for event manager role
9 = Check that shortlisted event managers are still available

project team are feasible. Again, a time-based contingency will need to be applied, which should be around 10 per cent of total project hours.

Critical path analysis

A critical path analysis (sometimes referred to as a CPA) is also a great way to manage the project activation milestones, and in turn manage client expectations when milestone deliverable dates need to be flexible. It maps milestones onto a timeline, and then an arrow starting from a milestone branches off to show tasks that cannot start until that milestone is complete. The relationships between interdependent tasks and task categories are therefore clearly defined. This process helps to ensure that a project – in this case a live brand experience – can be delivered on time. Many different project management programmes are available, allowing the easy creation of a CPA and Gantt chart.

A CPA can be set up to manage the timeline of a staff booker who was booking some *Brand Ambassadors* and an event manager for a live brand experience at short notice. The project manager who leads the activation team will now be able to closely monitor progress and identify any potential consequences for other deliverables following a delay in the completion of an individual task. If the individual task is interlinked with other tasks that depend on the completion of the original task, then it is crucial that it is achieved on time.

As an example, if the staff booker delayed steps 7 or 9 (confirming that shortlisted applicants are still available), then he or she would not be able

Table 14.2 Sample: basic GANTT chart

Legend:
- Sandra
- Bob
- Lica
- Matt
- Gallia
- Ramez

21–26th 07/09	21/07/2009	22/07/2009	23/07/2009	24/07/2009	25/07/2009	26/07/2009
PRODUCTION						
Complete set build	Sandra					
Take client to visit set		Sandra				
Make any changes			Sandra	Sandra		
Conduct safety testing					Sandra	
Deconstruct the set for transport						Sandra
SPACE HIRE						
Finalize rate negotiations	Bob					
Complete paperwork			Bob			
Pay deposit						
Sign contract						
Review site maps						Bob
STAFFING						
Check availability of relevant people	Lica					
Shortlist staff		Lica				
Send shortlist to client		Lica				
Receive input/preferences from client			Lica			
Book the selected staff				Lica		
Book reserves and backups				Lica		
Send briefs, manuals and contracts				Lica		
TRAINING						
Provide venue options to client						
Book selected venue						
Create agenda for training						
Ensure appropriate equipment is in place						
Create training presentation						
LOGISTICS						
Package kits for each staff member						
Arrange kits to be couriered to staff						
Ensure staff have received packages						Lica
Hire a lorry						
Hire a van						
Plan route for event manager and driver						

to send the shortlist to the client. If he or she did send the shortlist to the client without ensuring that all the people on it were available, and the client chose someone who was in fact unavailable, then the client would be disappointed.

Schedules

A schedule in calendar format is an essential part of the project. It is quite an obvious and basic tool, but without one an activation team or client could feel lost. The schedule should map out which parts of the experiential marketing campaign are happening on certain dates, at certain locations (Table 14.3). The agency that is responsible for activating the campaign, and the client, should put the campaign schedules up on a wall or somewhere visible, for easy reference.

Table 14.3   Sample: basic schedule

Monday	Tuesday	Wednesday	Thursday	Friday	Sat/Sun
27 April	28	29	30	1 May	2
					3
4	5	6	7	8	9
FRUIT JUICE CAMPAIGN AT EVENT 1	FRUIT JUICE CAMPAIGN AT EVENT 1	FRUIT JUICE CAMPAIGN AT EVENT 1	FRUIT JUICE CAMPAIGN AT FESTIVAL		10
11	12	13	14	15	16
			FRUIT JUICE CAMPAIGN AT EVENT 2	FRUIT JUICE CAMPAIGN AT EVENT 2	17
18	19	20	21	22	23 / FRUIT JUICE CAMPAIGN AT MALL 1
FRUIT JUICE CAMPAIGN AT MALL 1	FRUIT JUICE CAMPAIGN AT MALL 1	FRUIT JUICE CAMPAIGN AT MALL 1	FRUIT JUICE CAMPAIGN AT MALL 1	FRUIT JUICE CAMPAIGN AT MALL 1	24 / FRUIT JUICE CAMPAIGN AT MALL 1
25	26	27	28	29	30
		FRUIT JUICE CAMPAIGN AT BEACH	FRUIT JUICE CAMPAIGN AT BEACH		31

Risk analysis

Arguably one of the most important parts of the project plan is the risk analysis. With live brand experiences, many factors contribute to the success of each and every element of the campaign. If one cog in the campaign wheel is missing or jeopardized, then it is highly probable that a chain of undesirable events will occur.

How one mistake can escalate in consequences – example

For example, Frank was an account manager at an experiential marketing agency:

- He didn't have much work on, so when the agency was approached by a client to run a live brand experience roadshow for a sports channel at short notice, the agency took on the project and quickly assigned it to Frank who himself was an avid fan of the channel in question, and a sports enthusiast.

- The sports channel usually spent all its budget on digital and outdoor advertising, and it was the first time that it was running a live brand experience tour, hence the fact that the client unrealistically expected the project to be turned around with under two weeks' planning.

- The concept, which was designed by the sports channel's PR agency, involved a giant-sized interactive 'spot the ball' game, featuring a large set that looked like a real football pitch with grass and a goal. The live brand experience was scheduled to tour around a variety of shopping malls, for one day at each mall.

- There was a very short lead time for the campaign, and some things in the *Action* planning were rushed.

- As a result, an inexperienced driver was mistakenly hired to transport the set, without the staffing team completing their usual reference checks.

- He filled the van that was transporting the set with petrol instead of diesel.

- The van broke down late on a Friday evening, with the campaign due to be live in another city the following morning. As a result, every step of the plan, scheduled to occur directly after he picked up the set with the van, was considerably delayed.

- Consequently, the live brand experience was a disaster and the client was devastated and lost money.

- All the *Brand Ambassadors*, event managers, venues, suppliers and the experiential marketing agency suffered too, both financially and emotionally.

The reason that the inexperienced driver was hired in the first place was that the original driver had existing commitments with his church that Sunday. When he had been booked for the campaign, he was unaware that he would not be able to return in time for his commitments. This confusion was due to lack of proper communication from Jane (the agency staff booker) and the driver.

When he cancelled at short notice, Jane panicked because there was no back-up plan, and no contingency in place. This left Jane desperate, and so she sacrificed the quality of the replacement driver to try and lessen the impact of her original communication error by rebooking the position as quickly as possible.

The importance of the risk analysis

Sometimes these types of problems can occur without anyone being at fault, and without communication errors. The moral of this story is that it is the project manager's responsibility to carefully conduct a risk analysis during the *Action* planning stages, and then ensure that each activation team member (such as a staff booker) has appropriate contingencies in place early on. Something will always go wrong and someone will usually let you down, even if it is due to a genuine emergency, a weather issue or a legal factor. No client is interested in the detailed drama when their agency's driver has existing commitments to his church, or that a team leader's grandmother has died, or that their experiential set was not waterproof when it rained, because their brand's image – and their campaign – is potentially in jeopardy. Therefore, the only way to ensure flawless execution and client satisfaction is to check well in advance that all bases are covered, and that contingencies are in place at no additional cost.

Brainstorm your risk analysis with your production team

By conducting a risk analysis through a lengthy operational brainstorm between the members of the activation team, and then filling in a risk analysis form, some of these types of things may still happen, but there will be an effective solution, ready and on standby. In addition, many potential problems can be predicted with some careful thought and lots of experience. This process will shape the strategic creation of many elements of the campaign, aiming to prevent unnecessary problems and risks from occurring. A risk analysis form factors in both the likelihood and the impact that a problem can have, therefore showing the risk score. Risks with higher scores will need to be prioritized, though all risks will require a contingency plan and a person who is accountable and responsible for that contingency.

Risk analysis for an interactive catwalk experience

The risk analysis form was completed for a live brand experience for a designer clothing brand (Table 14.4). The campaign, featuring an interactive catwalk and models, was positioned outside 18 fashion stores and had the *Experiential Objectives* of bringing the clothing brand to life, driving footfall into the retail store and thereby increasing sales. Once each contingency element has been allocated to an activation team member, their responsibilities will need to be added to the campaign's Gantt chart and CPA.

Checklists

Checklists are a great way to manage small daily tasks. A good project manager should ensure that every team member is working from a comprehensive checklist that includes every task allocated to them on the Gantt chart. Each day, or week, the checklist should be handed in to the project manager for review, and the completed tasks should be 'scratched out' or changed colour (to the colour that represents a completed task) on the Gantt chart. It is advisable to create a checklist template for each team member, containing tasks that reoccur with the majority of live brand experiences, then add to it and adapt it on a campaign-by-campaign basis.

External analysis: PESTEL factors

PESTEL is an acronym that stands for:
Political
Economic
Social
Technological
Environmental
Legal analysis

Table 14.4 Sample: risk assessment

Nature of risk or uncertainty	Likelihood high/ medium/ low	Impact high/ medium/ low	Likelihood x impact [score]	Contingency required and who will take responsibility to manage the risk and backup plan
Rain	3	3	9	Order branded umbrellas or a canopy (Sam)
Vehicle breakdown	1	3	3	Have the vehicle checked out thoroughly prior to the campaign (Robert)
Staff 'no shows'	3	3	9	Ensure that reserves are at the location, and the back-ups are on standby (Christina)
Staff lateness	3	2	6	Book the staff to be at location 1 hour prior to campaign start time (Christina)
Low footfall on the street outside the shops	1	3	3	Ask the client for the footfall data of each store to ensure there is a benchmark point (Matt)
Uniforms not fitting	2	3	6	Order spare uniforms in every size (Sam)
Running out of merchandise	1	3	3	Ensure that there is 50% more merchandise than anticipated distribution estimates (Sam)
Client not liking the appearance of the set	1	3	3	Build in enough time for the client to view the set and potentially suggest changes prior to the campaign going live (Matt)
Event Manager mobile phone out of battery	3	2	6	Provide the Event Manager with two spare batteries (Christina)
Traffic on the route to location	3	2	6	Ensure that the Event Manager and driver arrive 1 to 2 hours early to allow for traffic (Christina)
Store managers not fully understanding when/if the campaign is happening	3	2	6	Ask the client for permission to contact store managers directly to liaise and ensure they are 'in the loop' (Matt)

About PESTEL PESTEL describes a framework of macro-environmental factors. This acronym is usually used for a different purpose early on in marketing planning, but it lends itself very nicely to this stage of the project plan. At the end of the *Action* stage of the *SET MESSAGE* planning system, it is important to state any legal (such as insurances), social (this includes health and safety, employment, public liability), environmental, economic and technological issues, and precautions for any such factors that the client or stakeholders should be aware of (including how these issues are addressed and covered). This external analysis should form your contingency planning and be formatted as a 'Potential PESTEL problem and solution' table (Table 14.5).

The external analysis is the final part of the project plans within the *Action* stage in *SET MESSAGE*.

Communication and collaboration

After the project plans, next comes the communication and collaboration plan. One of the most important rules in successful activation is not forgetting to plan the communication methods and review points between the agency, client and stakeholders into the *Action* stage. Include, in the *Action* part of *SET MESSAGE*, a clear outline of when and where client/agency meetings will occur and how information will be passed between relevant parties, and ensure that everything that is agreed is confirmed in writing or by e-mail to avoid people forgetting or being confused about what they, or others, did and did not agree to.

Part of good communication is the ability to share information and documents with ease. There are many ways to enable this, both within an agency activation team and between the activation team and the client. There are plenty of file-sharing applications available, such as Google or Microsoft's web-based

Table 14.5 PESTEL problem and solution table

Potential PESTEL problem	Solution
Environmental problem: Unwanted environmental waste	Build in a 'litter pick' at the end of each day
Social problem: Noise pollution and disturbance of local residents	Ask for the residents' permission before holding a music-based experiential event in a nearby park
Legal problem: Injury of small children	Ensure that the set is appropriately designed for small children and made from soft materials with no hard corners or edges. Also have a health and safety officer present

file-sharing applications, Google Docs and OneDrive. Alternatively, remote networking can also be a good approach. Rather than constantly e-mailing revised spreadsheets or files and risking the chance that someone will still be working from a wrong version, work on one collaborative file online.

If you can create a system that enables seamless communication and easy access to current versions of plans and documents, then the chances of communication problems occurring will be minimized.

Suppliers and third parties

Suppliers are a key part of the success of a campaign. Even if you are a client outsourcing to a specialist experiential marketing agency, it is likely that not every single part of the campaign will be managed or produced by the agency in-house. Even fully integrated experiential marketing agencies will still outsource some things, for example venue, space hire, props, uniforms and merchandise printing.

It is good to know that you can trust the suppliers involved in your live brand experience, and it is worth checking their references and making sure the agency that appoints them involves the client in the process. From an agency perspective, when planning the outsourced elements of a campaign, there are eight key steps to the process. These should be addressed in this part of the plan:

Eight key steps when sourcing suppliers

1 Identify the different types of suppliers you will need and your exact requirements.

2 Consider if you want to outsource to a company that will manage big chunks or small elements (for example, hiring one company for the truck and another company for the branding on the truck).

3 Identify two or three existing suppliers to whom you could potentially appoint each outsourced element, and score the anticipated pros and cons, based on past experience, of outsourcing to each one.

4 Send highly detailed briefs (with visual references and clear labelling) that specify the exact requirement, the budget and the deadline for production, as well as the preferred format and deadline for bids and proposals.

5 Carefully evaluate each supplier's bid and proposal, checking references and considering both the anticipated pros and cons, and scoring the pros and cons of each proposal.

6 Appoint a main supplier for each element and appoint a second supplier to be on standby for each element, in case you are let down or unhappy with the result and need to change supplier.

7 Allow enough time for unexpected delays, for switching suppliers if necessary, or for requesting changes to anything that is unsatisfactory.

8 Ensure that you have everything that is agreed in writing, and that the payment schedule with the supplier fits within the payment schedule agreed with the client.

Approvals schedule

In this stage of the plan, there should be a clear approvals schedule that clearly states the dates and deadlines for approvals that the client needs to make. It is important to any brand that the client has the opportunity to approve anything that goes to print with their logo, or approve any expe-riential set or content production or individual that represents the brand. To avoid any delays in the approvals process, clients should request any artwork components in the correct resolutions and formats from their crea-tive agency well in advance and at the beginning of the planning process.

The agency needs to be very clear about when they will be sending proofs or samples, or when the client can visit and preview the set to sign it off in person. That way, the client can inform any relevant stakeholders or decision makers that they will need to be available for approval on certain days. Also, the agency will not be stressed by worries that the schedule will be thrown off track due to the client not approving things on time or not providing the relevant artwork components. Time should also be factored in for the client not approving something and wanting it changed. Some things that will need client approval are listed in the box below.

Example elements to include for client approval:

- branded vehicles;
- branded merchandise or giveaways;
- branded uniforms;
- the set design, decor and multisensory elements (scents, lighting, music, materials, refreshments or food etc);

- the experience team (brand ambassadors, speciality staff, team leaders, event managers);
- the space hire or venue comprising the selected locations;
- competition prizes, legals and terms and conditions;
- social media content, micro-sites, apps and any other digital elements;
- any ads, press releases or amplification elements;
- the scripts and briefs given to the brand ambassadors/live brand experience team;
- the training (the approach, venue, training manual, face-to-face training presentation and training agenda);
- anything else that features the client's brand logo or imagery.

Also to be considered in the approvals schedule is that some of the printing may be in a much larger format than the client is used to, and therefore the clients' creative agency or design team may require additional time for reformatting or re-creating assets for scaling up. For example, a giant logo that needs to be printed onto vinyl to wrap a 40-foot trailer is not something that will necessarily already be handy or kept 'on file'. In addition, sometimes there will be elements that need to be approved by external or third parties, such as any partner logos or space-hire applications. These third-party approvals should also be factored into the timeline, as always, allowing for contingencies.

It is crucial to include notes on this approvals schedule that clearly describe any caveats, outlining potential negative implications of any delays. This approvals schedule can alternatively be formatted as a CPA.

Summary

In summary, the *Action* part of the *SET MESSAGE* planning system is of ultimate importance because there is no point in creating the most innovative and revolutionary *Experiential Strategy*, or in booking the highest footfall most desirable venues, or designing the best amplification and content plan for the live brand experience, if the execution is going to be flawed (often with devastating domino-like ripple effects).

The statement 'If you fail to plan, you plan to fail' is most apt at this stage, and is something that no one would choose to learn the hard way (though many, too often do!).

If the *Action* part of your *SET MESSAGE* plan contains the components, as summarized below, then you have covered all the bases.

Action plan components

- Recipe (consumer journey).
- Budgets.
- Project plans (WBS, Gantt chart, critical path analysis, schedules, risk analysis, checklists and external analysis).
- Communication and collaboration plan.
- Suppliers and third-parties plan.
- Approvals schedule.

Your *SET MESSAGE* plan is almost ready for activation, with only the *Gauging Effectiveness* and *Evaluation* stages left to come.

Note

1 Project Management Institute (2004) *A Guide to the Project Management Body of Knowledge*, PMBOK Guides, Project Management Institute, Newtown Square, PA

Gauging effectiveness

15

Creating a real-world test-and-learn approach for experiential marketing environments

As we have seen, there are many unpredictable events and variables that can contribute to the success or failure of a live brand experience. If you plan a TV advertising campaign, once the advert has been created, approved and scheduled there is not much that can come in the way of it being aired as planned. It is pre-recorded, controllable and reliable. A live brand experience, on the other hand, has people's free will (along with all the previously discussed risks and external factors) to contend with. Methods that allow you to gauge the effectiveness of the live brand experience element of the experiential marketing campaign during its progress are of ultimate importance, and allow you to monitor the results of the experience and react accordingly.

The unpredictable and dynamic real-world environment

Even though careful *Action* planning (as described in Chapter 14) can contribute greatly to the success of the activation of your plan, there will always be some completely unpredictable dynamics. Sometimes these dynamics are positive and sometimes they are negative. *Gauging Effectiveness* is about telling the difference and reacting appropriately. This is achieved by reviewing the results of the *Systems and Mechanisms for Measurement* and ensuring flexibility options are in place.

Live brand experiences, especially when implemented face-to-face IRL, can require a certain amount of improvisation. Because things can go wrong, and many unpredictable, positive opportunities can also be created during the process, it is wise to be mentally and emotionally prepared to mitigate or capitalize on those eventualities. If you are on the agency side, it is your duty to ensure that the client is also prepared for the unpredictable.

It is true that the more careful *Action* planning you do, the more you will be in control. But because so many factors come into play and relate to each other in a multitude of combinations, there will be things that are out of your control when you are *Action* planning and that will only be discovered during the live brand experience.

Monitoring results in real time to allow a flexible approach

The *Gauging Effectiveness* stage will ensure that not only do you plan methods that allow you to react quickly to the fluid reality of your live brand experience, but that you have a way to monitor the campaign while it is live, using those methods. Such methods include real-time reporting of results from the live experience team (*Brand Ambassadors*, team leaders and event managers) to the experiential marketing agency, and online real-time reporting from the experiential marketing agency to the client.

Test-and-learn approach to scaling up, down or 'rolling out'

Flexibility and options are important, allowing you to adapt according to the findings, such as ensuring scalability. The *Systems and Mechanisms for Measurement* that you built into the plan already will ensure that the people who are present at the live brand experience are feeding back all the relevant data.

During the final step in the *SET MESSAGE* planning system; 'the *Evaluation* stage', you will be estimating the outputs of those *Systems and Mechanisms for Measurement*. When you are *Gauging Effectiveness* during the progress of the live brand experience, you need to compare the data that is fed back with the estimates in the *Evaluation* segment of your plan. This way, if something turns out better than expected, the insights and learning that can be gained will be available instantly to allow you to scale up and leverage the positive results for the rest of the campaign or plan for future, larger-scale global roll-outs following the success of test markets. Likewise, if something is not working as well as expected, or if unpredictable circumstances arise, then instant changes can be made and damage is minimized. For this reason, it is always recommended to start small, with a 'test and learn' approach that will allow you to take on board results, and plan how you will react to several possible outcomes at the *Gauging Effectiveness* stage.

Nick Adams, Managing Director at Sense, told Event in the 2016 Brand Experience Report:

> Some brands who may not have previously thought about globally integrated campaigns may well do so now. The world is getting smaller, and social media and amplification techniques are making a global reach more possible.[1]

Technological advancements and the rise of global experiential activation platforms make *Gauging Effectiveness* more crucial than ever, and thinking ahead can mean planning even two to three years from an activation kicking off – right from the start – to ensure the right levers are in place – to dial up when it works, or pull the brakes just in time.

Global roll-outs are on the rise

Global ideas are becoming increasingly commonplace in the world of experiential marketing, and as content is accessible internationally it makes sense often to stick to broad global activation principles and then adapt for local tailoring and insights. Often some of the best ideas that are suitable for global roll-out stem from local markets. By creating a robust plan for *Gauging Effectiveness*, test data can be created to build a business case that can enable an idea to cross borders and even continents.

CASE STUDY

Coca-Cola – personalized bottles go global

Coca-Cola was far from the first to develop the idea of personalized packaging, and yet its *Share a Coke* campaign is one of the 'poster children' for famous personalization campaigns, along with Starbucks who famously introduced writing names on coffee cups, and Nutella who shot to cult gifting status after offering named jars for sale.

Coca-Cola did this by initially identifying local success in Australia, followed by a ruthless display of organizational efficiency to fast-track its roll-out in more than 70 countries across the world. This wouldn't have been possible if they hadn't built in a robust method of gauging the effectiveness that enabled it to immediately correlate high sales with fast adaptations for what eventually became one of the largest-scale personalization campaigns ever rolled out around the globe.

In a 2013 report on food and drink marketing, Lucky Generals' Andy Nairn cites a quote from a 2002 IPA Effectiveness Award Submission from the Olivio brand. It reminds us to 'focus not on realities that divide, but fantasies that unite... the secret is not necessarily to think global but to think big. Consumers do not know whether an ad is global – only whether it is great.'

In Event's 2016 Brand Experience Report, Phil Carter, board director at Iris Culture, says:

> The drive for this has been motivated by the desire for consistency and quality in the execution of work all across markets. Clients are increasingly aware of the benefit gained from activation plans being delivered in sync, as opposed to local markets attempting large-scale projects individually.[2]

Systems and Mechanisms for Measurement and how they enable *Gauging Effectiveness*

For a *System and Mechanism for Measurement* to be of any value, there must be a way to accurately define and quantify it. After you complete the *Evaluation* scorecard, which will be covered in the *Evaluation* stage of the *SET MESSAGE* planning system, quantifiable estimates will be associated with each of the *Systems and Mechanisms for Measurement* that you have built in to your plan already (each corresponding with an *Experiential Objective*, as previously discussed in earlier chapters). The quantifiable estimates will act as targets and will allow continuous *Gauging Effectiveness* of the live brand experience during its progress.

Washing-powder brand – example

A live brand experience for a washing powder held in shopping malls across Europe had a mechanism for measuring word of mouth that was based on the number of interactions. The estimated number was 2,000 participant interactions per location, per day. This was calculated by dividing the total number of interactions (as logged in the experiential scorecard during the completion of the *Evaluation* stage) by the number of locations and days. In this case the estimate of 2,000 participant interactions per location, per day became a target. The event managers at all the locations would fill in a digital survey every few hours, each day, and there was a real-time feed of the number of interactions as every participant had to sign-in to the experience before participating. When the number of interactions was far higher or lower than expected, the agency and client would become aware immediately, get to the bottom of why there had been a dramatic variation, and be able to react quickly and appropriately.

As previously discussed, the *Systems and Mechanisms for Measurement* relate to the *Experiential Objectives*, which in the case of the washing-powder brand included 'driving word of mouth'. In some instances, such as this one, two of the project's systems are linked to each other.

For example:

1 the system for measuring the word-of-mouth reach (multiplying the number of direct interactions by an estimated number of people who would hear about it from each participant, and then adding the initial number of interactions) is interlinked with the system for measuring the participation of the live brand experience (counting the number of interactions). See Chapter 16 for formula for calculating word-of-mouth reach.

2 Therefore, since the word-of-mouth reach cannot be estimated or measured without the number of interactions, it would not be beneficial to set the *Experiential Objective* of driving word of mouth, without following through by planning how you would go about *Gauging Effectiveness* of the live brand experience in that respect.

Planning and anticipating results to define success and failure in advance

Deciding in advance how the data gathered from the *Systems and Mechanisms for Measurement* will be communicated quickly, and establishing what percentage of positive or negative variation is considered to be poor, acceptable or exceptional, is crucial. Defining how far above or below the estimate you should go before adapting, scaling up/down or rolling out the live brand experience is very important.

The experiential scorecard (to be detailed in Chapter 16) will provide the estimate across the whole campaign, and you will need to divide that estimate by the number of locations and days to get the unit estimates (which act as targets). Then, during the actual campaign, you will need to know how the real results compare to those targets. This process is especially useful when planning global roll-outs and ensuring each respective market has access to benchmark data from previous markets, enabling them to benefit from previous learnings.

Allowing for comparative analysis

Whether these targets are to be measured qualitatively, quantitatively or both should have already been specified during the *Systems and Mechanisms for Measurement* part of the plan. Moreover, it is important that both the experiential marketing agency and client stick to these definitions of acceptable or unacceptable variations in results during all ongoing live brand experiences. These variations can be used for numerous comparisons, from month to month, or year to year, to allow for benchmarking and realistic comparisons (between campaigns, projects phases, regions or markets). Likewise, if a client is switching experiential marketing agencies, it should ensure that the new agency applies many of the same *Systems and Mechanisms for Measurement* to its plans as the previous agency, facilitating the *Gauging Effectiveness* stage during a campaign and enabling clear understanding of what is a positive or negative result. If the actual results of several *Systems and Mechanisms for Measurement* on a specific day or location of a campaign are poor, then the agency should quickly try to gauge why and, if relevant, propose adequate changes to the client. An agile, and speedy approach, changing and adapting quickly is essential to the positive outcome of a live brand experience programme. Often technology and reporting systems can help with speeding up this process.

Real-time reporting and online dashboards

Speed is crucial for *Gauging Effectiveness*. By monitoring the results of your live brand experience in real time, you can continuously aim to improve and adapt it by learning from the variations between the actual outputs of the *Systems and Mechanisms for Measurement* (such as consumer feedback and data collected) and the estimated outputs. You can also learn from the event manager's feedback. The *Brand Ambassadors* and team leaders should give feedback to the event managers, who should regularly and systematically communicate with the experiential marketing agency.

There are a couple of ways that technology can enable this process to happen efficiently and reliably:

- The event managers report the feedback and data into survey forms on their smartphones, tablets or reporting app, and instantly transmit from the devices to the online client access page or dashboard, which should be hosted online somewhere secure, like the experiential marketing agency's website.

- If your experience features interactive technology such as motion sensors, those can detect participation volumes in different parts of your experience and automatically transmit that data to your reporting dashboard for analysis.

It is important that the internal agency team, the client and its stakeholders are able to view the results of the *Systems and Mechanisms for Measurement* with ease throughout the live brand experience's progress. This is why it is important that the experiential marketing agency designs bespoke online client reporting dashboards, and tailors them for each individual campaign's reporting needs. That will allow the internal agency staff and the client to log on to the dashboard remotely, *Gauging Effectiveness* of the campaign during its progress, and reacting and adapting as necessary.

Dashboards and reporting portals

There are many types of reporting dashboards, but all should allow users to log on with a unique password and view results. These can include sampling data, interaction figures, consumer feedback, participant demographics, and all the qualitative and quantitative results from *Systems and Mechanisms for Measurements*.

The experiential marketing agency should have the facilities to adapt their reporting methodology for each project and ensure event teams are trained to upload results in real time so that the client is always up to date. As well as results in real time, the experiential marketing agency should be able to upload visual evidence (such as photos and video clips) onto the same client access page where the reporting dashboard is hosted, within 48 hours of a campaign going live.

Flexibility and change management solutions

There may be areas that need quick adaptation, scaling up, down, amending or rolling out, depending on the variations between *actual* results (discovered through the real-time reporting) and *estimated* results (calculated from the broader *Evaluation* estimates in the experiential scorecard). If the experiential marketing agency notices a variation that is either a problem or opportunity, and wants to propose a change to the client, then there needs to be a planned and agreed procedure for doing so, with scope of work being revised and billed accordingly.

At this point in the plan, it is important to include procedures for approving changes during a live brand experience's progress. The recommended method of doing this is to create forms like those shown in this chapter and to ensure that all relevant members of the client decision-making team are aware of the possibility of a change request during the campaign (see Table 15.1).

Table 15.1 Sample: change request form

CHANGE REQUEST FORM		
LIVE BRAND EXPERIENCE NAME:		
PROJECT MANAGER NAME:		
LIVE BRAND EXPERIENCE LOCATION:		
Agency originator name and phone:	Date of request:	Change request no.: allocated by Change controller
Items to be changed:		Reference(s):
Description of change (reasons for change, benefits, date required):		
Estimated cost and time to implement (quotation attached? Yes/No):		
Will this cost be additional, or part of existing contingencies?		
Priority/constraints (impact on other deliverables, implications of not proceeding, risks)		

The change request form can be uploaded onto the online client access page or e-mailed, as long as it is sent in a way that facilitates quick decision making and an agile reaction. The chances of the live brand experience succeeding can directly relate to the speed with which the results and any corresponding change requests are shared (by the agency) and the speed with which the receivers can react (the client).

Table 15.2   Sample: change evaluation form

CHANGE EVALUATION			
What is affected:	Work required (resources, costs, dates):		
Related change requests:			
Name of evaluator:	Date evaluated:		Signature:
CLIENT CHANGE APPROVAL			
Accepted/Rejected/Deferred	Name:	Signed:	Date:
Comments:			

Once a change request form has been approved, there will need to be a log of that change and any other changes that are requested and approved.

These changes can easily be logged in a form such as a change control log, which will prove useful when conducting the final *Evaluation* of the campaign.

Summary

The ever-changing environment of the real world and the force of individual free will are bound to create unexpected circumstances. Just imagine if, during a live brand experience that was being executed face-to-face IRL, a group of radical political protesters decided to march with picket boards in the same location. Would the client be happy for its brand to be affiliated with this radical and polarizing cause? Would the experience's *Brand Ambassadors* and participants be safe in such a volatile environment? The answers are 'probably not'. Though the client may not want to move

Table 15.3 Change control log

		CHANGE CONTROL LOG			
Live brand experience:		**Date (from/to)**			
Project manager:		**Client:**			
Change number	**Description of change**	**Date Received**	**Date Evaluated**	**Date Approved**	**Date Completed**

Table 15.4   Change control record

Live brand experience:			Date (from/to):		
Project manager:		Client:			
Change number	Description of change	Reason	Impact	Comments	

the campaign, they would not be happy if they were not informed of what was going on, and they didn't have the opportunity to participate in deciding on the solution. If the proposed solution were to change locations, they surely would want to be involved in that decision.

Managing expectations and planning for success

If a client hoped that their live brand experience channel – with the *Experiential Objective* of increasing sales – would result in a big sales uplift in the stores where the experience was positioned, and some of those stores ran out of stock during the first hour of the experience, the client would want to know about the problem and decide on an appropriate solution. Depending on circumstances, they might want to have a mechanic to drive to e-commerce, attempt to transport stock from other stores to the affected stores, relocate the experience to a store that had sufficient stock, or postpone the experience to another day.

Regardless of which solution they would have preferred, the client would not have been happy if their experiential marketing agency had not informed them of the problem until it was too late to react, and if further planning could have prevented this loss in potential sales. If the experiential marketing agency did not have real-time reporting in place, then it is not likely that the client would be informed in time.

Unpredictable circumstances require forward consideration

There are plenty of examples of unpredictable circumstances, which when addressed swiftly can be dealt with in a manner that optimizes the results of the live brand experience and ensures maximum achievement of *Experiential Objectives*. By building *Systems and Mechanisms for Measurement* in the plan, completing the experiential scorecard in the *Evaluation* stage, and *Gauging Effectiveness* of the campaign by comparing actual outputs with estimated targets and using a combination of real-time reporting facilities and change management solutions to adapt and react, optimum results can be achieved.

The *Gauging Effectiveness* part of the *SET MESSAGE* plan will enable you to create a smooth and clear process for optimizing the live brand experience part of your experiential marketing campaign for agility and best results. This stage helps you to plan how you will adopt a 'test, learn' roll-out approach that can work locally or globally, and on small- or large-scale programmes alike!

Notes

1 *Event Magazine*, Brand Experience Report 2016 PDF (2016), Haymarket
2 *Event Magazine*, Brand Experience Report 2016 PDF (2016), Haymarket

Evaluation   16

Interpreting and monitoring tangible results from experiential marketing

The *Evaluation* stage, which begins during the *SET MESSAGE* planning process and is completed after the experiential marketing campaign is implemented, is arguably one of the most important stages of the campaign cycle: planning, activation and *Evaluation*.

Even if your strategy was fabulous and your activation was flawless, if you do not effectively evaluate the campaign results then there is nothing tangible to indicate that the campaign was indeed successful. It is very important to remain results-oriented when planning, activating and evaluating experiential marketing campaigns. It is true that there are many 'fluffy' benefits to experiential marketing, but, as previously discussed, there are also many tangible and quantitative benefits to be gained. By using the same metrics and *Evaluation* approaches across all your experiential marketing campaigns, you will enable benchmarking and comparison, and LROI measurement, not only in regard to comparing one experiential marketing campaign with another, but also in terms of comparing an experiential marketing campaign with a previous marketing communications campaign run without an experiential approach.

An integrated approach is the way forward

As previously discussed, live brand experiences should be placed at the core of experiential marketing campaigns. The unfounded myth that they cannot be evaluated properly arose for a number of reasons, including the fact that non-experiential marketing specialists are a popular choice for clients that want to plan and activate high-profile live brand experiences. Some of these campaigns have been managed by full-service agencies for big clients without thinking about how to evaluate until after the campaign is finished.

Be experiential

Experiential marketing can essentially include any marketing channel applied in an 'experiential' way, and if the live brand experience is at its core, and the other selected channels are designed to amplify the live brand experience as the message or content. The traditional channels can still be measured and evaluated using the common metrics that are accepted across the industry, while the live brand experience channel lends itself especially well to easy and comprehensive *Evaluation*, due to the *Two-Way Interaction* with consumers.

The human interface and direct engagement and relationship building with participants that characterize live brand experiences are reasons why they are in fact often easier to measure than many other channels. However, it is true that there is not one consistent method used by all experiential marketing agencies for measuring and evaluating live brand experiences. As a result, it makes it harder to benchmark the results of a live brand experience implemented by one agency against the results of a similar live brand experience implemented by a different agency.

Consistency over time

It should be acknowledged that this lack of a widely accepted *Evaluation* approach does contribute to a difficulty in comparison and benchmarking of live brand experience results. As live brand experiences become a more established part of the marketing landscape, *Evaluation* methodologies will become increasingly sophisticated and responsive. In time there will be more consistency in the metrics. This *SET MESSAGE* planning system aims to unify the ways in which experiential marketers evaluate their experiential marketing campaigns, with a strong emphasis on how to evaluate live brand experiences.

This chapter covers two different steps: 1) how to complete the *Evaluation* part of your *SET MESSAGE* plan, where you will plan and summarize the ways that you will evaluate *during* the campaign (the *Gauging Effectiveness* stage); 2) the actual *Evaluation* stage, which is how you will evaluate the experiential marketing campaign once it is over or at agreed intervals in an ongoing programme.

Learning objectives by this stage in the planning process:

- It is hoped that from reading previous chapters you have already built in *Systems and Mechanisms for Measurement* into your plan, and already know how you will go about *Gauging Effectiveness* during the campaign's progress.

- Therefore, by the time that you come to evaluate the campaign post-activation, you will have acquired plenty of qualitative and quantitative data to be formatted and analysed.

- If the experiential marketing campaign is ongoing, then you may want to break it up into chunks and complete the *Evaluation* stage at the end of each chunk (for example, quarterly).

- After the campaign is over, the results from the amplification channels (such as social media, PR and broadcast media) should be straightforward, as those channels have common metrics and built-in analytics.

- The results from the live brand experience channel that were collected in real time when you were at the *Gauging Effectiveness* stage of the activity should be combined into a report that includes the results of the amplification channels.

- The two sets of data form the body of information and intelligence that you will then dissect to evaluate the experiential marketing campaign as a whole.

- Your *Systems and Mechanisms for Measurement* should have been built into the live brand experience.

- The *Gauging Effectiveness* stage should have been completed during the campaign process.

- Even if this is all handled by an experiential marketing agency and their live brand experience team, you may want an external market research agency to complete a formal independent audit.

- The combined results should form the basis of information and data that you (or your experiential marketing agency) will work with when evaluating the campaign.

Do brand experiences and events drive ROI and LROI?

A widespread study of consumer data from large companies (70 per cent have total revenue over $500 million) in IT, medical and pharmaceutical, financial services, automotive, entertainment, media and consumer products

Figure 16.1 Most effective social channel for viral impact pre-event, onsite and post-event

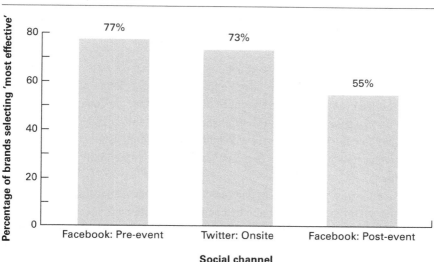

SOURCE Freeman XP and The Event Marketing Institute (2015) [Online] http://freemanxp.com/
insights/insights-papers/the-viral-impact-of-events-best-practices-to-amplify-event-content/

was conducted by *Chief Marketer* in 2014. They found that slightly more than half of consumers (54 per cent) would make a purchase of a promoted product or service during an event, with women significantly more likely to open their wallets (63 per cent) than men (45 per cent). And of those who don't, 57 per cent ultimately would buy the product or service at a later date.

The study was also in favour of connecting events to LROI, or long-term ROI – as 84 per cent of the consumers who bought the product or service, either at an event or afterwards, would make a repeat purchase. In fact, 74 per cent become regular customers. Men were more likely to report themselves as regular customers: 88 per cent versus 67 per cent of women.

While women appeared to contribute more to short-term ROI, men could be viewed as more important to long-term return. Freebies were much more important to the female respondents: notably 92 per cent cited them as a motivating factor, compared with 73 per cent of men. Discounts or special offers were important too, with 52 per cent of all respondents – 56 per cent of the women and 48 per cent of the men – citing them as a reason to participate.[1]

CASE STUDY

Glacéau Vitaminwater Shinebright Studio

Glacéau Vitaminwater wanted to communicate its *Message – Key Communication* that it 'helps creative people shine bright'. Experiential specialist agency Sense created the Shinebright Studio pop-up that took over an east London gallery space with creative workshops from creators and influencers that would help the brand connect with innovative millennials and tastemakers. Vitaminwater needed to appeal to the community with authenticity and credibility.

Sense achieved great scale (a combined over 52 million impressions) for the Vitaminwater brand experience by combining creative production, and partnering with the right influencers for makers workshops and masterclasses, to appeal to the audience with resonance and natural appeal.

The pop-up succeeded in generating over 35 million PR and content coverage, over 17 million social impressions, an estimated word-of-mouth reach (WOM) of 65,000, and 10,000 direct immersed participants.[2]

The experiential scorecard

This section of the *SET MESSAGE* plan should outline the ways in which you will evaluate the campaign once it is over. If you refer back, you checked which *Systems and Mechanisms for Measurement*, corresponded with your selected *Experiential Objectives* (by checking the table provided), then you prepared your own table detailing the *Systems and Mechanisms for Measurement*. That table acts as the basis for the 'experiential scorecard'.

The experiential scorecard will be featured in the *Evaluation* part of the *SET MESSAGE* plan. It is a table that acts as a quantitative measure of both quantitative and qualitative *Systems and Mechanisms for Measurement*. It should be formatted as a table that shows the appropriate measurement mechanism or system and its corresponding *Experiential Objectives*, the estimated results (which you will fill in at this stage of planning), and two blank columns for the actual results and comments, detailing theories on why any positive or negative variation occurred (Table 16.1). This will be filled in during the *Gauging Effectiveness* stage. After completing the written *Evaluation* part of your *SET MESSAGE* plan, your experiential scorecard should therefore include estimates that show the anticipated results.

Table 16.1 Sample: an experiential scorecard

Car X Experiential Campaign Q2			
Measurement mechanism + corresponding objective	**Estimate**	**Actual**	**Comments**
OTS (opportunity to see) [Objective: Raise awareness]	658,000		
Word of mouth reach [Objective: Drive word of mouth]	2.56 million		
Number of interactions [Objective: Drive word of mouth]	150,000		
Increase in awareness of key communication message (survey Q1) [Objective: Communicate complex brand messages]	30%		
Increase in perception of Car X as a stylish as well as capable vehicle (survey Q2) [Objective: Position the brand as x]	65%		
Number of visitors to Car X website that clicked from micro-site [Objective: Drive traffic to website]	40,000		

Making estimates

These estimates should be completed based on past experience and should always be realistic. The location agents or space owners for the live brand experience (whether it is face to face, IRL or remote through virtual or digital tech) selected locations (as described in earlier chapters) should be able to provide footfall or visitor data that can help to determine how many people might be present. If the live brand experience is designed as a destination and has mechanics to invite people to it, then the number of people who have confirmed attendance should also be able to guide these estimates.

It is important to factor in the length of time that it takes for participants to complete their interaction in the live brand experience, as well as the maximum number of participants who *can* possibly be involved at any one time, namely the total maximum capacity of the brand experience. Other things to factor in when estimating include the number of *Brand Ambassadors*, the number of locations in which the brand experience is occurring, and the number of days that the experience is taking place. It is also important to include the estimates for the results of the amplification channels (such as combined social media, influencers, PR and broadcast reach).

The *Evaluation* part of your plan should also list and describe the documents or presentations that will be shown to the client at the end of the campaign for review, from either the experiential marketing agency or other agency partners to the client, or from an in-house team directly to internal and external stakeholders.

The campaign evaluation (post-campaign, or at agreed intervals)

The '*Evaluation* Pack' will be prepared after the campaign and should be presented in the agreed format that was specified when you completed the written *Evaluation* part of the *SET MESSAGE* plan. It is likely to contain:

Evaluation Pack: the TRACK acronym (or TRACKronym!)

The completed experiential scorecard
ROI and LROI analysis
A change analysis
Content and visual evidence review
KPIs and an SW+I report (strengths, weaknesses and insights)

All of the above will be explained in detail over the course of this chapter.

The order in which the elements in the *Evaluation* Pack are listed is a recommended order in which to conduct the post-campaign *Evaluation* process. The remainder of this chapter will explain how to perform each step.

TRACK stage #1: The completed experiential scorecard

The experiential scorecard is based on the same table that you created when you completed the written *Evaluation* part of the *SET MESSAGE* plan, but at this stage should also show the completed '*actual* results' and 'comments' columns (see Table 16.2).

Table 16.2 Sample of a completed experiential scorecard

Car X Experiential Campaign Q2

Measurement mechanism + corresponding objective	Estimate	Actual	Comments
OTS (opportunity to see) [Objective: Raise awareness]	658,000	700,000	Based on mall footfall data
Word-of-mouth reach [Objective: Drive word of mouth]	2.56m	3.15m	Higher than planned, due to a higher number of interactions than anticipated
Number of interactions [Objective: Drive word of mouth]	150,000	175,000	It was higher than anticipated due to a higher footfall than usual
Increase in awareness of key communication message (survey Q1) [Objective: Communicate complex brand messages]	30%	50%	Survey results showed a 50% increase in awareness of the key communication, when participant data was compared to non-participant data, collected during the campaign
Increase in perception of Car X as a stylish as well as capable vehicle (survey Q2) [Objective: Position the brand as X]	65%	40%	The increase in perception was not as big as anticipated due to Car X's existing positioning as capable, along with a common view among both participants and non-participants that the car was stylish
Number of visitors to Car X website who clicked from micro-site [Objective: Drive traffic to website]	40,000	72,650	The number of hits to the micro-site was higher due to the number of participants and word-of-mouth reach being higher

The experiential scorecard's purpose is outputs; even qualitative questions have been quantified to show an increase or decrease in a common response. As long as the previously defined *Systems and Mechanisms for Measurement* were chosen in line with the *Experiential Objectives* (using the chart provided), then the experiential scorecard should facilitate easy *Evaluation* of whether those objectives and their targets were met. The comments should throw some light on why a positive or negative variation occurred between estimated and actual results.

The experiential scorecard quantifies results in a tangible way that can justify the spend on experiential marketing initiatives. The process of tailoring the metrics to the *Experiential Objectives* during the *Systems and Mechanisms for Measurement* stage, then facilitating the *Gauging Effectiveness* stage of the campaign in relation to those metrics, and finally formatting the results into the experiential scorecard during *Evaluation*, is a full-cycle process for measuring the *desired* outcomes against the *actual* outcomes whilst learning from any variations.

TRACK stage #2: ROI or LROI analysis

ROI

'Return on investment' originated as an accounting term but is usually regarded as a grey area in marketing, often being loosely referred synonymously to what 'results were generated' from a campaign. The term 'ROI' can be used as a financial measure of the actual percentage of profit made, as a direct measurable result of a campaign. For that to be instantly possible in the case of a live brand experience, the experience would need to be either near to a store that sold the product being promoted, or there would need to be a traceable mechanism and incentive in place, such as redeemable sales promotion vouchers or online promotional codes or other trackable links to e-commerce. All this clearly points towards short-term thinking. This also implies that the goal of the investment is an instant sales uplift and suggests that it is necessary for sales promotion to be involved.

LROI

Another way to look at the return is in the context of a long-term experiential marketing strategy, where the ultimate objective of the live brand experience channel is to convert participants into customers and, beyond the idea of 'loyalty' or repeat purchase, into brand advocates, and finally into brand evangelists. In this case, the return can be measured by how far the live brand experience succeeds in moving the consumer through the 'advocacy pipeline'.

With that said, it is clear in business that good healthy sales and market share are the ultimate goals. There is no reason to think that the goalpost is moving – in fact, far from it. The value of a customer who talks about your brand as if it were a trusted friend, and considers his or her relationship with your brand to be a two-way street, is priceless. 'People trust people', and there is nothing that could be more desirable from a business perspective than your *Target Audience* spreading positive word of mouth about your product to their peers, thus creating the coveted golden bond. It is proven that personal recommendations are the most likely factor to influence and drive purchase consideration, and the lifetime value of the customer is far greater than the value that any instant sales uplift campaign could generate.

The advocacy pipeline

The impact of a positive live brand experience can be so great that a participant can move through the advocacy pipeline stages very quickly, but to make a long-lasting impact across a whole *Target Audience* group, those reached by the word-of-mouth, influencers and other amplification channels of the experiential marketing campaign should be factored in to the equation.

For long-term return on investment (LROI), a long-term experiential marketing strategy is required. The core of your creative concept *Two-Way Interaction* (the live brand experience, as outlined in the *BETTER* creative process) should be at the core of the overall marketing communication strategy, thus allowing all the marketing communications channels to work in alliance with each other and amplify the live brand experience. Amplifying and supporting the live brand experience improves results dramatically across the board.

This amplification of real-world or event-based activities can be applied in many ways. Whether the amplification is in the form of branded content broadcast on TV or YouTube, social media influencers, digital ads promoting your experience, digital out-of-home advertising (DOOH), or through a radio broadcast of a live brand experience, the unified channels work together to create the complete and integrated experiential marketing campaign that uses relevant storytelling to build long-lasting relationships with the members of the brand's *Target Audience* with whom it reached.

The aim is that those *Target Audience* members then become brand advocates and evangelists who proceed to take the positive brand *Message – Key Communication* to their peers through personal recommendations and ultimately generate or share content that reaches the masses, increasing awareness and sales in the process.

Calculating LROI for live brand experiences

The sales generated from a live brand experience should be seen to be symptomatic of the word-of-mouth reach generated from that positive, brand-relevant *Two-Way Interaction*.

Interview excerpt: driving purchase consideration through immersive product trial and education

Rodolfo Aldana, Director of Tequila, Diageo

Trial with mentoring has at least two and a half to three times higher conversion rate than trial without mentoring. So, if you sample 10 people, let's say, only two people are going to go and purchase the product later in the process in the following weeks (one in five). If you sample those people *and* mentor, you are going to double or almost triple that number in terms of conversion.

When you see what the conversion is, you see that it (mentoring) absolutely makes more sense. The challenge is that of course the cost of mentoring is very high so you have to know.[3]

By creating a link between the number of 'immersed participants', namely the number of interactions of the live brand experience that turned into brand advocates, and the long-term word-of-mouth reach – while taking into account, that word of mouth generates sales better than any other channel – we get closer to correlating it (the number of interactions generated from the live brand experience) with the number of sales generated. The ultimate aim is to estimate the LROI of live brand experiences.

Interview excerpt: evaluating experiential marketing and the ROI associated with *Two-Way Interaction*

Barbara Bahns, Head of Regional Marketing Planning and Communications CEE, Visa Inc

Experiential marketing is absolutely something that we are doing more and more of in a broader sense and increasingly connecting other channels to it. The measurement piece is a bit tricky and if we do something we should be able to demonstrate we can engage millions of people. Experiential marketing is where it is problematic if you speak to the numbers people, that is, the finance guys etc within a company, who are saying, 'Well, how much was it, and was it worth doing?' They just look at the figures and say 'that should have been more people'.[4]

It is proven that the long-term effect that word of mouth has on sales is greater than with any other approach. This is why, by using a model that calculates LROI, which factors in the word-of-mouth reach of a live brand experience, we can quantify the impact that the live brand experience has on sales (which should be at the core of the integrated experiential campaign and combined with the results of the amplification channels).

Four simple steps for calculating LROI

The formula for calculating the LROI for live brand experiences consists of four simple steps:

Step 1. Calculating the WOM *Reach*.

Step 2. WOM to sales conversion.

Step 3. Profit (value).

Step 4. Profit (percentage).

Step 1: calculating the WOM reach

Each person who interacts in a live brand experience is likely to tell their friends or peers. For this example we will base our calculations on each person telling 17 others. Therefore, the word-of-mouth (WOM) *Reach* would be calculated as the number of interactions multiplied by 17, plus the number of interactions.[5] You can conduct research during your live brand experience programme to estimate this number in specific relation to your project, audience and their propensity to spread WOM, as this will vary depending on the characteristics of your audience. In addition, bear in mind that first-hand peer-to-peer recommendations versus WOM on social media will vary in volume and impact.

Step 2: WOM to sales conversion

This (estimate) can be calculated as a percentage of the WOM *Reach* of the live brand experience (for this example we will apply an entirely conservative 2.6 per cent, based on the average conversion to sales from direct mail campaigns), not forgetting it is proven that word of mouth is more likely to generate purchase consideration than any other marketing channel (especially direct mail!).

Step 3: profit (value)

The profit generated from the live brand experience can be calculated by multiplying the profit per sale by the number of sales (estimate). Then subtracting the cost (or loss if the experience is partially revenue-generating) of the live brand experience.

Step 4: profit (percentage)

In order to calculate the LROI you divide the profit generated by the cost of the live brand experience and multiply by 100 (as you would in any standard percentage calculation).

The example that follows shows how we apply the LROI formula (based on each live brand experience participant telling 17 others, and based on 2.6 per cent of those reached by the word of mouth converting to sales).

LROI = the long-term return on investment estimate

LROI = $(X/C) \times 100$

This is the profit estimate (X) divided by the cost (C), multiplied by 100 to get a percentage. Note:

C = Cost (or loss, if revenue-generating) of the live brand experience

X = the profit estimate

X = $SxP-C$

As generated from the live brand experience, based on subtracting C (the cost of the campaign) from S (number of sales) multiplied by P (profit per sale). Note:

S = number of sales estimate (based on a percentage of W, the word-of-mouth reach)

P = profit per sale

C = campaign cost

Estimating total WOM reach

This calculation simply adds the total number of people who will hear about an experience to the number of people who participated:

W= WOM *Reach* estimate

W = 17N+N

Based on an estimate from research conducted by Jack Morton Worldwide that found each participant of a live brand experience tells 17 others on average, but you can replace with your own estimate, if you have one.
Note:

N = the number of consumer interactions with the live brand experience

W = the word-of-mouth reach, based on 17N+N

A small-scale example

Hamed is the marketing manager for a website selling customized greeting cards that can be ordered online:

- His cards sell at £4 and his profit per greeting cards is £1.50.

- He approached an experiential agency to create an integrated experiential campaign, featuring an interactive greeting card roadshow and amplification of the activity using PR and digital advertising.

- The live brand experience channel's total cost was £50,000 and generated 115,000 interactions.

- He wanted to estimate the LROI and used this model to predict what his LROI could be.

Estimating LROI in four easy steps:

Step 1: calculating the WOM *Reach*.

Step 2: WOM to sales conversion.

Step 3: profit (value).

Step 4: profit (percentage).

Step 1: calculating the WOM reach He multiplies the number of interactions in the live brand experience (115,000) by 17 (the average number of people he estimated each participant could tell about the experience) and then adds the original number of interactions to get the word-of-mouth reach estimate, 2.07 million (W).

Step 2: WOM to sales conversion To get the estimated number of sales resulting from the word-of-mouth reach, he used the conservative direct mail stat and calculates 2.6 per cent of 2.07 million (the word-of-mouth reach). This produces an estimated 53,820 sales (S).

Step 3: profit (value) To get the profit generated from the live brand experience, he multiplies the profit per greeting card, which is £1.50 (P), by the estimated number of sales, 53,820 (S) to get £80,730. Then he subtracts the cost of the campaign, £50,000 (C) to get the profit generated of £30,730 (X).

Step 4: profit (percentage) He calculates the LROI of 161 per cent by dividing the profit generated from the live brand experience by the cost of the live brand experience, and multiplies the result by 100.

The method Hamed used is summarized in the formula below:

LROI = 61 per cent, based on (X÷C) x100.

S = 53,820 number of sales (estimate) based on 2.6 per cent of W (word-of-mouth reach).

P = £1.50 (profit per sale).

X = £30,730 the total profit estimate, based on S (number of sales) x P (profit per sale) – C (campaign cost).

C = £50,000 (cost of the live brand experience).

N = 115,000 (the number of consumer interactions with the live brand experience).

W = 2.07 million (17N +N, the estimated word-of-mouth reach).

Estimated results In this case, Hamed can predict that 161 per cent will be the LROI from the live brand experience activity, because he used the formula that factors in the long-term effect of the campaign, taking into consideration the estimated word-of-mouth reach.

This is actually a very conservative estimate because the 2.6 per cent return is based on an average return from a direct mail campaign, while word-of-mouth has been proven to be around 10 times more effective, and has been voted above traditional media as most likely to drive purchase consideration.

Factoring in the impact from amplification channels To calculate the ROI of the integrated experiential marketing campaign in full, it is important to include measurement and returns from the amplification channels. The other marketing communication channels that Hamed used to amplify the live brand experience for his online greeting cards were interactive digital ads and PR.

The interactive online ads featured slideshows showing some of the cards made by consumers who had participated, and an invitation to submit a card design to be shown on future ads. The amount of people who clicked on an online advert and then purchased a card measured the success of the online channel.

The PR channel was based on a photocall of all the *Brand Ambassadors* and consumers engaging in the live brand experience, which went on to feature in a number of national and local newspapers and magazines. The PR channel, which achieved print coverage, was measured by column inches (how much the space would have cost if it were paid advertising space). The online and PR metric he used are commonly used measures, though obviously approaches vary.

Hamed combined the LROI generated from the live brand experience with the generic measures that he placed on the PR and online advertising channels, allowing him to evaluate the success of the integrated experiential marketing campaign as a whole.

A larger-scale example

Jane is a senior planner at an experiential marketing agency. Her client is a high-end white goods manufacturer:

- When the client approached Jane with the task of launching a new brand of luxury energy-saving washer-dryers, Jane designed a strategy that featured a six-month live brand experience tour.

- The tour involved an energy home, which toured around the United States. Consumers were then invited to walk around the energy home, and learn how to save energy in their own homes, while creating their own 'energy-saving tips binder' and having their 'aura photo' taken.

- The 'aura photo', which mapped out the energy around their head and shoulders, was linked to social media, and an instant print-out was slotted into the front cover of their energy-saving binder as a souvenir.

- The live experiential marketing strategy was a major hit amongst the *Target Audience* of affluent families.

- Jane's client was exceptionally pleased, but wanted Jane to provide a method of demonstrating that the constant rise in sales since the start of the experiential marketing campaign was directly linked to the activity.

- Jane proposed looking at the LROI of the live brand experience, and calculated it using the same formula.

The formula is: **LROI = 953 per cent, based on (X/C) x100** (this is the profit generated from the live brand experience divided by the cost of the live brand experience, multiplied by 100).

S = 140,400 estimated number of sales based on 2.6 per cent of W (word-of-mouth reach).

P = \$150 (profit per sale).

X = \$19 million is the estimated total profit generated based on S (number of sales) x P (profit per sale) – C (campaign cost).

C = \$2 million (cost of the live brand experience).

N = 300,000 (number of consumer interactions with live brand experience).

W = 5.4 million (17N +N, the word-of-mouth reach estimate).

High and low involvement purchases

As you can see, whether the investment is small or large, and whether the product is a high-involvement purchase like an energy-saving washer-dryer or a low involvement purchase like a personalized greeting card, live brand experiences can generate a high LROI. By aiming also to combine the ROI of each amplification channel, you can endeavour to evaluate the complete integrated experiential marketing campaign.

LROI

The LROI gives you the figure for the longer-term financial return you can expect to gain from the live brand experience. Depending on whether it is a high-involvement purchase (usually expensive or infrequent purchases such as a car) or a low-involvement purchase (usually impulse buys or FMCG products such as a candy bar), the time frame can vary from one day, to one week, to five years. By using the LROI formula, it is easy to evaluate and estimate the long-term effect that the live brand experience part of the experiential marketing campaign will have.

By combining the LROI of the live brand experience (using the formula) and the ROI of the amplification channels (using standard metrics) to contribute to the *Evaluation* stage of the *SET MESSAGE* planning process, we can begin to predict the combined effects of the complete campaign.

Customer lifetime value

It is important to also factor in the customer lifetime value (CLV), especially in specific industries where the long-term profit to be gained from each customer is greater down the line. One example is the gaming industry, where the profit margin on a console is far lower than the profit margin on the consumer buying video games on an ongoing basis. The same applies to the home capsule-coffee-machine business, where units are often sold at a loss due to the lucrative profits to be had from the future revenues of coffee-capsule club subscriptions.

If you would like to generate LROI from experiential marketing, you must invest in a long-term experiential marketing strategy. By placing live brand experiences and the experiential philosophy at the core of your long-term marketing strategy, the LROI will be far greater than if you approach it as a tactic for a quick sales uplift.

TRACK stage #3: A change analysis

The next part of the *Evaluation* stage is the 'change analysis'. This is a careful examination of what differed between the original plan and the delivered plan. This should encompass changes in timing, cost and outputs. The data that should form the basis of this will have already been collected during the *Gauging Effectiveness* stage using the change control log. The purpose of the change analysis at this stage is to determine the reasons behind any changes and to gather any insights, useful in future planning.

Note: the change number shown in this stage of the *Evaluation* should correlate with the change number shown on the change control log that was used during the *Gauging Effectiveness* stage of the *SET MESSAGE* planning system.

TRACK stage #4: Content and visual evidence review

Content opportunities are plentiful when it comes to live brand experiences, from consumer-generated content that has been organically captured and shared socially, to carefully curated influencer and 'top-down' brand-generated content and media coverage.

Compiling and reviewing all the best content and 'visual evidence' is a crucial part of ensuring stakeholders internalize the positive results of an experiential marketing campaign. The live brand experience (both the set and every stage of the consumer journey) itself should be captured in both moving and still pictures, which in turn forms the 'visual evidence' component to be reviewed alongside the broader, far-reaching content generated.

Visual presentation of data

This segment of the 'TRACK' part of your *Evaluation* should be appealing and well presented, therefore any images and video should be edited and displayed in a concise, attractive format for all to see exactly how it worked and, most importantly, how consumers reacted and participated in the brand-relevant interaction. From a marketing perspective, there is nothing more fulfilling than to see the *Target Audience* happy and appreciative of your brand.

Visual content

One minute of edited video footage and a slideshow of photography taken from a live brand experience can say more than 1,000 words' worth of data and analysis. The visual evidence from the live brand experience (assuming that it was executed face-to-face IRL) can also be used to amplify the campaign – forming content for digital messages, TV adverts, and a platform for future relationship building.

Sharing

The participants themselves usually love to be able to rewatch the clips of the experience they so much enjoyed, being tagged in this footage, which should be available to share socially on platforms such as Facebook, Instagram or Snapchat. This is even more effective when the process is handled with enough sophistication to enable the matching up of sections of the visual evidence with the details of the consumers who are featured in it.

Along with the edited live brand experience footage and images, there should be visual evidence of the amplification channels as well. For example, if part of the experiential marketing campaign featured a YouTube series that was branded and based on interactive audience participation and audience-generated content, then an edited 'best bits' from the show would be great to use in the 'content and visual evidence' section of the 'TRACK pack' within your *Evaluation* report.

Amplification-channel coverage should be included

Say, for example, a PR amplification initiative invited consumers to attempt to break a world record. A compilation of the consumers' competition entries and the resulting news coverage should be included in the visual-evidence part of the *Evaluation* packet.

No matter which amplification channels you used, or whether the live brand experience was held online, in person or through some other method of remote communication technology, the content and visual evidence that capture it present a far more vivid picture and understanding of what took place than any black-and-white data can. The visual evidence of the experiential marketing campaign provides a souvenir that reminds the participants and/or stakeholders of the experience, thus keeping the vivid memories of the campaign alive for far longer than in the mind alone.

TRACK stage #5: KPIs, strengths, weaknesses and insights

The KPIs, strengths, weakness and insights report is stage 4 of the TRACK model and the final part of the post-campaign *Evaluation* process.

Brand advocacy and KPIs

Marketing departments operate across multiple channels. From social media, to e-mail marketing, to advertising, to lead generation, to digital marketing, to events and experiential marketing, all which will include a number of activities. With such a wide variety of channels being used and often integrated around a live brand experience, it is important for marketing teams to actively track progress and performance in real time with the right marketing metrics and KPIs that bear in mind that personal recommendations, the golden bond and brand advocacy are the ultimate goals.

Cautious when comparing metrics between channels

When comparing the marketing metrics results between channels, you should keep in mind that the impact on 1,000 'advert exposed' people compared to the impact on 1,000 immersive event participants, for example, is massive. Therefore, when comparing the CPT between both, this should be taken into account. Namely, how impactful has that reach really been? The cost per thousand (CPT) opportunity to see (OTS) on a media campaign will be far less valuable to the brand than those deeply engaged in a brand experience.

Placing varying scales of value on each unit when analysing your results is crucial and at this stage in your *Evaluation* you can apply creative and bespoke research that aims to establish in greater depth how your KPIs and metrics have worked within your campaign, with the view that the cost per thousand brand advocates (CPTBA) is enormously valuable to your business in comparison to CPT media exposures per se.

Explore how successful you have been at moving participants (live brand experience participants, and those second- and third-degree consumers reached via word of mouth or amplification channels) through the 'advocacy pipeline' towards being a brand advocate and ultimately an evangelist.

Strengths, weaknesses and insights

The body of this report should be formatted as a table, with two columns, one for 'strengths' and one for 'weaknesses'. It should be split into three sections: 'planning', 'implementation' and 'results'. Following the table, there should be a summary of 'insights' for the future.

The purpose of the report is to summarize everything that was good, bad, adequate and outstanding about each of the three stages, as well as how these stages could be improved upon. This will facilitate better performance when conducting the next stage of the experiential marketing programme. It should take into consideration all data gathered during the *Gauging Effectiveness* stage, an analysis of the KPIs in view of brand advocacy and evangelism being the ultimate goal, including a careful analysis of why the targets affiliated with the *Systems and Mechanisms for Measurement* were met or even exceeded.

Summary

In summary, it is important to outline exactly how the experiential marketing campaign is going to be evaluated during the planning stages following the *SET MESSAGE* planning system. Then, during the *Evaluation* stage, post-campaign, a detailed *Evaluation* TRACK pack should be prepared. It should be clear that every client and brand is different and different people and budgets demand different levels of *Evaluation*. A fully comprehensive *Evaluation* TRACK pack should contain the sections summarized in the framework box below.

The TRACK pack

The completed experiential scorecard.

ROI and/or LROI analysis that takes into account both the live brand experience and any other amplification channels that comprised the experiential marketing campaign, taking into consideration the customer lifetime value (CLV).

A change analysis.

Content and visual evidence review (combining edited video footage, photos and media).

KPIs, strengths, weaknesses and insights reports that elaborate on the impact of each customer impression or engagement across every 'campaign touchpoint' and the positives and negatives from both the client and agency perspectives during the planning, implementation and results, while looking at extracting insights and practical ideas on what can be drawn from them for the future.

Notes

1 Event and Experiential Marketing (2014) [accessed 23 April 2016] Chief Marketer B2C Special Report [Online] http://cdn.chiefmarketer.com/wp-content/uploads/2014/08/24571_CM-Special-Report_Consumer_web.pdf

2 Sense (2016)

3 Smilansky, S (2017) Excerpt from an interview with Rodolfo Aldana, Director of Tequila, Diageo

4 Smilansky, S (2017) Excerpt from an interview with Barbara Bahns, Head of Regional Marketing Planning and Communications CEE, Visa Inc

5 The Viral Impact of Events (2015) [accessed 13 April 2016] Freeman XP and The Event Marketing Institute [Online] http://cdn.freemanxp.com/documents/1382/the_viral_impact_of_events_study_freemanxp_and_emi_final.pdf

Conclusion 17

Planning for the future of experiential marketing

An experiential revolution

Experiential marketing is revolutionizing marketing and business practice around the world. To survive tough competition, to avoid participating in price wars, and to reap the benefits of loyal customers and *Target Audiences* driving word of mouth, experiential marketing is the answer. This book has looked at experiential marketing from both philosophical and practical perspectives, allowing readers to come away with a clear understanding of how to brainstorm, strategize, plan, activate and evaluate integrated experiential marketing campaigns.

How an experiential approach fits into marketing communications

The context is marketing communications, so we began by looking at how many long-standing approaches to marketing, such as traditional advertising, are losing effectiveness rapidly. We demonstrated how experiential marketing and customer experience are key differentiators in competitive business environments, paving the way for a new economic playground where brands and consumers enjoy interacting together.

Placing *Two-Way Interactions* at the heart of campaigns

Though experiential marketing is a pioneering approach and has therefore been subject to confusion and scepticism, this book has elaborated on the notable shift in business and marketing towards the new era of communications it represents. This book has positioned the big idea, always in the form of live brand experience, at the core of the experiential marketing programme, inspiring its readers to amplify real experiences in the form of *Two-Way Interactions* using a combination of 'amplification channels'.

Forecast for the future

The forecast for the future of experiential marketing is that its philosophy will filter through every aspect of brand communication with *Target Audiences* and there will eventually be a shift towards a predominance of permanent, arranged or requested *Two-Way Interactions*, rather than spontaneous or 'pop-up' experiences that traditionally bank on *Target Audiences* happening to be at the right place at the right time.

A practical creative model and planning system

For a successful experiential marketing concept to be born, the right research, creative development processes and planning systems are needed. This book explained how to develop experiential ideas using the *BETTER* creative model, and then refine and structure the plan for best results and effective measurement using *SET MESSAGE*.

Be the start of the change you want to see in your organization

As a reader and an experiential marketer, it is up to you to pass on what you have read and share experiential marketing philosophies with other people throughout your organization. You must participate in this exciting three-dimensional revolution where customers, employees and brands work together as partners, mutually satisfying each other's needs.

INDEX

Note: The index is arranged in alphabetical, word-by-word order. Numbers in headings and 'Mc' are filed as spelt out in full; acronyms are filed as written. Locators in *italics* denote information within a Figure or Table.